T0418922

Improvising Fugue

Improvising Fugue

A Method for Keyboard Artists

John J. Mortensen

OXFORD
UNIVERSITY PRESS

Oxford University Press is a department of the University of Oxford. It furthers the University's objective of excellence in research, scholarship, and education by publishing worldwide. Oxford is a registered trade mark of Oxford University Press in the UK and certain other countries.

Published in the United States of America by Oxford University Press
198 Madison Avenue, New York, NY 10016, United States of America.

CIP data is on file at the Library of Congress
ISBN 978–0–19–764524–6 (pbk.)
ISBN 978–0–19–764523–9 (hbk.)

DOI: 10.1093/oso/9780197645239.001.0001

To my father, Joseph I. Mortensen, Th.D: –
the original Dr. Mortensen, and the best.

When I tread the verge of Jordan,
Bid my anxious fears subside;
Death of death, and hell's Destruction,
Land me safe on Canaan's side;
Songs of praises, songs of praises
I will ever give to Thee.

Contents

Acknowledgments

The members of the Improv Planet community give me hope that improvisation is accessible and rewarding to people all over the world. They are curious and funny, thoughtful, and kind.

My friends Mykolas Bazaras of Lithuania and Louise Boll of Denmark arranged tours in their respective nations. Many of the ideas in this book began to take shape in the concert halls, conservatories, and cafés of those countries.

I am indebted to Professor Giorgio Sanguinetti for his important book *The Art of Partimento*. All contemporary study of partimento relies on Sanguinetti's work.

Professor Robert Gjerdingen has given to the world not only his valuable books *Music in the Galant Style* and *Child Composers in the Old Conservatories*, but also the crucial resources at partimenti.org.

Professor Peter van Tour's research has shed new light on the practices of the partimento tradition. I am grateful for his generosity and encouragement.

Professor Beth Porter's support of my projects has been indispensable.

Nikhil Hogan is surely the foremost chronicler of the improvisation revival.

The Board of Delegates of Oxford University Press and editor Michelle Chen championed the idea for this book.

My wife Linda will not read this book. But she has read me cover to cover, knows the good chapters and the wretched, and keeps me on the top shelf just the same.

My cat Clive sat looking patiently over my shoulder as I wrote. Among many other accomplishments, he has proved conclusively that inability to improvise a fugue is no barrier to companionship.

Prelude

This book will show you how to improvise fugues at the keyboard. Eventually.

It's a climb. Before you can scale the cliffs of fugue improvisation, you must first follow the forest pathway of consonance, dissonance, cadences, and Rule of the Octave. Then come the rising foothills of partimento and diminution. Next you encounter the twisting switchbacks of imitation and partimento fugue. After that you must scramble up the boulders of bicinium, leading to the vertiginous heights and thinning atmosphere of invertible counterpoint. Only then does the sheer vertical rock face of fugue come into view.

Fugue improvisation requires that one must first journey through ever-ascending landscapes of musicianship. You can only reach the higher regions by passing through the lower. This book ventures through the Italian partimento tradition as this preparatory landscape—the approach route to the mountain. It does so because partimento provides a broad, nearly comprehensive experience of the harmony and counterpoint of the eighteenth century. Partimento is above all *practical*; one does it primarily at the keyboard rather than on paper. Practicing partimento means inventing music while playing music while hearing music while thinking about music while solving problems about music. Partimento is keyboard skills and ear training and voice leading and harmony and diminution and invertible counterpoint, all at the same time. Furthermore, partimento study is beneficial long before one ever gets to fugue, simply because it shows the player how music actually works. It demystifies how music is made, and is therefore useful for training in theory, composition, figured bass, and many other skills. A chronic illness of the modern method of "classical" performance training is that students learn to play music without the faintest idea what's going on. For this ailment, partimento is the cure.

The history of fugue spans hundreds of years and untold thousands of compositions. So many diverse pieces of music have been called fugues that it is difficult even to say what a fugue is or isn't. This book does not attempt to circumnavigate the entire fugal globe, but is limited to music for keyboard in styles ranging from the mid-seventeenth through the early nineteenth centuries. Simply to keep a manageable length, the book pays no attention to vocal or instrumental fugue, or to more recent contributions in modern harmonic languages such as those of Shostakovich. Further, by necessity certain common phenomena are ignored completely. (One such item is the *soggetto servile*, an optional secondary voice that may begin simultaneously with the main fugue subject.) We already have enough on our plates.

In the eighteenth century, improvisation was one skill among many that were expected of a competent keyboardist. Improv was viewed less as a unique and impressive skill and more as a necessary practical tool for the accomplishment of daily work. That era's practices of improvisation existed along a continuum. At one end we find pieces mostly scripted, leaving only little bits that were completed spontaneously, such as on-the-fly ornaments added to a written sarabande. In the middle of the continuum stand longer extemporaneous sections within composed pieces, such as cadenzas or *Eingänge*, or music composed only partially, such as anything with continuo (that is, accompaniment from figured bass). On the far end are those pieces created without notation, which could be partly or mostly unpremeditated.

I say "mostly unpremeditated" because any fugue requires at least a moment of thought, unless the player is experienced and the subject is trivially easy. In this moment of thought, the capable improviser will scan the subject for inherent harmonic and contrapuntal possibilities as well as potential problems, and quickly formulate plans for developing a coherent piece. Fugue improvisation as presented in this book will draw freely from practices along the full length of the continuum. Some of the exercises may require much more than a moment of thought—perhaps days of thought, or even some written-out work. Nevertheless, the overall direction of the book is toward independence from the page, so that readers move ever closer to the unpremeditated end of the continuum. The goal is that readers would be not merely reciters of the music of others, but creators of their own.

I am primarily a pianist, but I have tried to make everything in this book useful for all keyboard artists. I have tried to say very little about things idiomatic to the piano, and I hope that harpsichordists, organists, and players of digital keyboards do not find their instruments marginalized in these pages. With broad access in mind, all examples are notated on two staves with modern clefs, even if the original sources are otherwise configured. Those who wish to dive deeply into primary sources will need to deal with all the old clefs, but I thought that in a book that already presents many challenges to the reader, making the musical examples inscrutable might be a bad idea.

In order to make your way through this book, you will need significant musical background. The material is not for beginners or casual dilettantes. I tried to calibrate the material to the level of an intelligent, motivated undergraduate conservatory student. (Such creatures are rare, but one meets them occasionally.) From my experience on Improv Planet, I have been gratified—nay, gobsmacked—to learn of the great number of devoted amateurs around the world who can keep up at that level.

Specifically, you will need adequate keyboard skills to read two staves and play independent parts with two hands, but you will not need to play spectacularly difficult things like Chopin études. Knowledge of the basic workings of figured bass will be necessary—that is, what the little numbers mean, and how to play them. You should know key signatures and details about major and minor keys, like raised leading tones and the alteration of the melodic minor scale as it ascends and descends. You will also have to transpose hundreds of times.

Those who have never improvised will find my previous book *The Pianist's Guide to Historic Improvisation* (Oxford University Press, 2020) to be a more gradual, gentler introduction to the agonizing process of morphing from a musician who is exclusively "on page" to one who is capable of going "off page." One might say that both books in tandem form an improvisation course in two parts—like a prelude and fugue.

I am a teacher, and so I cannot resist admonishing you in advance on the importance of doing all the exercises. Fugue improvisation involves not merely intellectual knowledge but a kind of haptic wisdom that only develops through prolonged interaction with the keyboard. Each skill rests upon the solid foundation of other skills. Work on each level until you are very good at it. If you can play an exercise in various keys at a steady tempo with musical expression, you are ready to move on. If you stumble and fumble and bumble, you are not ready. If you can't play it in rhythm, you can't play it. It don't mean a thing if it ain't got that swing. Do not underestimate the foundational material; after teaching hundreds of improvisation lessons to students around the world, I have found that the most common problem is that players have not adequately mastered the entry-level skills of Rule of the Octave.

Another of my compulsions as a teacher is to name things. I do it to make concepts vivid and memorable, and to make it easy to refer to them. In the eighteenth century no one named bass motions, but referred to them by interval (up a fourth, down a third). This takes a long time to say, and requires one to reconstruct the motion by playing those intervals in one's head. It's clumsy. Some bass motion names I have taken from others (Monte Principale, Romanesca) and some I have made up (Cascade, Über-Lamento, Dolareti). This practice is completely unscholarly and unhistorical, for which my flimsy and monosyllabic excuse is that folks learn more when things have names.

In tandem with this book I suggest that the reader revive the ancient practice of keeping a *zibaldone*, a notebook of personal observations, themes, musical techniques, admirable passages, and so on. Writing on paper by hand slows you down and compels you into sustained interaction with musical materials. At various points throughout the book the reader is encouraged to write things in a zibaldone.

I have in mind no specific time frame for how long it will take to learn everything in this book. Obviously, this will depend on the reader. Very roughly, I imagine that a dedicated, talented conservatory student could do it in two years. An avid amateur might take five. When I was a student, it would have taken me twenty.

To indicate scale degrees I follow the new practice of showing melody or upper voices with solid black circles and white numbers, and bass scale degrees with black numbers on white circles. The tonic and dominant notes in an upper voice are ❶ and ❺, and those in the bass are ① and ⑤. Those who wish to adopt this style will find the circled numbers in the font Wingdings 2.

Readers are invited to check out improvisation resources hosted at johnmortensen.com. The same website presents numerous videos of concert improvisations, lectures, my touring schedule, and the usual self-aggrandizing promotional puffery you would expect.

I wrote this book out of a lifelong fascination with fugues. Love preceded understanding by many years. In fact, I can recall trying to write one as a teen, with no idea whatsoever how to do it. I knew just enough to start with a theme in a single voice, after which the music quickly deteriorated into agonized incoherence. Mercifully, I was too inept as a pianist to play it for anyone. I dearly hope that piece of paper has disintegrated and returned to the soil whence it came.

Even as a young person with no serious musical training, I heard something special in fugues. Like a chain reaction, such music exudes energy when melodic ideas collide under the pressure of thematic density. Time is timeless; moments are momentous. Out of an unpromising string of unaccompanied notes unfolds an entire world of sound, of logic and feeling, meaning and myth. A fugue is a scale model of the universe.

Let us begin.

Chapter 1

Introduction to Furno

We begin with a study of *Metodo facile breve et chiaro delle prime ed essensiali regole per accompagnare partimenti senza numeri* (Easy, short, and clear method on the first and essential rules of accompanying unfigured partimenti) of Giovanni Furno (1748–1837). Furno was a leading teacher in the conservatories of Naples. While he is forgotten today, one of his students was Vincenzo Bellini (1801–1835), the opera composer who deeply influenced Frédéric Chopin (1810–1849).Though Furno's *Method* is but one among many treatises from that era, I find it to be the most approachable for modern players just beginning their journey into the wonders of partimento and improvisation.

A partimento is a bass line that contains clues about how it could become a complete piece of music. The most important clue is how the bass moves.

We study partimenti in a three-step process: *recognize, realize, and stylize.*

To *recognize* to is see what harmonies are required by the motion of the bass notes. The idea of motion is very important. Often a single note does not provide enough information to determine its harmony. In most cases we have to look at two or more bass notes, as the motion between them, along with their rhythmic characteristics, will provide the clues we need to complete the harmony.

To *realize* is to play the bass and appropriate harmonies in a simple chordal texture. In doing so we explore a range of intended harmonic possibilities of the partimento.

To *stylize* is to transform the partimento into a specific kind of piece, such as figuration prelude, fantasia, toccata, allemande, and so on. Before we can do any stylizing, we must lay the foundations of recognizing and realizing. And before that, we must understand consonance and dissonance, the very bedrock of eighteenth-century music.

Consonance and Dissonance

The first statement in the *Method* is "Primieramente si deve sapere, che la musica è composta di consonanze, e dissonanze" (First, you have to know that music is made of consonance and dissonance). The fact that these are the opening words, and that Furno does not say music *contains* these things but is *made of them*, should indicate the foundational importance of this idea.

Furno's terminology is in some cases obsolete and confusing (for instance, he calls perfect fourths "major fourths" and diminished fourths "minor fourths"), and he explains everything with long streams of intervals that may sound perplexing. Nevertheless, once you have practiced and heard it all, you will find that all the concepts are simple, intuitive, and harmonious.

Furno states that thirds, sixths, octaves, and tenths (and their additional transpositions) are consonant, and seconds, fourths, sevenths, ninths (and so on) are dissonant. Dissonances are prepared in advance by common tone, and resolve (usually downward) by step to a consonance. In the majority of cases the upper note is considered dissonant against the lower note. For example, an octave from C up to another C is a consonance. If the bass moves up to D, the upper C becomes a dissonant seventh against the bass, and must fall to B, which is a consonant sixth against D in the bass. The upper voice is "prepared" (that is, it exists previously as a consonance), becomes dissonant when the bass moves, and resolves downward to another consonance. While we will encounter some exceptions later, this principle is central to tonal music: dissonances are prepared by common tone and fall by step to consonances.

If we begin with a third, such as C to E, the interval is consonant. If the upper note E moves to D, now the lower C is dissonant and must step down to resolve. Thus, in some cases the lower note is dissonant against the upper. These principles are illustrated in Example 1.1.

The reason this is so important is that music of the eighteenth century derives its narrative power in part from the interaction of dissonance and consonance, and the rules for handling these interactions are precise. As you play partimenti, you will need to predict when dissonances are likely to happen, and figure out how to prepare and resolve them correctly.

EXAMPLE 1.1 Preparation and resolution of dissonances

Root Position and Inversion

To play partimenti and learn to improvise, you will need to set aside some of your ideas about chords. The idea of root position and inversion is foreign to the world of partimento, in which one does not think of chords as having a theoretical root that may or may not appear as the lowest sounding tone. This is a theory introduced by Rameau, and is useful for some things (abstract analysis, playing jazz and popular music) and not as useful for other things (playing partimenti and improvising contrapuntal textures). If you took a music theory class, you encountered this idea in the form of Roman numerals. In *The Pianist's Guide to Historic Improvisation* I sometimes used Roman numerals to describe musical situations. I did so as a compromise, since the Roman system is very familiar to today's musician. In partimento, however, Roman numeral analysis is frequently unnecessary and sometimes downright counterproductive. We still use them to describe broad key areas, but rarely to explain individual chords and almost never to describe chord progressions.

Eighteenth-century musicians thought of chords not as triads that could be inverted, but as existing in two main types: *chords of the fifth* (what we would call a root position triad) and *chords of the sixth* (what we would call first inversion). Other chords are described by intervals above the bass, as well. What we would call a third inversion of a seventh chord, they would describe as the bass taking a second, fourth, and sixth.

This distinction may seem pedantic, but it is not. Thinking of harmonies as inverted triads forces you to "uninvert" chords to figure out what the root supposedly is. This extra step, required on almost every beat of every partimento or improvisation, thus accumulates to swarms of momentary mental calculations, placing an unbearable drag on the performer's thinking. In improvisation, thinking too much is just as bad as not thinking enough.

This will take some getting used to. A chord with E in the bass and C and G in upper voices *is not a first-inversion C major triad.* It is the bass note E taking a chord of the sixth. Yes, eighteenth century musicians knew that the sonority was the same as a "root position" chord on C. Any idiot would know that. But its function—the way it will behave in music, the places it is likely to go—are much more a result of the fact that its bass is E. The bass is the important thing in partimento; the upper voices result from the note in the bass. The bass tells you most of what you need to know about the rest of the harmony. This is why it is so important not to "de-legitimize" the bass note and declare that some theoretical root is actually the main note to consider.

I know that this all sounds theoretical and useless. Not so. It is the difference between fluency and hesitancy. As we move forward with partimenti, you will understand why, and you will find that thinking in partimento terms—chords of the fifth and chords of the sixth—becomes intuitive and rapid.

A little farther down the road, partimento will introduce you to contrapuntal improvisation. Counterpoint absolutely requires that one think of music as made of intervals, not chords with theoretical roots. Again, the reasons for this will become clear in time.

Figured Bass

Figured bass, also known as thoroughbass or continuo, is a shorthand system for describing harmony. It is indispensable in studying partimento and fugue. Along with a bass line notated on a staff, Arabic numbers (not Roman) above or below the staff provide important information about what the upper voices are doing. Each number represents an interval above the currently sounding bass note. If the number has no sharp, flat, or natural, the interval will fall within the diatonic scale. Numbers may be adapted to represent a chromatic alteration of a note. For example, the dominant chord in a minor key will always have a raised third, shown as ♮3 or ♯3, depending on the key signature. This book will assume the reader's knowledge of figured bass. Those who have no prior experience may wish to undertake a separate study of this topic.

Rule of the Octave

Furno next introduces the Rule of the Octave (although he does not call it that; it got its name elsewhere). The Rule of the Octave (RO) is so important that in many treatises it appears as one of the first topics. (In Francesco Durante's treatise, it appears *before any explanatory text.*) RO is foundational because it is a simple yet broadly useful harmonic system. One could compose a variety of pieces only with RO, and if artfully done, they would not sound boring or harmonically impoverished. Once you have mastered RO, you can improvise credible, stylistically legitimate music, even before going on to higher levels of harmonic training.

The RO is a system in which every bass note within a major or minor scale takes a given set of intervals. Some scale degrees always take the same intervals no matter what, but others take different intervals depending on the way the bass is moving. Example 1.2 shows one way to play ascending and descending RO in major and minor.

EXAMPLE 1.2 Rule of the Octave

Minor RO uses the melodic scale, so 6 and 7 must be raised or lowered as appropriate.

Ascending in major and minor, ① takes $\begin{smallmatrix}5\\3\end{smallmatrix}$, ② takes $\begin{smallmatrix}6\\4\\3\end{smallmatrix}$, ③ takes $\begin{smallmatrix}6\\3\end{smallmatrix}$, ④ takes $\begin{smallmatrix}6\\5\\3\end{smallmatrix}$, ⑤ takes $\begin{smallmatrix}5\\3\end{smallmatrix}$, ⑥ takes $\begin{smallmatrix}6\\3\end{smallmatrix}$, and ⑦ takes $\begin{smallmatrix}6\\5\\3\end{smallmatrix}$. Descending in major and minor, ① takes $\begin{smallmatrix}5\\3\end{smallmatrix}$, ⑦ takes $\begin{smallmatrix}6\\3\end{smallmatrix}$, ⑥ takes $\begin{smallmatrix}\#6\\4\\3\end{smallmatrix}$, ⑤ takes $\begin{smallmatrix}5\\3\end{smallmatrix}$, ④ takes $\begin{smallmatrix}6\\4\\2\end{smallmatrix}$, ③ takes $\begin{smallmatrix}6\\3\end{smallmatrix}$, and ② takes $\begin{smallmatrix}6\\4\\3\end{smallmatrix}$. Alternatively (and as shown in Example 1.2), ⑥ descending may take $\begin{smallmatrix}6\\3\end{smallmatrix}$ without the ♯6. (This equivocal phenomenon will be explained presently.) Note that ①, ②, ③, and ⑤ are always the same, no matter what. ④ and ⑥ take different intervals depending on whether they ascend or descend.

Guess what? You have to memorize all this! Unfortunately, this series of numbers is almost impossible to remember! But do not be dismayed. RO is easy once we know it at the keyboard by rote, because the intellect, ear, and hand all work together. We learn RO not by memorizing all the numbers but by playing it.

When I teach university-level improvisation courses, I require students to learn RO thoroughly before the first meeting of the class. They have to send me a video of themselves playing RO with a metronome at 80 (one chord per click), ascending and descending, with no errors, in every major and minor key up to

EXAMPLE 1.3 Furno's melody for Rule of the Octave

three sharps or flats. If this task isn't done, they are not allowed to join the class. Why would I do something so draconian? Because RO must be effortless. It lies behind thousands of split-second decisions improvisers have to make. Any hesitation results in an instant train wreck.

RO is to improvisation what katas are to karate. I don't practice any martial arts and am a menace to no one, but for a short time my children took karate lessons. Karate students begin by learning the first kata, which is a series of basic moves that they will draw upon later as they develop a karate "vocabulary." They repeat the moves of the first kata a ridiculous number of times, and then have to do them in front of judges. Eventually they can do the katas without thinking, which is important, because things happen rather quickly in karate fights.

Furno taught specific, strict melodic lines to use with RO. The shape of the melody unfolds in part from the soprano's starting note, that is, the *position* of the first chord. (Don't confuse position with inversion. Position refers to the note in the top voice.) You can learn RO that way if you want. Example 1.3 shows Furno's prescribed melody for first position in major.

I have no objection to learning Furno's, or anyone else's, melodic lines for RO. However, since each master taught different melodies, obviously there is not one correct answer. While I like the additional challenge of improvising a melody with good voice-leading, and encourage my students to try it, nevertheless if improvising the melody overtaxes your mind, there is nothing wrong with using prescribed melody. You will outgrow it very soon.

Voice Leading and Parallels

Anyone who has taken a course in classical music theory knows the headache of finding and exterminating parallel fifths and octaves between all combinations of voices. I was taught to go through a four-part exercise and check every combination of parts. (In a four-part texture there are six combinations of voice pairs.) This was about as fun as hunting and squishing cockroaches in my college apartment. I always missed something so my papers came back with red ink all over them.

The process of checking every pair of parts works on paper, but not in improvisation, so I concluded that the great improvisers of history had a superhuman power of foreseeing and correcting all these combinations while playing in real time. Perhaps their hands were playing the beginning of a phrase while their minds were seven measures down the road untangling some ugly parallels between inner voices. For two reasons, this was never the case.

First, RO training limits concerns about parallels to soprano and bass only, because inner doublings and parallels are usually imperceptible on keyboard instruments. When moving in parallel motion between outer voices, use sixths or tenths. That will solve your problem. Also, when in doubt about a voice-leading situation, move the hands in contrary motion. Just send the right-hand chord in the opposite direction from the bass. Voice-leading problems will be solved instantly!

Second, voice-leading is like good manners, which require that we memorize solutions to various situations. I only speak a little bit of bad street Russian, but one time I was to be introduced to the administration of the Tchaikovsky Conservatory in Moscow, so in advance I learned to say, "It is a pleasure to meet you" in Russian and thus navigated an important social interaction without embarrassment. As you study RO, you will eventually memorize voice-leading solutions to many situations.

Our improvisation heroes of the past were probably not checking pairs of voices in their heads. They were using bass motions with solutions that were inherently correct, which had become effortless habits of ear, hand, and mind.

Simple RO

You may learn *Simple RO* before working on the full version described above (which we might call *Complete RO*). Simple RO uses only chords of the fifth on ① and ⑤, and chords of the sixth on every other bass note, with one exception: ④ descending from ⑤ takes a second and a fourth. The harmonies of Simple RO have the same function as those in the complete version, but do not sound as rich. One advantage is that all harmonies use only three voices, whereas some in Complete RO require four. With only three voices, the task of keeping track of them will be easier. Simple RO appears in Example 1.4. Note that the F in measure 7 may be natural or sharp.

EXERCISE. Practice Simple RO ascending and descending, major and minor, in as many keys as you can handle. Go slowly enough so that the notes

EXAMPLE 1.4 Simple RO

really sink into your awareness. Continue practicing until you can play Simple RO flawlessly.

EXERCISE. After you master Simple RO, continue with Complete RO. You can begin practicing in any key, but many treatises show it in G, and follow up with partimento exercises also in G. You may try to improvise the melody or simply copy one of the previous examples in this chapter. Eventually you should learn RO in every major and minor key. For now, if you can manage all major and minor keys up to three sharps and flats, you will be ready for everything Furno will throw at you.

4-6 Exceptions

Before continuing, however, we must learn the 4-6 Exceptions, which are different intervals for ④ and ⑥ under certain conditions. Example 1.5 shows the way Furno actually presented his RO examples (in this case starting in third position); they keep going after ascending and descending. He goes leaping around for some reason. This leaping motion demonstrates the 4-6 Exceptions.

Dauntingly, ④ and ⑥ already require different harmonies depending on whether they ascend or descend. Under the rules of 4-6 Exceptions, each also has the option of taking a chord of the fifth (${}^{5}_{3}$) at times. If ④ does not touch ⑤ at all (neither ascending to it nor descending from it), it can take ${}^{5}_{3}$. If ⑥ does not descend to ⑤ or ascend to ⑦, it can take ${}^{5}_{3}$. Note that ⑥ may still take ${}^{5}_{3}$ when it comes

EXAMPLE 1.5 Furno's RO with 4-6 Exceptions

from ⑤, which is sort of like a deceptive cadence. (⑤ to ⑥, with both taking $\frac{5}{3}$, is possibly the most perilous RO situation for parallels: two chords of the fifth a step apart. In this situation, keep the soprano on the same note, or move the right hand downward as the bass rises.)

These rules seem hopelessly confusing when written out in verbal form. Just play the patterns from Furno and it will all make sense after a while. Also, Furno will provide many 4-6 Exceptions in his ten partimenti, so we will have repeated opportunities to practice.

Practicing

As you practice RO, do not play in strict rhythm at first, but rather give yourself time to take note of the intervals, the feel of the chords under your hand, and hear the sonority. When you are ready, begin to play in rhythm, using a metronome. Practice in various meters so you become accustomed to chords landing on different beats. And you can start with an anacrusis (upbeat) of various lengths so that ① does not always land on a downbeat. It is important to learn RO as a flexible pattern, not locked into any specific metrical configuration.

The descending major scale requires a chromatic alteration on ⑥. This is the raised sixth above the bass. Furno's descending minor scales give ⑥ a chord of the sixth *without* the raised sixth above the bass. However, many masters, including the revered Fenaroli, taught that ⑥ descending in minor should take a raised sixth. This is the "augmented sixth" chord you may have encountered in theory class. If you merely play a natural sixth above the bass without chromatic alteration, you will get an older, more Baroque sound, while the raised sixth will create a more Galant (or even Mozartean) sound, in my opinion. Even though Furno teaches the natural sixth, both options will work in his partimenti. You should learn to play and hear both versions, and chose between them to obtain the musical effect you want.

Take particular care to manage the changing notes of the minor scale on ⑥ and ⑦ as the scale rises and falls. These are the same as the melodic minor form of the scale.

Proceed through more keys in any order. You may wish to create your own practice regimen of various keys at different tempi. Your ultimate goal should be effortless mastery of RO in every key, beginning in any position on the first chord.

When you get to Furno's first partimento in the next chapter, you will see immediately that he does not allow the bass to run straight up and down the scale. He begins leaping around from the start. While we learn RO first as a rising and falling scale, it will usually not confine itself to stepwise motion in real music. In fact, a complete ascending or descending scale, harmonized by RO, is exceedingly rare in written music. Don't get attached to playing RO in the same order every time because Furno is going to shatter that cozy little world very soon.

Chapter 2

Furno's Ten Partimenti

In order to solve Furno's first two partimenti, you need only Rule of the Octave—but you need it very thoroughly. As mentioned in the previous chapter, Furno teaches RO in a stepwise manner, up and down the scale. In these partimenti, the bass skips around, requiring you to think outside the parameters of your initial practice regimen. You will also need to figure out when to apply the 4-6 Exceptions.

Furno #1

Furno's first partimento, seen in Example 2.1, is in G major. The first step is to figure out where you should use the 4-6 Exceptions, and where to use the usual RO procedures.

EXERCISE. Copy the bass line of Furno #1 into your zibaldone. Figure out what harmonies to use over each bass note, and play them. Write them in if you need to, but try to solve them at sight, without any help beyond the written bass line. Begin playing, taking the bass with the left hand and all upper voices

EXAMPLE 2.1 Furno's first partimento

5

with the right. Start in any position of the first chord; all three positions will work. Remember that *position* refers to what note is in the top voice, and is not to be confused with *inversion*. Find the 4-6 Exceptions and harmonize them appropriately. Do not let the soprano move in parallel fifths or octaves with the bass. As a general rule, if the right hand moves in contrary motion with the bass, you probably won't get any parallels. Don't worry about creating an interesting tune, though; at this stage all you need to do is keep the voice-leading correct. Boring is allowed. If your hands get too close together, play the bass down one octave. For now, don't worry about playing in rhythm. Once you have found your way through, go back and try starting in the other two positions of the first chord.

In carrying out the exercise above, you should have discovered instances where the bass indicates important alterations of the harmony. The E in the third measure is ⑥, and since it descends to ⑤ it must take a raised sixth in one of the upper voices. The C in measure 5 is ④ and does not touch ⑤, so it can take $^{5}_{3}$. The E in measure 6 is ⑥ and does not descend to ⑤ or ascend to ⑦, so it can take $^{5}_{3}$, and the same is true of the E in measure 7.

Example 2.2 shows solutions to Furno #1 starting in all three positions, and with 4-6 Exceptions marked with an X. Note that the solutions freely change between three and four voices. This would get you into trouble in theory class, but was considered necessary and correct in partimento style.

EXERCISE. Write out transposed versions of the bass from Furno #1 in your zibaldone. Try at least three other major keys. Practice these in the same manner explained in the previous exercise, using all three positions of the starting chord. As you are able, keep a steady rhythm. Always play slowly enough so that you are accurate. If you are playing a piano, bring out the top line the same way you would voice chords in any composition.

Furno #2

Furno's second partimento, shown in Example 2.3, consists only of RO in a minor key.

EXERCISE. Copy the bass line of Furno #2 into your zibaldone. Play it, figuring out all the harmonies, including 4-6 Exceptions. Don't forget that ⑥ and ⑦ are lowered when descending.

Furno taught that ⑥, descending in minor, should take $^{6}_{3}$. As mentioned in the previous chapter, many other teachers harmonized this same bass note differently. Furno certainly knew the work of Fedele Fenaroli (1730–1818), who preceded him in Naples and whose treatise was famous. Fenaroli taught that ⑥ descending in minor should take $\begin{smallmatrix}\sharp 6\\ 4\\ 3\end{smallmatrix}$ —essentially what we would call an augmented sixth chord. Either option will work, but they sound very different.

EXAMPLE 2.2 Solutions to Furno #1

EXAMPLE 2.3 Furno #2

Try them both so you can decide which one might be appropriate in a given musical situation.

Example 2.4 shows a solution for Furno's second partimento beginning in second position and with Fenaroli's harmony for ⑥ descending in minor. 4-6 Exceptions are marked with an X.

After recognizing the correct harmonies and realizing them at the keyboard, the final step in partimento playing is to stylize. Stylizing can be as

EXAMPLE 2.4 Furno #2 with 4-6 Exceptions marked

modest or ambitious as you like. In this chapter we will study two modest forms of partimento stylization.

Figuration Prelude

A figuration prelude is just a series of chords broken up into a consistent pattern of shorter notes. A good example is the first prelude from *The Well-Tempered Clavier* of J. S. Bach (1685–1750). Figuration preludes are easy to create because you only need two things: a series of chords with good voice-leading in (usually) three or four voices, and a figuration pattern that is stylistically appropriate. For a comprehensive study of figuration preludes, see my book *The Pianist's Guide to Historic Improvisation* (Oxford University Press, 2020).

Figuration preludes require a specific number of voices in each chord, since the figuration pattern has to be consistent and cannot add or drop voices. The easiest way to begin is to use three voices, which will result in Simple RO. With three voices (bass and two upper voices) it is not too difficult to break each chord into a pattern. In eighteenth-century music the most common pattern for a three-voice texture is what I call the "umpadeeda." The first few measures of Furno #1, stylized with umpadeedas, are shown in Example 2.5

EXERCISE. Go back through the first two partimenti of Furno and play them in Simple RO, starting in any position. Remember that Simple RO uses only chords of the fifth on ① and ⑤, and chords of the sixth on every other bass note, with one exception: ④ descending from ⑤ takes a second and a fourth. (And note that the 4-6 Exceptions apply to Simple RO.) Play the bass note on the beat, then add the upper voices in the umpadeeda pattern. If you repeat the pattern two or more times for each harmony, you can extend the duration of the partimento quite a lot. It also gives you more time to think!

Example 2.6 shows the first two partimenti of Furno stylized as figuration preludes in three voices. Note that any chords with four voices must be reduced to three.

The umpadeeda pattern uses four sixteenth notes per beat. By dropping the last note, the pattern becomes a group of three, suitable for pieces in compound meters. Thus you can easily modify the two partimenti to be in 6/8, 9/8,

EXAMPLE 2.5 A stylization of the opening bars of Furno #1

EXAMPLE 2.6 Furno #1 and #2 as figuration preludes

and so on. While it is possible to play the pattern only once per bass note, this would result in a very fast harmonic rhythm, which may not be desirable. In 9/8, for example, you could easily play the pattern three times, thereby filling each measure with a single harmony. When repeating the figuration of a chord to stretch the harmonic rhythm, remember that the bass may hop up or down an octave to generate additional interest.

EXERCISE. Play Furno's first two partimenti in compound meters, trying out various harmonic rhythms. Vary the positions of the starting chord. Transpose them to several other keys.

While three-voice textures have only a few options for figuration patterns (umpadeeda being the most common), four-voice textures allow for greater variety. Example 2.7 shows a few.

Playing partimenti in four voices with figuration will allow for the fuller harmonic sound of Complete RO, but comes with the responsibility to keep track of more voices, and the obligation not to drop any.

EXERCISE. Go back through Furno's first two partimenti and complete each harmony with three voices above the bass (four voices total), playing in block chords. On most of the chords, you will have to double a note, since only a few of them require four notes. Avoid doubling ⑦ if possible. Once you can play the block chords in four voices, apply a figuration to the partimento. Because you may choose various meters, harmonic rhythms, and figuration patterns, these partimenti may be played in countless ways. Remember that you should also transpose and try all three positions of the first chord. Example 2.8 provides ambitious four-voice, compound-meter solutions for each partimento, both transposed to a new key.

EXAMPLE 2.7 Figurations in four voices

EXAMPLE 2.8 Compound meter stylizations of Furno #1 and #2

Unmeasured Fantasia

The unmeasured fantasia style lives on among harpsichordists but is barely known to pianists today. Usually notated in long values (either half or whole notes), the style is rhythmically very free, sometimes lacks bar lines, and may not follow the notated written rhythm fastidiously. Passages in this style are sometimes marked by *Arpeggio*, *Harpeggio*, or some similar term, meaning that the chords are to be freely arpeggiated up and down at the discretion of the performer. Often, though, no specific directions are provided, as the performer was expected to understand the style. It is in good taste to vary the pacing so that one dwells upon significant or poignant harmonies, while at other times generating a sense of forward momentum. The unmeasured fantasia style appears in the Chromatic Fantasy of J. S. Bach, although some editions, such as that of Hans von Bülow (1830–1894), notate those sections in specific rhythmic values, obliterating Bach's intended moments of freedom.

In order to play partimenti as unmeasured fantasias, you will need to get a sense of the style. Listen to harpsichordists perform passages of this kind; their timing and number of repetitions of the rising and falling

EXAMPLE 2.8 Continued

EXAMPLE 2.9 Furno #1 as unmeasured fantasia

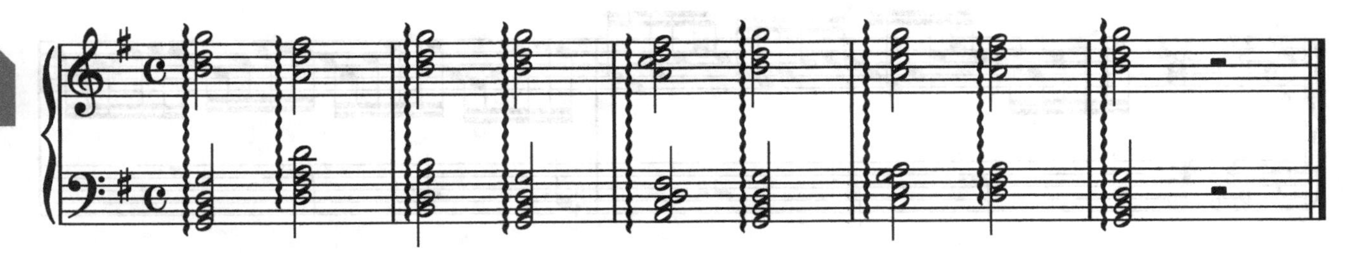

arpeggios will give you enough guidance to get started. Unlike ordinary partimento playing, in which the left hand takes only the bass, in unmeasured fantasy style each hand takes as many notes as possible (usually three to five). Inner doublings may be unlimited, while good voice leading must govern the outer voices.

Each chord may be rolled once, twice, or even three times, and the arpeggios may be made into a continuous rising and falling pattern.

Example 2.9 illustrates how Furno's first partimento might be played in unmeasured fantasia style.

EXERCISE. Play Furno #1 and #2 as unmeasured fantasias. Make them rhetorically interesting and dramatic by varying the pacing of arpeggios. Employ acciaccaturas at appropriate moments.

Cadences

Furno's third partimento introduces cadences. If you have taken a music theory course, you may have learned about all kinds of cadences like perfect authentic, imperfect, deceptive, and so on. In the world of partimento, we will ignore those definitions for now; instead, we have just three distinct cadences types: simple, compound, and double.

A cadence occurs when the bass moves from ⑤ to ①, and ① is on the stronger beat. Nothing else counts as a cadence: not ② to ①, not ⑦ to ①, not ④ to ③. We tell the three types apart by how long they are.

The simple cadence takes one beat for ⑤ and one or more beats for ①. ⑤ takes $^5_3$ and ① takes $^5_3$.

The compound cadence takes two beats for ⑤ and one or more beats for ①. ⑤ takes $^6_4$ or $^5_4$ then $^5_3$, and ① takes $^5_3$.

The double cadence takes four beats for ⑤ and one or more beats for ①. ⑤ takes $^5_3$, $^6_4$, $^5_4$, and $^5_3$, and ① takes $^5_3$. The last beat over ⑤ may also take $\substack{7\\5\\3}$.

Importantly, all cadences work in any position of the soprano. Example 2.10 shows the three cadences according to Furno.

EXAMPLE 2.10 Furno's three cadences

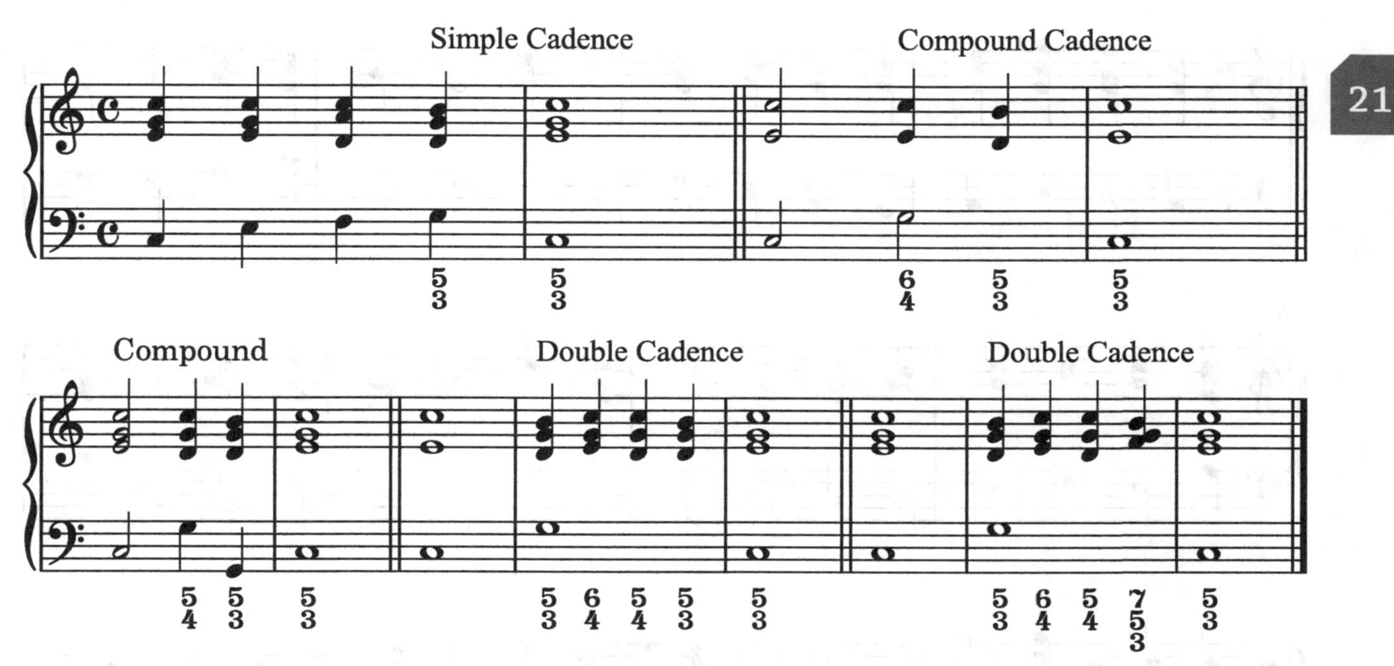

EXERCISE. Practice the three cadences in all positions, transposed to many major and minor keys.

Furno #3

You are now ready for Furno's third partimento. To solve it, first find every instance in which the bass moves from ⑤ to ①, and ① is on the stronger beat. Based on the duration of ⑤, determine what type of cadence should take place. The rest of the partimento is then solved with Rule of the Octave (or, as I often find myself saying when teaching, "everything else is RO").

EXERCISE. Play Furno #3, applying RO and cadences at the appropriate locations. Don't forget about 4-6 Exceptions. Start in every position of the soprano. Copy the bass into your zibaldone, and add transposed versions, which you should then solve in the same manner. As an additional challenge, stylize Furno #3 as figuration preludes and unmeasured fantasias. Example 2.11 includes the partimento along with a possible realization.

Terminations

Terminazioni di tono means "conclusion of the key"—that is, modulation. One of the skills of partimento is recognizing modulations. These often take place through two events. The first is the termination itself, which is the moment at which the music departs from the previous tonality and enters the new key. The second event is a cadence confirming the new key. The cadence, however, may never arrive, since music sometimes visits tonalities without committing to them by means of a cadence.

EXAMPLE 2.11 A realization of Furno #3

In Furno's fourth and fifth partimenti (the ones that demonstrate terminazioni), most keys are confirmed with cadences, with just two exceptions to be noted later.

Furno indicates that terminations may be initiated by four motions of the bass: a rising half step, a rising whole step, a descending half step, and a descending whole step. However, his description makes it sound as though a termination happens any time one of these motions occurs, which is not the case. Obviously, the bass may ascend and descend by half and whole steps at various places within a scale without leaving the key. What he means is that these steps are possible places where terminations *may* occur. I believe that today's musicians need more clarity than Furno provides, so I will recommend a specific procedure for identifying modulations shortly.

Before going further, we should review the typical range of modulations. With some exceptions, we may generalize that eighteenth-century harmony moves conservatively between tonalities. The most careful modulations are to the five neighboring keys: the relative of the key of the moment, those one accidental in either direction in the circle of fifths, and their relatives. Much of the time, modulations add or subtract just one accidental, or none if moving to the relative. Example 2.12 shows the five neighboring tonalities.

EXAMPLE 2.12 The five neighboring tonalities

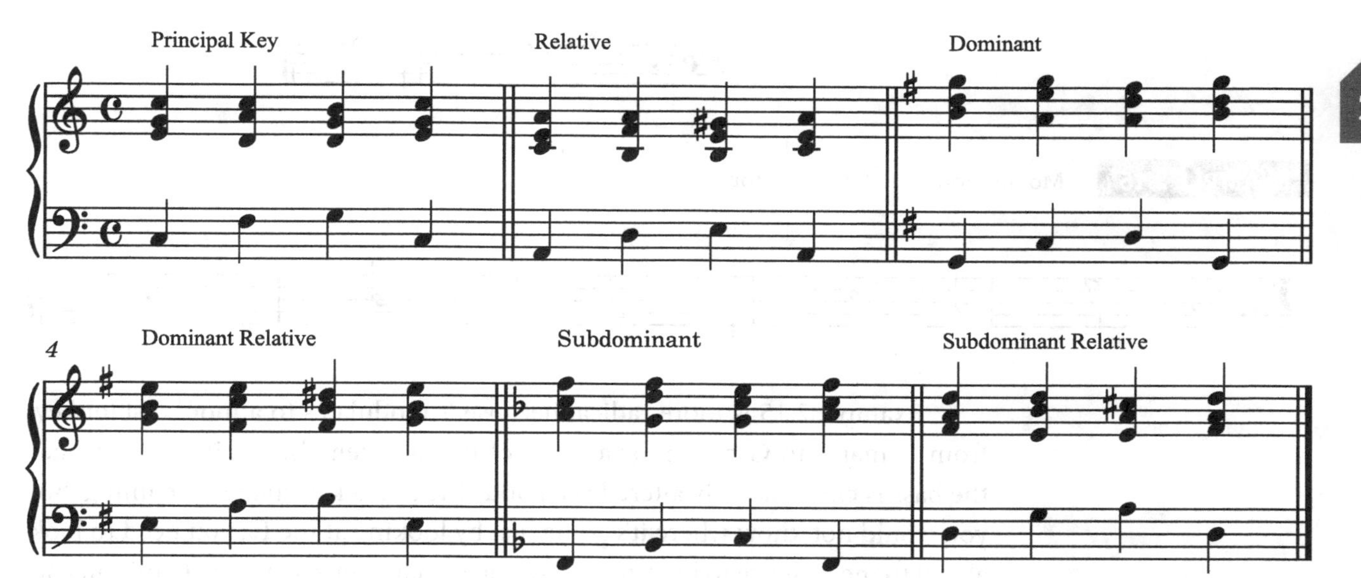

It is also possible to move to the parallel key, although this is a more striking move and may suggest a somewhat later style. Every harmonic decision evokes an historical era. Because the partimento tradition began in the seventeenth century and persisted well into the nineteenth, we will see wide stylistic variety as we study a range of partimenti.

To realize a partimento with modulations, I recommend an orderly and systematic process. Find all the cadences first, noting the key of each. Then back up and locate the *earliest possible* moment of termination, when the old key ended and the new key began. At the moment of termination, you have to change from the old scale to the new scale. Sometimes this is rather obvious, as in the second measure of Example 2.13, where the termination is on F♯.

Since F♯ does not exist in the previous key of C major, it is easy to see that this note will now serve as ⑦ of G major, and you should harmonize it with RO in that key.

Less obvious is the next modulation. In Example 2.14, the bass creates a cadence in E minor. The termination happens on the A on the downbeat of the second measure. Previously the A would have served as ⑥ of C major, but now is ④ of E minor. Therefore, on the A, you should harmonize with RO in E minor.

EXAMPLE 2.13 Locating termination in a partimento

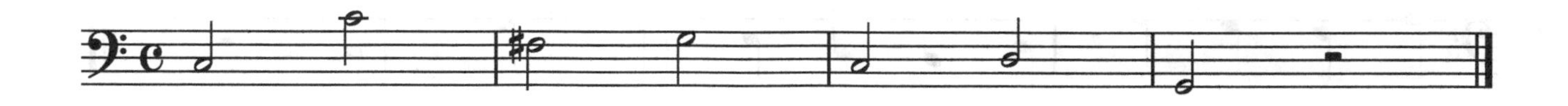

EXAMPLE 2.14 A cadence in E minor

EXAMPLE 2.15 Modulation from C to G minor

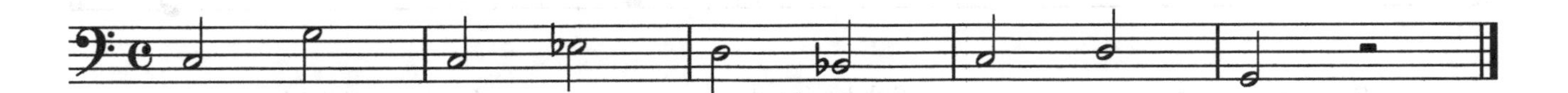

Example 2.15 is more radical because it modulates to a more distant key, from C major to G minor, or a jump of two accidentals. Again, the fact that the bass is chromatically altered is a good clue that a key change is coming, but you would not know where it's going just by looking at the E♭; you need to look ahead to the cadence to be sure. The E♭ will be harmonized as ⑥ of G minor, and from there you can move forward to the cadence.

Furno #4

Sometimes the exact moment of termination is not possible to determine with certainty. Instead, we see a range wherein the actual key change might occur. In the seventh measure of Furno's fourth partimento, seen in Example 2.16, a cadence confirms D minor on the downbeat. It is possible to take the very next note, the F, as having moved to A minor, and harmonize it as such. It is also possible to wait until the absolute last possible moment, the downbeat of the eighth measure. Thus we see that we have *earliest and latest moments* of possible termination.

EXAMPLE 2.16 Furno #4

Furno's explanation of terminations is very brief and may be confusing because he does not distinguish between stepwise motions that do and do not initiate terminations. Usually you can solve your modulation problems by looking ahead to find the cadence, and then backing up to locate the termination.

Furno #5

In the fifth partimento, shown in Example 2.17, two terminations are *not* followed by cadences. In measure 20, B♮ moves to C, but immediately back to B♭. This should be obvious as a momentary visitation of C major without the confirmation of a cadence. Similarly, near the end, B♮ once again approaches the C, which is a whole note and therefore a probable location of a double cadence. Again, the unconfirmed, brief visitation of C major is not confusing.

EXERCISE. Copy Furno's fourth and fifth partimenti into your zibaldone. Find every cadence. Then back up and find the terminations. Label these events. If there is a range of possible terminations, label these and prepare to harmonize in more than one way, exploring the implications of locating the

EXAMPLE 2.17 Furno #5

termination in different places. You may even wish to notate what RO scale is in effect throughout each piece. Provide solutions for the upper parts that use good voice-leading, and play them. Correct anything that does not sound like music. Transpose to other keys. Stylize as figuration prelude and unmeasured

EXAMPLE 2.18 Furno #5 as a figuration prelude

EXAMPLE 2.18 Continued

fantasia. Example 2.18 shows one possible solution of Furno #5 as a figuration prelude.

Bass Motions

Beginning with Furno #6, we enter the world of bass motions, which are the improviser's formidable weapons. As you work through Furno's remaining partimenti, you will come to understand how bass motions work.

Curiously, Furno taught only six motions, leaving out many that he certainly knew and would have heard on a daily (perhaps hourly) basis. Similarly, Fenaroli's predecessor Francesco Durante (1684–1755) taught a certain set of motions, but then others appear in his didactic compositions. The same could be said of almost any teacher: they taught some, but used many more. From this scattered approach, I speculate that most treatises were intended to give a broad idea how bass motions work, and students were expected to pick up the remainder on their own.

Once you understand how much information bass motions convey, you will see that Roman numerals are of limited value for improvising. All the important news comes from bass motions. Roman numerals concentrate on each bass note *in isolation*, completely missing the point of the partimento tradition. Roman analysis is not wrong; it tells you true things. But it doesn't tell you the things you need to know when you improvise. When flying an airplane, you need an altimeter, not a stock market ticker.

Cascade

In his sixth partimento Furno introduces a bass motion that descends a third and rises a second. When extended, this motion creates a pattern of cascading thirds, so we will call it the Cascade. The first (higher) note takes a chord of the fifth. The second (lower) note takes a chord of the sixth. However, it is more common for the second chord to take $\substack{6\\5\\3}$ or simply $\substack{6\\5}$ if in three voices (four are required to create $\substack{6\\5\\3}$).

Furno also shows how to add suspended ninths to the chord of the fifth, so that each chord of the pattern contains dissonance that is resolved in the following chord, even as a new one is prepared. These overlapping chains of dissonance and consonance give the Cascade a rich and intriguing sound. What is more, the dissonances vary in intensity between each chord, as some seconds, sevenths, and ninths (depending on the position and voicing of the right hand) are minor and some are major. Example 2.19 shows Furno's ideas for Cascade with some additional options. Note the parallel fifths between inner voices; Furno doesn't care.

Furno #6

The sixth partimento includes everything we have studied so far: Rule of the Octave, cadences, terminations, and the Cascade. Furno #6 appears in Example 2.20.

EXERCISE. Copy Furno #6 into your zibaldone. Find and label all the cadences, and note what key is confirmed. Back up from each cadence and find the earliest and latest possible moments of termination, and label them. Highlight each key area so you always know what scale and RO pattern to use at any given time. Find the Cascade motions in the partimento, and label them. Everything left over, that is neither cadences nor Cascade, is RO. Realize the partimento with right-hand chords, avoiding parallels between outer voices. Transpose the partimento and play it in other keys. Example 2.21 shows a possible solution.

EXERCISE. Stylize Furno #6 as figuration preludes in three and four voices, and as an unmeasured fantasia. Transpose these stylizations to other keys.

EXAMPLE 2.19 Cascade

Ascending 5-6 and Descending 7-6

Furno's seventh partimento introduces two new stepwise bass motions, Ascending 5-6 and Descending 7-6, which are shown in Example 2.22.

Ascending 5-6 is amusing when you think of it as a way to avoid parallel fifths. We do not use parallel stepwise chords of the fifth between exposed voices,

EXAMPLE 2.20 Furno #6

of course, but if the fifth moves up to a sixth and the other voices follow later, it would dodge the accusation of parallels. While this may seem like a sneaky way to follow the letter of the law while violating its spirit, in fact Ascending 5-6 sounds very beautiful and contains no hint of parallels.

Descending 7-6 contains a dissonant seventh and so it must always be prepared. A common way to prepare is to begin with a chord of the fifth, raise the fifth to a sixth, and then drop the other voices. Normally when a 7-6 goes from ② to ① the upper voices will resolve according to the manner shown in Example 2.23. Likewise, when moving from ⑥ to ⑤ the upper voices will resolve as if treating ⑤ as ①.

In Furno's teaching, 5-6 and 7-6 happen over longer note values in the bass. Furno is showing that each bass note supports two harmonies, so it makes sense that the bass note should be two beats long. In real music, things don't necessarily work this way. For example, a quarter note in the bass note could support a 5-6 if the upper voices consisted of eighth notes. But for the sake of simplicity, Furno assumes in these partimenti that the harmonic rhythm always moves in quarter notes.

The upper voices are invertible in 5-6 and 7-6 motions. This simple capability has profound implications; in most bass motions, the upper voices may readily trade places, resulting in the same harmony but a new texture. Further, while this technique has the appearance of a sophisticated feat of counterpoint, in fact it is almost effortless. Anyone who understands partimento can do it on the spot.

EXAMPLE 2.21 A realization of Furno #6

EXAMPLE 2.22 Ascending 5-6 and Descending 7-6

EXAMPLE 2.23 Beginning and concluding Descending 7-6

EXAMPLE 2.24 Furno #7

Furno #7

EXERCISE. Furno #7 appears in Example 2.24. Copy it into your zibaldone. Find and label all the cadences, and note what key is confirmed. Back up from

EXAMPLE 2.25 A realization of Furno #7

6

11

16

22

each cadence and find the earliest and latest possible moments of termination, and label them. Highlight each key area so you always know what scale and RO pattern to use at any given time. Find the 5-6 and 7-6 motions in the partimento, and label them. Everything else is RO. Realize the partimento with right-hand chords, avoiding soprano-bass parallels. Transpose the partimento and play it in other keys. Example 2.25 shows a realization for reference.

EXERCISE. Stylize Furno #7 as figuration preludes in three and four voices, and as an unmeasured fantasia. Transpose these stylizations to other keys.

C5 and Monte Romanesca

Furno's eighth partimento introduces two new motions. Both require a good deal of explanation, which Furno does not provide.

Furno describes the first motion as rising a fourth and falling a fifth. Of course, a rising fourth and falling fifth are the same thing. Many people refer to this motion as falling fifths or circle of fifths, but since one cannot fall too many fifths without dropping off the edge of the keyboard, in typical practice the motion alternates falling fifths with rising fourths in order to maintain a manageable range. In this book we will call this motion C5 (short for circle of fifths).

Each bass note of the C5 motion takes a chord of the fifth—sort of, but not really. While it is possible to accompany C5 with complete triads, most masters preferred a more agile and interesting harmonization with two upper voices. One voice takes a third above the bass and the other takes a seventh. The upper voices then take turns dropping by step. This pattern provides every bass note with a third and seventh, but the two upper voices take turns being the third and seventh. Their alternating stepwise motion nicely complements the leaping bass, and allows each dissonant seventh to be prepared by common tone.

Because sevenths are dissonant, each must be prepared by common tone. When a C5 motion begins, it may or may not be possible to prepare the first seventh—it depends on what happens before the start of the C5. In many cases the first bass note of the motion might have to take a third and fifth instead of a third and seventh.

It does not matter whether the third is in the middle or top voice; as with many bass motions, the upper voices may be traded. Because fifths invert to fourths, the upper voices don't look different on the page or keyboard when they trade parts. C5 may begin with the bass anywhere in the scale and continue as long as you like. If you keep going, you will end up where you began. Sometimes Antonio Vivaldi (1678–1741) likes to go around the circle twice, but most composers use shorter segments of C5.

C5 works in major and minor. In minor, the leading tone is normally lowered until the end of the motion. C5 is colorful, interesting, and harmonically powerful, and its voice-leading is idiot-proof. For these reasons it is among

EXAMPLE 2.26 The voice-leading of C5

the most frequently employed bass motions in eighteenth-century music. Example 2.26 shows how C5 works.

The other new motion in this partimento rises a fifths and falls a fourth. As these are the same thing, we can think of this motion as rising fifths. In his book *Music in the Galant Style* Robert Gjerdingen named this motion Monte Romanesca, so we will call it that, as well.

Just like C5, Monte Romanesca has a specific upper-voice solution. While it is possible to give each bass note chords of the fifth, this is not the most interesting or most common solution. Rather, the masters preferred a solution with a series of suspensions in both upper voices.

Monte Romanesca only works in major keys, and always starts on ①. It may go as far as ③ (①-⑤-②-⑥-③), and occasionally continues to ⑦. If it does go to ⑦, you will be forced to modulate.

The upper voices may trade places, in which case all the suspensions change in character. While all the suspensions are fourths against the bass, they also

EXAMPLE 2.27 The voice-leading of Monte Romanesca

create dissonant intervals between the upper voices: either sevenths or seconds. When the voices trade places, the seconds become sevenths and vice versa.

Most intriguingly, the Monte Romanesca solution taught by the masters arranges the upper voices in canon: one voice is an exact imitation of the other, either a fourth below or a fifth above. We will encounter more instances of "built-in canon" later in this book. Example 2.27 shows how the Monte Romanesca works.

Because the Monte Romanesca normally proceeds to ③ but no further, the motion requires an "exit strategy."

Furno's strategy in the partimento is to apply a scale mutation over ③ (in this case, a sharp third or A♯), moving the partimento into B minor for a while.

Furno #8

EXERCISE. Copy Furno #8, shown in Example 2.28, into your zibaldone. Find

EXAMPLE 2.28 Furno #8

and label all the cadences, and note what key is confirmed. Back up from each cadence and find the earliest and latest possible moments of termination, and label them. Highlight each key area so you always know what scale and RO pattern to use at any given time. Find the C5 and Monte Romanesca motions in the partimento, and label them. Everything else is RO. Realize the partimento with right-hand chords, avoiding soprano-bass parallels. Transpose the partimento and play it in other keys. Example 2.29 shows a transposed realization.

EXERCISE. Stylize Furno #8 as figuration preludes in three and four voices, and as an unmeasured fantasia. Transpose these stylizations to other keys.

EXAMPLE 2.29 A transposed realization of Furno #8

EXAMPLE 2.30 Furno #9

Furno #9

Furno's ninth partimento appears in Example 2.30.

Tied Bass

In the ninth partimento Furno introduces the Tied Bass motion, so called because it often involves notes tied across bar lines. In many cases, ties are a reliable visual cue that a Tied Bass is in play, as the motion requires the bass to sustain from a weaker beat to a stronger beat. However, it does not actually matter if the bass is tied; it can also be dotted, syncopated, or rearticulated, as long as the same pitch continues from a weak to a strong beat.

The stronger beat takes $\begin{smallmatrix}4\\2\end{smallmatrix}$ (or $\begin{smallmatrix}6\\4\\2\end{smallmatrix}$ if enough voices are present) but the second and fourth above the bass need not be prepared because they are not dissonances; *the bass is the dissonance!* The Tied Bass is unique among motions because the bass contains the dissonant notes, which we are accustomed to finding in the upper voices.

EXAMPLE 2.31 The voice-leading of Tied Bass

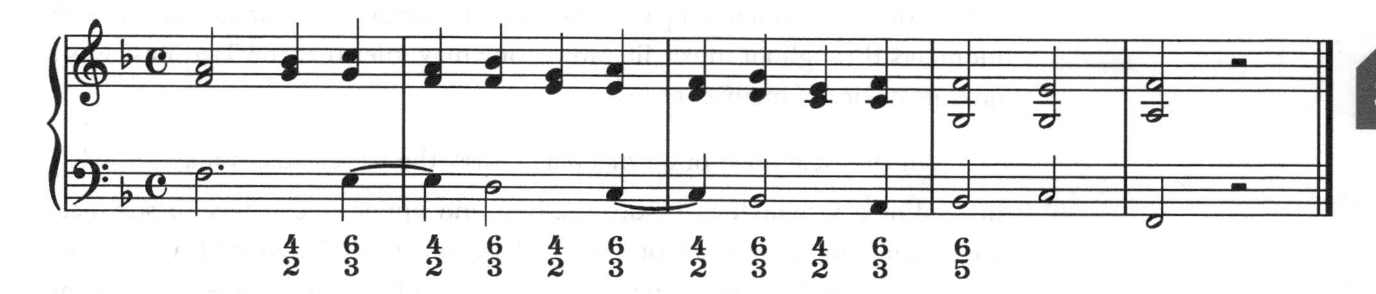

The bass falls by step to resolve the dissonance, and takes $^{6}_{3}$. If the Tied Bass motion continues, this same bass sustains and the upper voices provide the next $^{4}_{2}$. Example 2.31 shows the basic voice-leading model for the Tied Bass motion.

Furno explains three instances in which a syncopated bass results in a shorter series of events, not the typical extended Tied Bass motion shown in Example 2.31.

1. The bass is syncopated but does not descend a step after the syncopated note. This is not a real Tied Bass motion at all, and should be harmonized with consonant intervals.
2. The bass is syncopated, descends a half step, and returns to the original note. In this case the bass should be considered as ①-⑦-①. The syncopated note takes $^{4}_{2}$ (with a perfect fourth) on the strong beat, $^{6}_{3}$ or $\substack{6\\5\\3}$ on the weak beat, and $^{5}_{3}$ on the return.
3. If the resolution is not syncopated and continues down by step to another note after the resolution, the strong beat of the syncopated note will take $^{\#4}_{2}$ and the bass should be considered as ④-③.

Example 2.32 illustrates each situation described above.

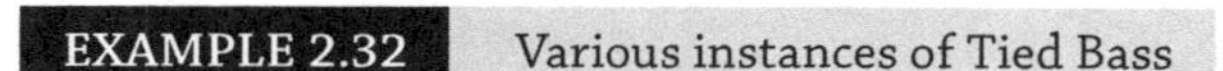

EXAMPLE 2.32 Various instances of Tied Bass

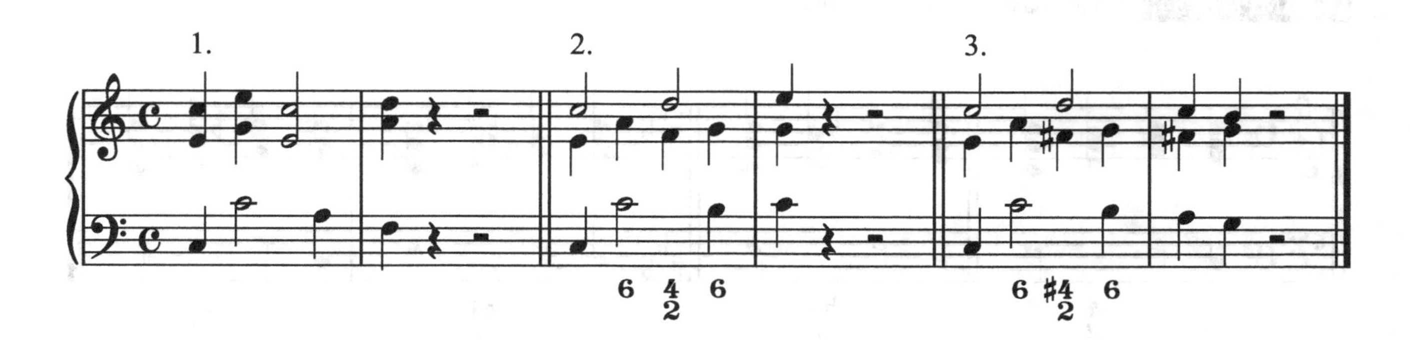

Furno includes all these situations in the ninth partimento. However, for purposes of improvisation, the most important use of the Tied Bass is in more extended, sequential passages. From its frequent appearance at dramatic moments throughout music literature, one may infer that the Tied Bass was a favorite device of many composers.

On the weak beat of a syncopated bass, the upper voices may provide $\substack{6\\5\\3}$ instead of $\substack{6\\3}$, in which case both the bass and upper voices have dissonance-consonance pairs, but out of sync with each other. This voice-leading plan, which requires four voices, results in two pairs of consonant intervals moving by turns: one holds while the other moves, as seen in Example 2.33.

Furno details further uses of the Tied Bass. When descending from ④ to ③, an augmented fourth will preserve the current tonality, but a perfect fourth will instigate a departure to a new key. Note that in minor, this second case will also require a lowered sixth above the bass. Major and minor instances of this idea appear in Example 2.34.

EXAMPLE 2.33 Tied Bass in four voices

EXAMPLE 2.34 Tied Bass in major and minor

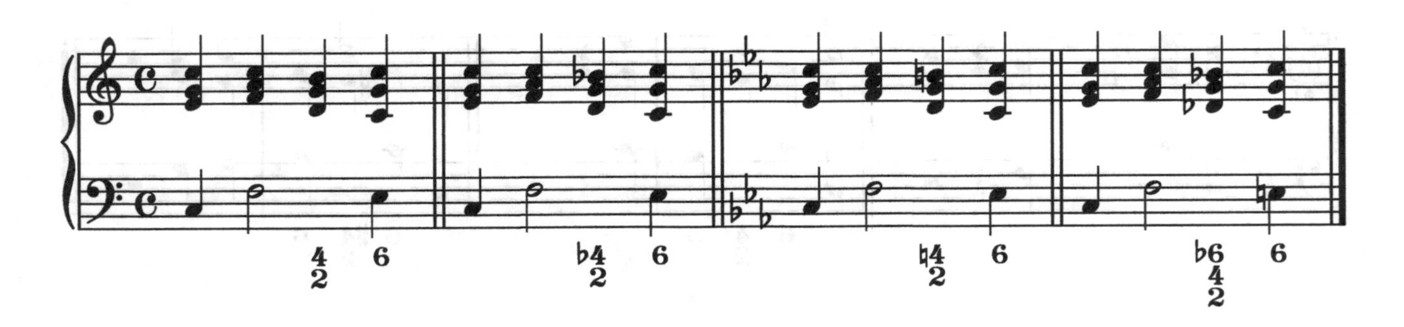

EXAMPLE 2.35 Furno's Tied Bass on ⑥ and ⑤ in minor keys

Example 2.35 shows Furno's recommendations for Tied Bass motions beginning on ⑥ and ⑤ in minor keys.

It is also possible to realize a Tied Bass motion with descending thirds or sixths in parallel motion above the bass. In this model, $\genfrac{}{}{0pt}{}{4}{2}$ resolves to $\genfrac{}{}{0pt}{}{5}{3}$. It is not as colorful as the usual $\genfrac{}{}{0pt}{}{4}{2}$ to $\genfrac{}{}{0pt}{}{6}{3}$(or $\genfrac{}{}{0pt}{}{6}{5}$) but does appear in real music sometimes. Two versions appear in Example 2.36.

While Tied Bass has no absolute stopping point at which it cannot continue, descending a full octave from ① to ① does not work well because the arrival at the lower ① is on a chord of the sixth, which is not the strong conclusion one hoped for. Unlike C5, which can travel all the way from ① to ① and sound good, Tied Bass usually breaks off at ③. Example 2.37 illustrates the situation.

EXAMPLE 2.36 A variant of Tied Bass

EXAMPLE 2.37 Concluding a Tied Bass motion

When initiating a Tied Bass motion (especially from ① or ⑤), Furno prefers the use of an augmented fourth, although this is not strictly necessary according to the rules of harmony. Fenaroli also recommends this. Example 2.38 shows one of Fenaroli's solutions in which ① takes the augmented fourth. In fact, two other bass notes also take the augmented fourth, yet they do not cause a departure from the key.

EXERCISE. Before working on Furno #9, practice the variants of the Tied Bass motion explained previously. Do so in many major and minor keys. Practice in rhythm, as the metric placement of $\frac{4}{2}$ on strong beats is absolutely required. Remember that you cannot easily extend Tied Bass for a full descending scale, so you should practice exiting the motion, which is normally done at ③. When you are confident in playing Tied Bass, work through Furno #9 in the usual way: recognize, realize, stylize.

EXAMPLE 2.38 Fenaroli's solution for starting Tied Bass on ①

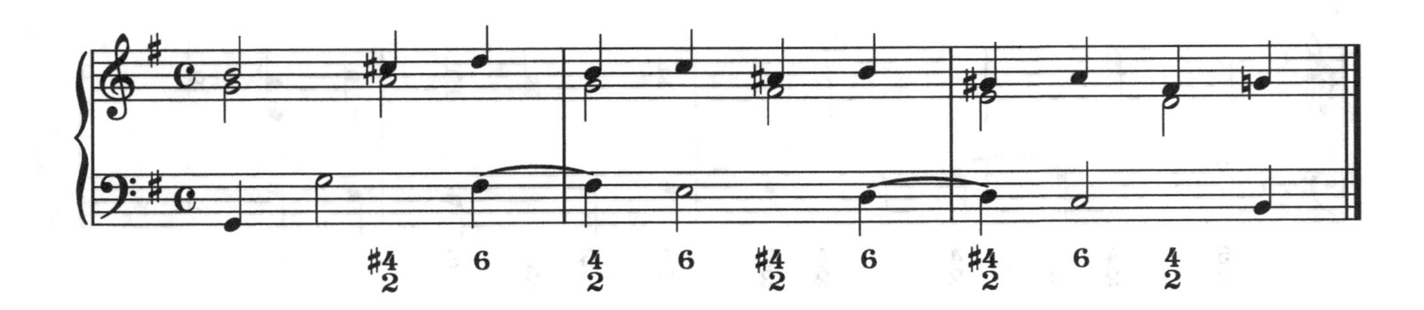

Furno #10

Furno's tenth partimento puts everything from the treatise together in one big puzzle. While the other nine required RO, cadences, and one or two bass motions, the tenth employs every concept Furno has presented—almost. He leaves out one, with no explanation. I will leave it to you to figure out which.

EXERCISE. Since we have no new bass motions to learn, we can begin solving the partimento right away. Example 2.39 presents, in graphic form, the first step of partimento work: to recognize. The example shows the partimento with indications of cadences and key areas above the staff, and bass motions below. Any region not marked as a bass motion is RO. Example 2.40 shows one possible realization. Consult these examples if necessary, but try to solve the partimento on your own first.

EXAMPLE 2.39 Furno #10

EXAMPLE 2.40 A realization of Furno #10

EXAMPLE 2.40 Continued

Chapter 3

Bass Diminution

Having studied Furno's partimenti, you have learned to use Rule of the Octave, cadences, terminations (also called modulations or scale mutations), and a few bass motions to solve a partimento. An important concept, found in almost all partimento collections but not in Furno, is *bass diminution*. Furno passes over the idea completely in his treatise, but most other partimenti assume knowledge of it, so we must pause here to discuss it.

Bass diminutions are extra, decorative notes in the bass line. In Furno one becomes accustomed to regarding every bass note as requiring harmonization in the upper voices, which is a good first step. But real music usually does not work that way. In real music, the bass may be elaborated with all manner of passing tones, neighbors, arpeggios, and other "non-essentials." They are non-essential because they do not determine the upper voice harmonization. Only *structural* bass notes do that. Some columns hold up buildings, while others are cosmetic. Sometimes the cosmetic elements are quite visible, while the structural ones may be concealed. However, an experienced engineer can immediately tell what is really holding the building up.

The purpose of working with bass diminutions is twofold. First, you must learn to look beyond them to discern the structural notes that determine harmony. Second, you must develop a sense of taste and style so that you can add diminutions to a bass to make it more interesting. You must learn both to add and to take away diminutions. We will begin by working on some partimenti of Fenaroli, learning to see beyond the bass diminutions to the structural notes.

Bass Diminution in Partimenti

In Fenaroli's third partimento (Gj 1303), shown in Example 3.1, the bass moves sometimes in quarter notes and sometimes in eighths. Some of the eighths are diminutions. It is possible to consider the first and third eighths of each

EXAMPLE 3.1 Fenaroli's partimento Gj 1303

four-note group as structural. Following Rule of the Octave, in most cases, the first note will require $\frac{5}{3}$ and the third will take $\frac{6}{3}$. Alternatively, one could take only the first note as structural, and the remaining three as diminutions. There is not much difference between these two solutions; they will sound similar.

EXERCISE. Work through Fenaroli's third partimento, recognizing cadences and modulations and identifying structural notes in the midst of diminutions. Realize it with chords. Then stylize it as a figuration prelude. Fenaroli's original has figures, but I have removed them in the example because at this point you should not need them.

Fenaroli's first and second partimenti (Gj 1301 and 1302), shown in Example 3.2, will now seem very simple in comparison with his third, since the first uses no bass diminutions and the second has very few. Again, I have removed Fenaroli's figures because you already know too much.

EXERCISE. Recognize, realize, and stylize Fenaroli's first and second partimenti.

Fenaroli's fifth partimento (Gj 1305), shown in Example 3.3, employs RO, cadences, modulations, and bass motions. Its quirkiness lies in the delay of the bass on many strong beats, and also in the uncommon tonality of B major, a bit unusual for that era. Fenaroli's purpose is to show that even

EXAMPLE 3.2 Fenaroli's partimenti Gj 1301 and 1302

though the "late" bass changes the character of the piece, the rules for realization are unaffected.

EXERCISE. Recognize, realize, and stylize Fenaroli's fifth partimento. The stylization should be neither figuration nor unmeasured fantasia. Develop your own, taking cues from the character of the bass. Once again, the original figures have been removed.

Fenaroli's sixth partimento (Gj 1306), shown in Example 3.4, introduces no new problems and provides further experience with bass diminutions.

EXERCISE. Recognize, realize, and stylize Fenaroli's sixth partimento.

EXAMPLE 3.3 Fenaroli's partimento Gj 1305

Adding Diminutions to Bass Lines

Now that you have learned to "take away" bass diminutions by seeing past them to structural notes, we will reverse the process and begin adding diminutions to unadorned bass lines.

Bass diminutions take many forms, but generally consist of repeated notes, nonharmonic tones, scale segments, or arpeggios. Repeated notes may be all of the same rhythmic value, or of varied durations. Nonharmonic tones include passing, neighbor, and escape tones. Scale segments may be a section of a scale, or may encompass a full octave or more. Arpeggios may appear as a pattern involving the structural note and a third above, or as an outline of a complete harmony. Most partimenti include several different kinds of bass diminution, and the style of diminution may also hint at the formal structure. For example, when a diminution pattern from earlier in a partimento appears near the end, quite possibly this is a signal to recapitulate thematic material used previously.

Masters seem not to have permitted students the comfort of "quarter-notes-only" partimenti for very long; by the third example from Fenaroli's Book I, most bass notes are decorated with diminutions. (Furno is an exception to this

EXAMPLE 3.4 Fenaroli's partimento Gj 1306

tendency.) By the way, you should not assume that just because a partimento is written in quarter notes that those notes are structural; some of them just might be diminutions.

Partimenti of Cotumacci

Examples 3.5–3.7 are partimenti of Carlo Cotumacci (1709–1785) from his *Partimenti, Fughe e Disposizioni al Contrapunto*. All are in the unadorned style you encountered in Furno, where each bass note is to be taken as structural.

EXAMPLE 3.5 A partimento of Cotumacci

EXAMPLE 3.6 A partimento of Cotumacci

EXAMPLE 3.7 A partimento of Cotumacci

These partimenti (which Cotumacci calls *Lezzione*—same thing) are presented under the heading *Regola di Seconda e Quarta Sul basso Sincopato, Legato, Puntato, o Raddopiato* (Rule of Seconds and Fourths on Syncopated, Tied, Dotted, and Repeated Basses). That should tell you something about what motions to expect.

EXERCISE. For each partimento in Examples 3.5–3.7, recognize the cadences and key areas. Determine what bass motion applies to each passage (there may be multiple correct answers). Realize the partimento in block chords. Then elaborate the bass with diminutions, drawing on those you have encountered in Fenaroli. Add interesting features to the upper voices when possible, such as occasional passing tones or suspensions. Once you have created a satisfactory stylization, transpose it.

Example 3.8 presents one possibility for adding diminutions to Cotumacci's third partimento from Example 3.7. The right-hand part is limited to simple chords so that you may give your attention to the diminutions in the bass.

EXAMPLE 3.8 Diminutions for a Cotumacci partimento

EXAMPLE 3.8 Continued

Chapter 4

After Furno

In Furno, you learned about bass motions such as Cascade, 5-6, 7-6, C5, Monte Romanesca, and Tied Bass. These are only a few of the many standard bass motions from the eighteenth century. Our work has hardly begun! This chapter explains more standard motions beyond those in Furno.

The bass motions that follow are organized according to how they move, and each is accompanied by a partimento for practice. You should take a long time with these, practice them in multiple ways, and get to know them thoroughly. Don't worry if you can't retain them all in your mind and hands after working through this chapter just once; absorbing a vast repertoire of motions requires sustained practice. Though in some cases I have named motions after specific people, that does not mean that the person invented the motion. All these motions were taught and played by countless musicians.

For this chapter I wrote the partimenti that accompany each bass motion, because real partimenti almost always mix multiple motions together, as you saw in Furno #10. As each new motion is introduced, it is better if you can practice it initially in isolation and not have to untangle it from others. Therefore, each of my made-up partimenti includes the new motion in question, bits of RO, modulations, and cadences. In good time we will move on to far more complex challenges, including partimenti with many different motions.

Stepwise Ascending and Descending Motions

Fauxbourdon, shown in Example 4.1, moves by ascending or descending step. It is the only motion that freely ascends and descends in the same way, every bass note taking a chord of the sixth. The motion is unlimited as it has no specific point past which it cannot continue, either rising or falling.

The origin of Fauxbourdon goes back to the dawn of harmony, and it is one of the oldest chord patterns. It is not perhaps the most interesting bass motion, since it consists only of chords of the sixth, and may sound bland. However,

EXAMPLE 4.1 Fauxbourdon

EXAMPLE 4.2 Fauxbourdon in music of Alessandro Scarlatti

its simplicity and flexibility (and the fact that it is unlimited) make it an ideal tool for improvisation. Falling Fauxbourdon is somewhat more common in music than rising, but both are possible. In minor keys Fauxbourdon typically uses the natural form of the scale to avoid augmented seconds. Alessandro Scarlatti (1660–1725) was completely addicted to this motion and used it for extended passages in his keyboard toccatas, a selection from which is shown in Example 4.2.

EXERCISE. Examples 4.3–4.8 show my Six Boring Perfunctory Stepwise Partimenti in which the rising and falling bass lines may be realized with any

EXAMPLE 4.3 Boring Perfunctory Stepwise Partimento #1

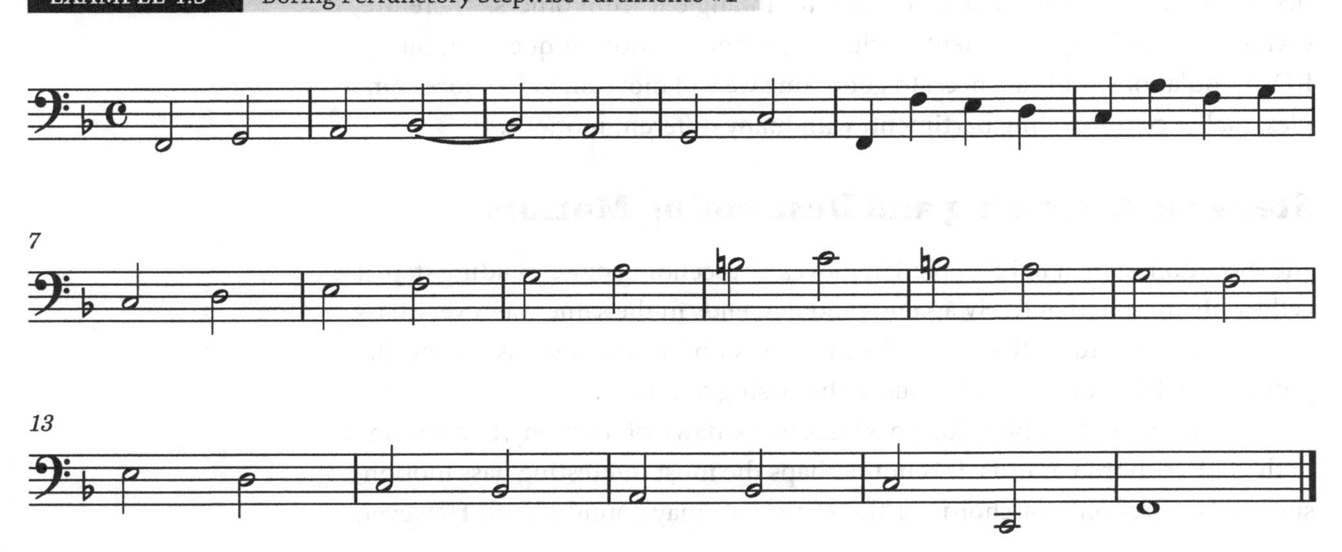

EXAMPLE 4.4 Boring Perfunctory Stepwise Partimento #2

combination of stepwise motions. For now, use Fauxbourdon. Realize them first in block chords, and then stylize them with interesting figuration. Finally, transpose them to other keys.

Stepwise Ascending Motions

Along with Rule of the Octave and 5-6 (which you learned from Furno), three more standard ascending stepwise motions are available.

As the name implies, 8-7-6 takes place in three stages. The bass takes a third and an octave. The bass and the third rise a step, turning the octave into a seventh above the bass. The seventh resolves to a sixth, but to set up for the next iteration of the motion, jumps up to an octave before the bass moves again. The upper voices are interchangeable. Fenaroli taught 8-7-6, as seen in Example 4.9.

EXAMPLE 4.8 Boring Perfunctory Stepwise Partimento #6

EXAMPLE 4.9 Fenaroli's 8-7-6

10-9-8 works exactly like 8-7-6 except that the voice that shall become dissonant starts a tenth above the bass rather than an octave. In a lovely variant, both the 10-9-8 and 8-7-6 may be played at the same time. That is, the bass will rise by step accompanied by a third above. The two highest voices will take an octave and tenth above the bass, which become dissonant as a ninth and seventh when the bass rises. These two dissonances resolve, then jump up a third before the next step in the bass. The bass and its third may be spaced apart as a tenth, and the upper voices may be similarly spaced (although most hands won't be able to reach this configuration). The upper third (or tenth) may also be inverted to a sixth. Interestingly, the configuration with both pairs in tenths may be "interlocked" so that bass and alto move together, and tenor and soprano move together. These motions appear in Example 4.10.

EXAMPLE 4.10 10-9-8 and variants

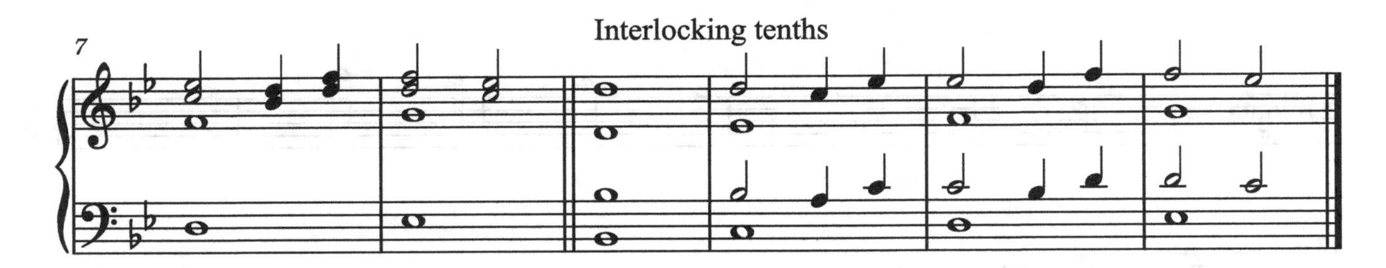

EXERCISE. You previously realized Examples 4.3–4.8 with Fauxbourdon. Now solve the rising bass lines with 8-7-6, 10-9-8, and the 10-9-8 variant, while continuing to use Fauxbourdon (or RO or 7-6) for the falling lines. After you have realized them, stylize them and transpose to several keys.

The Corelli Leapfrog is a glorious example of how a sneaky scheme to stay within the letter of the law of voice-leading can result in sublime music. This motion is named for Arcangelo Corelli (1653–1713) who used it frequently and beautifully, especially in his trio sonatas. The Leapfrog begins with a tenth and ninth above the bass. (The ninth must be prepared by common tone, of course.) The dissonant ninth resolves by step. The bass then rises a step, and the goal is to create another tenth with a prepared dissonant ninth against it. But there is no way to do this using normal voice-leading. Therefore, the upper voice remains in place to become the dissonance, and the lower voice *jumps over it* to form the consonant tenth. Then they trade again for the next stage. Sheer genius! One can invert the upper voices, as well, in which case they do not cross. Fenaroli offers a clever solution for the Leapfrog in which the voices do not cross, but in practice (on the keyboard, anyway) it differs only slightly from the standard Leapfrog. Example 4.11 illustrates all these versions of the Corelli Leapfrog. As you can see, Fenaroli's solution is not really so different from a 10-9-8.

Unfortunately, voices do not audibly cross on keyboard instruments (except on separate organ or harpsichord manuals with distinct registrations). On the piano, anyhow, there is no obvious way to communicate the successive climbing quality—each voice striving to outdo the other with intensity and longing—that is the essential aesthetic of the Leapfrog. As a further crushing disappointment, decorating this motion with typical keyboard figurations is

EXAMPLE 4.11 The Corelli Leapfrog

almost impossible due to the proximity of the voices (when arranged in seconds and thirds) or their distance (when inverted to ninths and tenths). For these reasons, the Corelli Leapfrog, though much favored in vocal and instrumental music, is rare in keyboard literature.

Another variant of the Leapfrog doubles the dissonances. Now each bass note will have a consonant tenth along with a dissonant ninth and seventh, resolving to an octave and a sixth. It is possible to configure this as a crossing motion by lofting the third voice from the top (the "tenor") above the soprano. I will call this motion the Doublefrog and get it in print before someone decides the name is too undignified for academic usage. Example 4.12 shows how the Doublefrog works.

EXERCISE. Develop another realization of the Six Boring Perfunctory Stepwise Partimenti from Examples 4.3–4.8 using Corelli Leapfrog for the ascending lines. Try all the variants. Use RO, Fauxbourdon, or 7-6 for the descending lines. Stylize the partimenti with simple diminutions and transpose.

EXAMPLE 4.12 The Doublefrog

EXAMPLE 4.13 A four-voice variant of 5-6

Just as the 8-7-6 and 10-9-8 may combined into a four-voice texture, the Ascending 5-6 may also have a fourth voice added. In this variant, the fourth voice begins by doubling the bass but delays moving, creating a dissonant seventh. This dissonance must fall to resolve, so just as in 8-7-6 and 10-9-8, this voice must descend by step and then leap up a third before the next movement of the bass. In other words, this variant combines 5-6 with 8-7-6, as seen in Example 4.13. There is almost no end to bass motion variants. For present purposes, those shown in this chapter will be enough. If you'd like to see many more, consult the *Marches d'harmonie* of Luigi Cherubini (1760–1842), available on partimenti.org.

EXERCISE. Work through the Six Boring Perfunctory Stepwise Partimenti, realizing ascending lines with the 5-6 variant. Use RO, Fauxbourdon, or 7-6 for descending lines.

Stepwise Descending Motions

Furno showed you the 7-6 and the Tied Bass for solving stepwise descending lines. Three more standard stepwise descending motions are available.

The Stepwise Romanesca walks down the scale alternating chords of the fifth with chords of the sixth. Most typically it begins on ① and descends as far as ③, although it may go to ②. It usually will not keep going to ① because that would result in ① taking a chord of the sixth, which sounds weird. So, unlike Rule of the Octave, a complete traversal of eight notes of the scale with Stepwise Romanesca does not result in a satisfying harmonic statement. The bass may always be accompanied by a third or tenth, while the other upper voice will alternate between fifths and sixths. The Stepwise Romanesca works in both major and minor, taking the natural form in the latter. Example 4.14 shows this motion.

EXERCISE. Realize Examples 4.3–4.8 using Stepwise Romanesca for the descending lines, and any motions you like for the rising lines. Stylize and transpose the partimenti.

3-#4-6, another stepwise descending motion, intersperses diatonic harmonies with chromatic ones. It typically begins on ① and descends to ③. ①

EXAMPLE 4.14 The Stepwise Romanesca

takes $\begin{smallmatrix}5\\3\end{smallmatrix}$ followed by a $\begin{smallmatrix}\#4\\2\end{smallmatrix}$. The bass descends a step and takes $\begin{smallmatrix}6\\3\end{smallmatrix}$. The bass descends again, taking first $\begin{smallmatrix}5\\3\end{smallmatrix}$ and then another $\begin{smallmatrix}\#4\\2\end{smallmatrix}$, resolving to $\begin{smallmatrix}6\\3\end{smallmatrix}$ as the bass drops. Like the Stepwise Romanesca, this pattern will result in ① taking a chord of the sixth if continued all the way down the scale, so most frequently 3-#4-6 terminates at ③. The motion works in major and minor, and the upper voices may be inverted. In minor, a melodic augmented second may result, and this is acceptable. Example 4.15 shows this bass motion.

EXERCISE. Realize Examples 4.3–4.8 using 3-#4-6 for the descending lines, and any available motions for the rising lines. Stylize and transpose the partimenti.

A variant of 7-6 adds a fourth voice. This variant may be configured as two pairs of tenths taking turns descending by step—double parallel tenths, so I call this variant DP10. It appears in the opening movement of Handel's suite HWV

EXAMPLE 4.15 3-♯4-6

EXAMPLE 4.16 Handel's DP10

429. This variant may also be reconfigured into two pairs of thirds or a tenth encompassing a third. Two voices will be on the beat, while the other two are off the beat. Example 4.16 shows Handel's original followed by a reduced version in structural notes only, along with additional versions.

EXERCISE. Apply DP10 to Examples 4.3–4.8, using it for descending lines. Use anything you want for ascending lines. Stylize and transpose the partimento.

Passacaglia occurs in minor only, beginning on ① and descending to ⑤. The bass motion we call Passacaglia is often found in pieces of music by the same name, which are sets of variations on the descending bass. ① takes a chord of the fifth, diatonic ⑦ takes a chord of the sixth, diatonic ⑥ takes a seventh resolving to a sixth, and ⑤ takes a raised third and an octave. The upper voices are invertible. The Passacaglia motion appears in Example 4.17.

EXERCISE. Example 4.18 is a partimento in which the descending lines may be realized by Passacaglia. Use motions you already know for the remainder of the bass.

EXAMPLE 4.17 Passacaglia

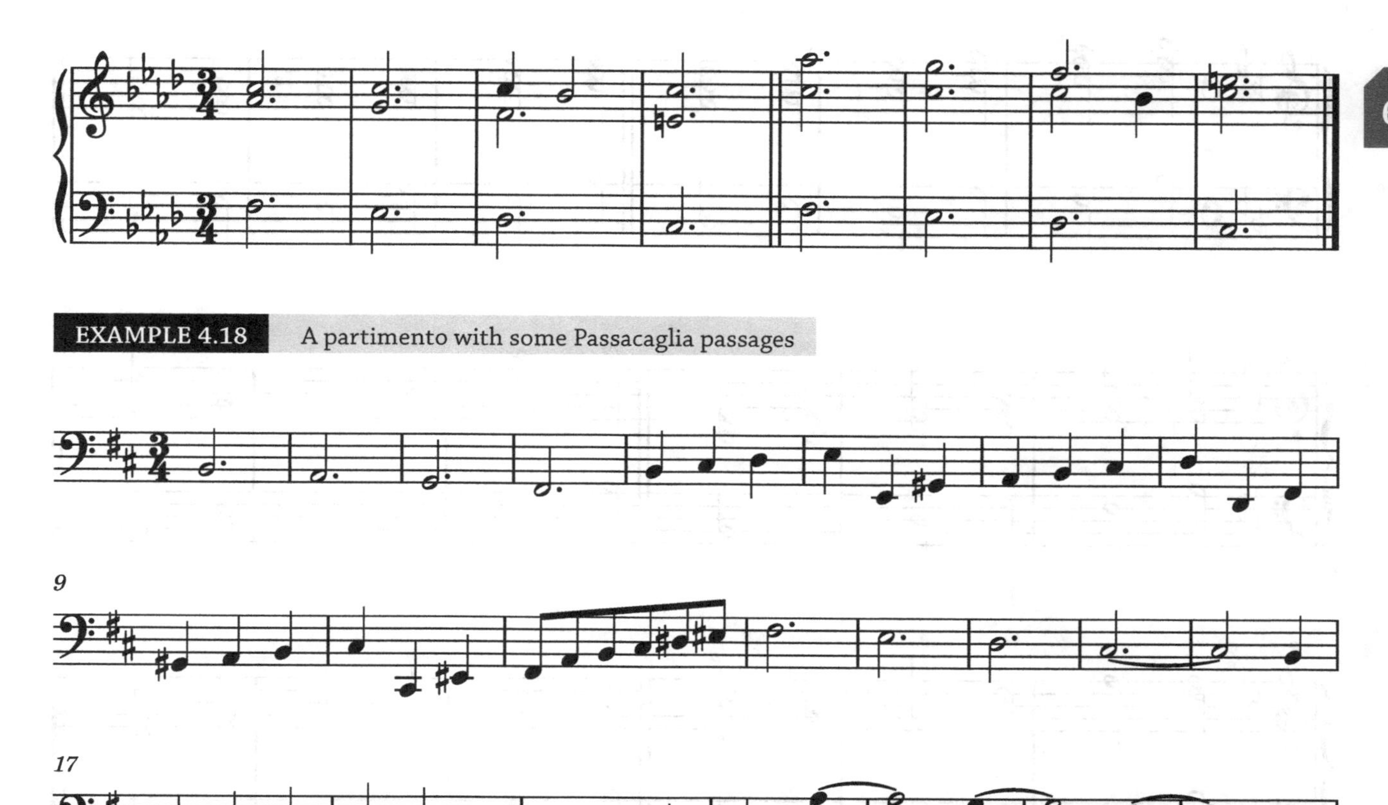

EXAMPLE 4.18 A partimento with some Passacaglia passages

Disjunct Motions

Disjunct motions, which consist of leaps or a combination of leaps and steps, are plentiful. Along with those taught in Furno (Cascade, C5, and Monte Romanesca), other standards include Leaping Romanesca, Perfidia, Monte Principale, Dolareti, Domirefa, and Falling Thirds.

The Leaping Romanesca falls a fourth and rises a second. It begins on ① and may continue until it reaches ① an octave lower, as follows: ①-⑤-⑥-③-④-①. Leaping Romanesca may take two or three upper voices, and it may begin

EXAMPLE 4.19 The Leaping Romanesca

with these upper voices in any position, resulting in several contrapuntal combinations, as seen in Example 4.19.

EXERCISE. Example 4.20 is a partimento that calls for a Leaping Romanesca. Realize, stylize, and transpose it.

Perfidia is simply a variant of Leaping Romanesca in which every bass note takes a suspension. In the prototypical form, the suspensions against the bass occur in a single voice, tied and descending by step, resulting in alternating suspensions of the fourth and ninth above the bass. Perfidia works with three or four voices in total. When in three, the two upper voices often move as 2-3 or 7-6 patterns. Perfidia functions equally well in major and minor. As you might expect, the upper voices may be inverted. Remember that the intervals in the bass may be inverted, so that a rising fifth may be substituted for a falling fourth, and a falling seventh may stand in for a rising second. Example 4.21 shows Perfidia in three and four voices.

EXERCISE. Return to Example 4.20, this time applying Perfidia as appropriate. Stylize and transpose the exercise.

Monte Principale rises a fourth and falls a third, all bass notes taking chords of the fifth, with an option for suspensions. The intervals are the same as Dolareti (to be explained shortly), but the rhythmic placement is different.

EXAMPLE 4.20 A partimento with some Leaping Romanesca passages

The partimento masters did not consider Monte Principale and Dolareti to be variants of the same motion. In a chromatic version, each pair of chords is major until the bass reaches ⑥ (which will be minor), creating a series of V-I relationships. This variant may also take 4-3 suspensions. Monte Principale begins on ①, always on a stronger beat. Because of the constant use of chords

EXAMPLE 4.21 Perfidia

EXAMPLE 4.22 Monte Principale

of the fifth, one must watch for parallels. While the motion may theoretically continue as far as you like (including hitting those diminished harmonies on ⑦ in major and ② in minor), in real music Monte Principale normally carries on for just a few stages, not a complete octave. Example 4.22 demonstrates several possible dispositions of this motion.

EXERCISE. Example 4.23 is a partimento that requires Monte Principale and some other motions you already know. Realize, stylize, and transpose it.

Rising Sixths leaps up a sixth and falls a fifth, so we might call it Dolareti, from the solfège syllables Do La Re Ti. As Fenaroli states, this is the same as falling a third and rising a fourth, which is like a backwards Monte Principale.

EXAMPLE 4.23 A partimento with some Monte Principale passages

Monte Principale and Dolareti are considered as separate motions in Fenaroli; the rhythmic placement makes them different. In Dolareti the first note takes a chord of the fifth and the second a chord of the sixth, with an option for a 7-6 suspension.

One reason Monte Principale and Dolareti take different solutions is that Dolareti will hit ⑦ as its fourth bass note (assuming it begins on ①). ⑦ will not work with a chord of the fifth but is fine with a chord of the sixth. Fenaroli's models for Dolareti appear in Example 4.24.

EXERCISE. Example 4.25 requires Dolareti and other familiar motions. Realize, stylize, and transpose it.

EXAMPLE 4.24 Fenaroli's Dolareti

EXAMPLE 4.25 A partimento for Dolareti and other motions

Rising Thirds leaps up a third and falls a step, and therefore we could call it Domirefa after the syllables Do Mi Re Fa. The motion has several solutions. The simplest would be merely to consider the second (higher) note as a diminution, and harmonize the lower notes with Rule of the Octave. This isn't really a solution to Domirefa per se, but a reimagination of it as RO. Fenaroli offers three solutions, the first of which does actually resemble RO in some ways. His second solution combines a rising chromatic line with a tied, suspended voice in the upper voices. His third idea creates a series of 7-6 suspensions. All these may be easily converted to function in minor keys. Example 4.26 shows Fenaroli's three solutions to Domirefa.

EXERCISE. Example 4.27 requires Domirefa and other familiar motions. Realize, stylize, and transpose it.

Falling Thirds does what it says: it falls by a third multiple times. It takes chords of the fifth on each note. This motion may continue until it arrives where it began, although the bass will likely transpose up an octave (perhaps more than once) to remain within practical range. The upper voices maintain smooth

EXAMPLE 4.26 Fenaroli's Domirefa

EXAMPLE 4.27 A partimento for Domirefa and other motions

EXAMPLE 4.28 Falling Thirds

EXAMPLE 4.29 A partimento for Falling Thirds and other motions

voice-leading and use common tones as available. Because all bass notes take chords of the fifth, one must use oblique or ascending voice-leading in the upper parts; otherwise one is in peril of parallels. A common use of Falling Thirds is the pattern ①-⑥-④-②, which then proceeds to ⑤. Example 4.28 shows this typical usage and a complete "cycle" of Falling Thirds.

EXERCISE. Example 4.29 is a partimento to be solved by Falling Thirds and other motions. Realize, stylize, and transpose it.

Shorter Chromatic Motions

Monte ascends chromatically, taking alternating chords of the sixth (or ${}^{6}_{5}$) and chords of the fifth. In modern theory, these would be regarded as a series of leading tones and tonics, tonicizing every other chord. From a certain point of view, this is true. But short chromatic bass lines are very common in eighteenth-century music, and often do not ultimately lead to new tonalities, so the partimento tradition of handling them as a single bass motion (rather than a series of separate modulations) is simple and practical.

In major Monte happens most typically from ③ to ⑥ but may also traverse ① to ③. In minor it may occur from ⑤ up to ① or ③ to ⑤.

Fenaroli taught several variants of these chromatic ascents in both major and minor, but they all use the same $\substack{6\\5}$ to $\substack{5\\3}$ motion as the driving force. Fenaroli's Montes are seen in Example 4.30.

EXAMPLE 4.30 Fenaroli's Montes

EXERCISE. Example 4.31 is a chromatic partimento requiring Monte. Realize and stylize it, and then transpose to several other keys.

Lamento descends from ① to ⑤ in minor and is often associated with music of lament. It is like a passacaglia but chromatic. Example 4.32 shows two possibilities for Lamento from Fenaroli.

EXAMPLE 4.31 A chromatic partimento for Monte and other motions

EXAMPLE 4.32 Fenaroli's Lamento

EXAMPLE 4.33 A partimento for Lamento and other motions

EXERCISE. Example 4.33 is a partimento that requires Lamento. Realize and stylize it, and then transpose to several other keys.

Longer Chromatic Motions

Ascending chromatic scales are often harmonized by Monte-like motion, but these must account for the diatonic half steps, where Monte is not possible. (There is no black key between E and F, I have found.) They do so in various ways.

Fenaroli taught a method of harmonizing the rising chromatic scale that does not include lowered ⑦. Where the diatonic scale has a half step, a typical chromatic 5-6 (which is a Monte) cannot occur because it needs the chromatic note that lies between the whole steps of the scale. So Fenaroli's chromatic ascent pauses at the half steps and reinterprets them as a new scale. Fenaroli avoided flat ⑦, so his solution is not a complete chromatic scale. The Fenaroli Chromatic Ascent is included in Example 4.34.

Saverio Valente (?–c. 1816) has three solutions for the rising chromatic scale, all of which cover the complete scale, unlike Fenaroli's. Valente's solutions are more likely to appear in the context of minor keys. As all these

EXAMPLE 4.34 The Fenaroli and Valente Chromatic Ascents

variants use similar or overlapping strategies, one may borrow techniques from each and mix them together. The Valente Chromatic Ascents are included in Example 4.34.

EXERCISE. Example 4.35 is a partimento in which you can use any of the chromatic ascents discussed previously. Realize and stylize the partimento, and then transpose.

Über-Lamento is an almost-complete chromatic descent. The name Über-Lamento reflects the fact that the first part of this pattern is the same as

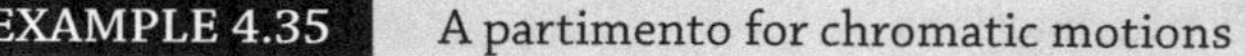
EXAMPLE 4.35 A partimento for chromatic motions

EXAMPLE 4.36 Über-Lamento

Lamento, but since this one is "über" (super) it keeps going past ⑤. It descends all the way to ① but avoids lowered ②. At this point in most musical situations, the bass would likely jump to ⑤, but it may also go straight from ② to ①. Über-Lamento is driven by 7-6 motions. The motion is shown in Example 4.36. The upper voices may be inverted.

EXERCISE. Example 4.37 is a partimento suitable for Über-Lamento. Realize and stylize and then transpose.

Valente taught multiple chromatic descents. One of them is the same as Über Lamento but includes flat ② (taking #6) to form a complete chromatic scale. Yet another of Valente's chromatic descents, which we might call Chromatic Fauxbourdon as it consists of chords of the sixth, appears in Example 4.38.

EXAMPLE 4.37 A partimento for Über-Lamento and other motions

EXAMPLE 4.38 Valente's Chromatic Fauxbourdon

Mozart's teacher Padre Martini (1706–1784) deployed another chromatic device in the Preludio to the third sonata from his *12 Sonate d'Intavolatura.* The bass descends chromatically, alternately taking fully diminished and $\begin{smallmatrix}6\\ \sharp 4\\ 2\end{smallmatrix}$ sonorities. The pattern makes up the entire Preludio except for the opening chord, the last few chords, and the cadence. We may call this technique the Martini. Valente taught it, as well, but Martini's use is audacious and earns him the naming rights. Example 4.39 illustrates this harmonization.

EXAMPLE 4.39 The Martini

EXERCISE. Return to the partimento in Example 4.37 and apply Chromatic Fauxbourdon or Martini to it. Realize, stylize, and transpose.

It is possible to ascend and descend chromatically simply by moving diminished triads or fully diminished seventh chords up and down the keyboard. Chromatic diminished chords are sometimes associated with defeat and humiliation when descending (as when one loses on a game show) and melodramatic suspense when ascending. Still, it is possible to use them without evoking a sense of the ridiculous. However, the other chromatic motions presented here are more common in real music.

EXERCISE. Example 4.40 is a partimento with several chromatic passages. Solve it using the chromatic motions explained in this chapter. Remember that you can combine elements of the different chromatic motions and need not keep consistently to any of them.

Mastery of the bass motions in this chapter will prepare you not only for more difficult partimenti but ultimately to begin improvising without the aid of a partimento at all. As always, each stage in the learning process must be strong and stable before anything new is built upon it. You may wish to return to this chapter many times whenever you need to reinforce your knowledge of specific bass motions.

EXAMPLE 4.40 A chromatic partimento

Chapter 5

Partimento Practice

This chapter presents a collection of partimenti from historical sources. These are for practice. The skills of partimento must be deeply internalized before going on to further, more difficult areas of study. The first eighteen have figures for the sake of review, but before long you should not need them anymore. In the simpler examples, the bass moves in simple values with no diminutions; these are easier to stylize into a different kind of music. Those with elaborately decorated basses already imply a certain established style; when working on them, cooperate with the given style of the bass as you provide upper voices.

Partimenti from Fenaroli's Book I (Gj 1301, 1302, 1303, 1307, 1310, 1314, and 1315) appear in Examples 5.1–5.7. They are quite easy. Nevertheless, try to make them into interesting pieces of music. Note that

EXAMPLE 5.1 Fenaroli's partimento Gj 1301

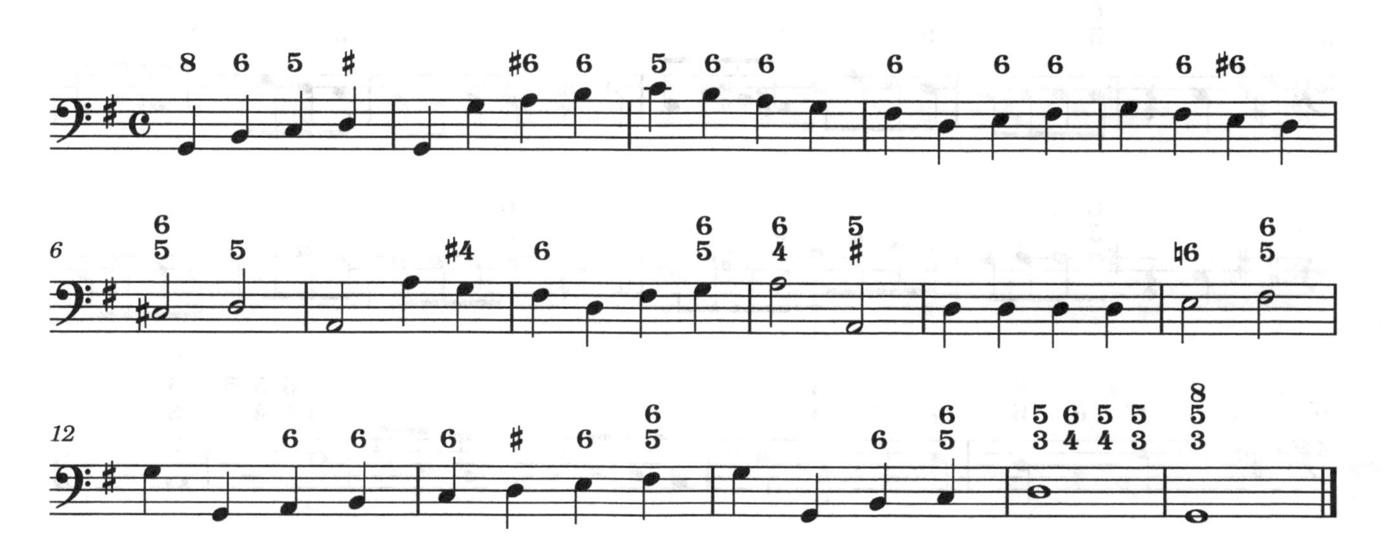

EXAMPLE 5.2 Fenaroli's partimento Gj 1302

EXAMPLE 5.3 Fenaroli's partimento Gj 1303

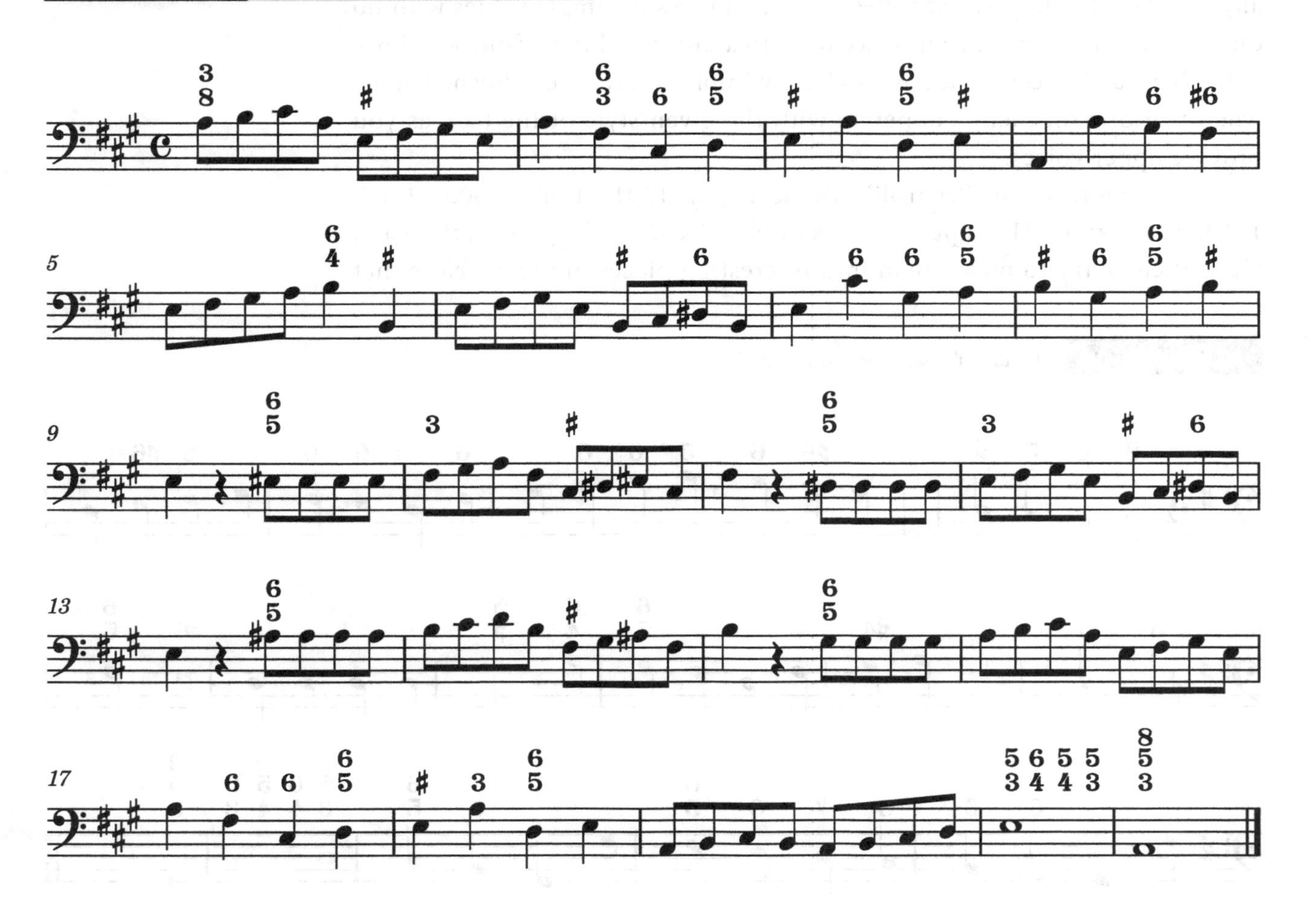

EXAMPLE 5.4 Fenaroli's partimento Gj 1307

EXAMPLE 5.5 Fenaroli's partimento Gj 1310

EXAMPLE 5.6 Fenaroli's partimento Gj 1314

EXAMPLE 5.7 Fenaroli's partimento Gj 1315

on occasion, figured bass numbers appear out of the usual descending order. This is usually an indication that the maestro has a specific order in mind for the voices.

A partimenti of Nicola Sala (1713–1801) appears in Example 5.8. When two notes are slurred together, Sala means that the second is passing and is not to be harmonized separately.

Examples 5.9–5.12 show partimenti of Cotumacci. Beware: sometimes Cotumacci does not include the required accidentals that should accompany certain figures. Apparently he expected students to understand that there were implied.

EXAMPLE 5.8 A partimento of Sala

EXAMPLE 5.9 A partimento of Cotumacci

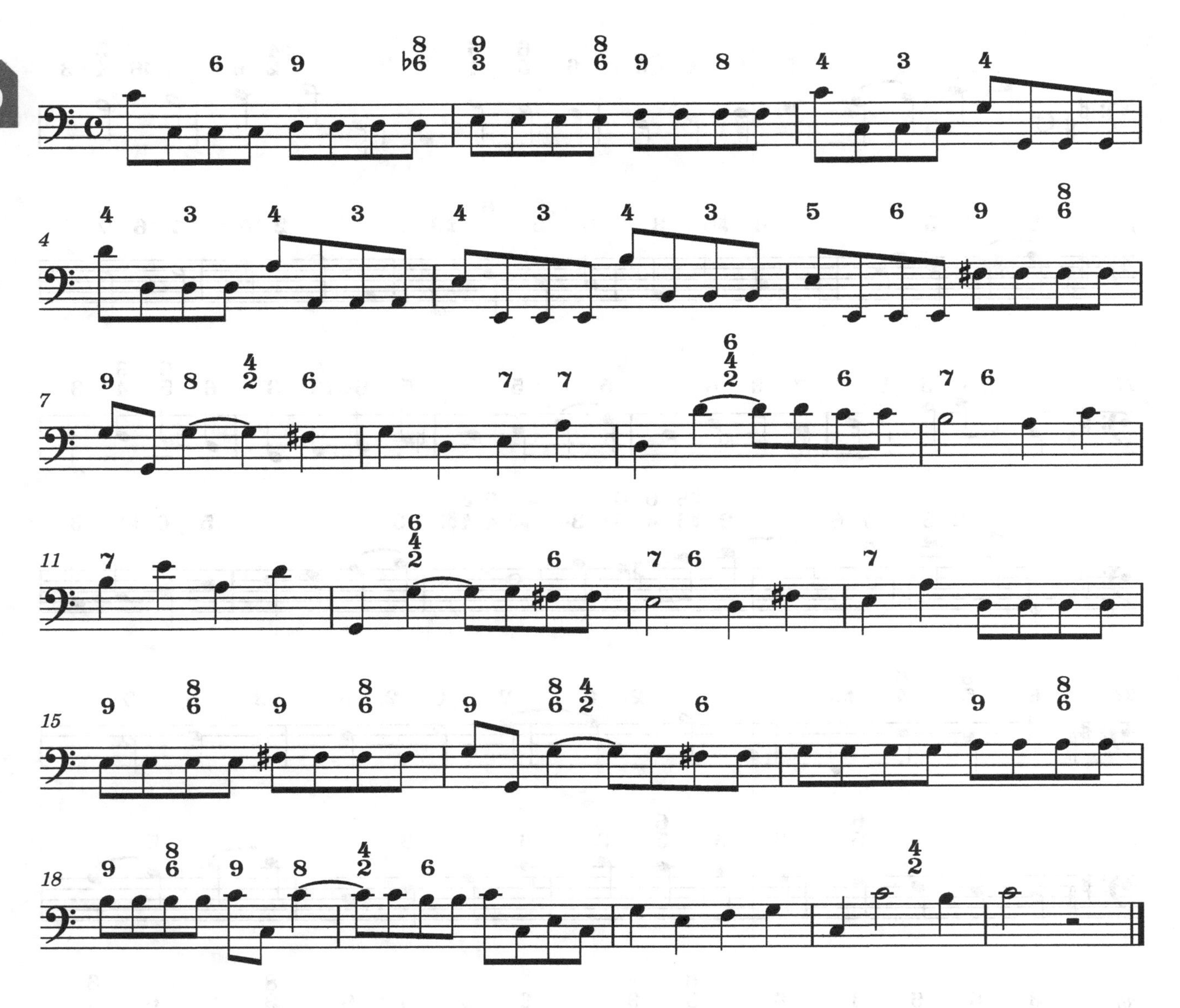

EXAMPLE 5.10 A partimento of Cotumacci

EXAMPLE 5.11 A partimento of Cotumacci

EXAMPLE 5.12 A partimento of Cotumacci

Example 5.13 shows a partimenti of Sala in which the 8-7-6 motion figures prominently.

In Example 5.14, Cotumacci presents opportunities to use the 7-6 motion.

Example 5.15 presents a partimento of Sala with Tied Bass motions.

Example 5.16 shows a partimento by Giacomo Insanguine (1728–1795) that includes C5 and Cascade motions.

Example 5.17 is from Durante's rules. The main topic is Cascade.

A partimento of Insanguine appears as Example 5.18. It teaches the use of C5.

Examples 5.19–5.21 show Fenaroli partimenti (GJ 1333, 1335, and 1359) from Book IV. From this point forward, the partimenti in this chapter will have no figures. You are on your own to determine bass motions.

EXAMPLE 5.13 A partimento of Sala with 8-7-6

EXAMPLE 5.14 A partimento of Cotumacci with 7-6

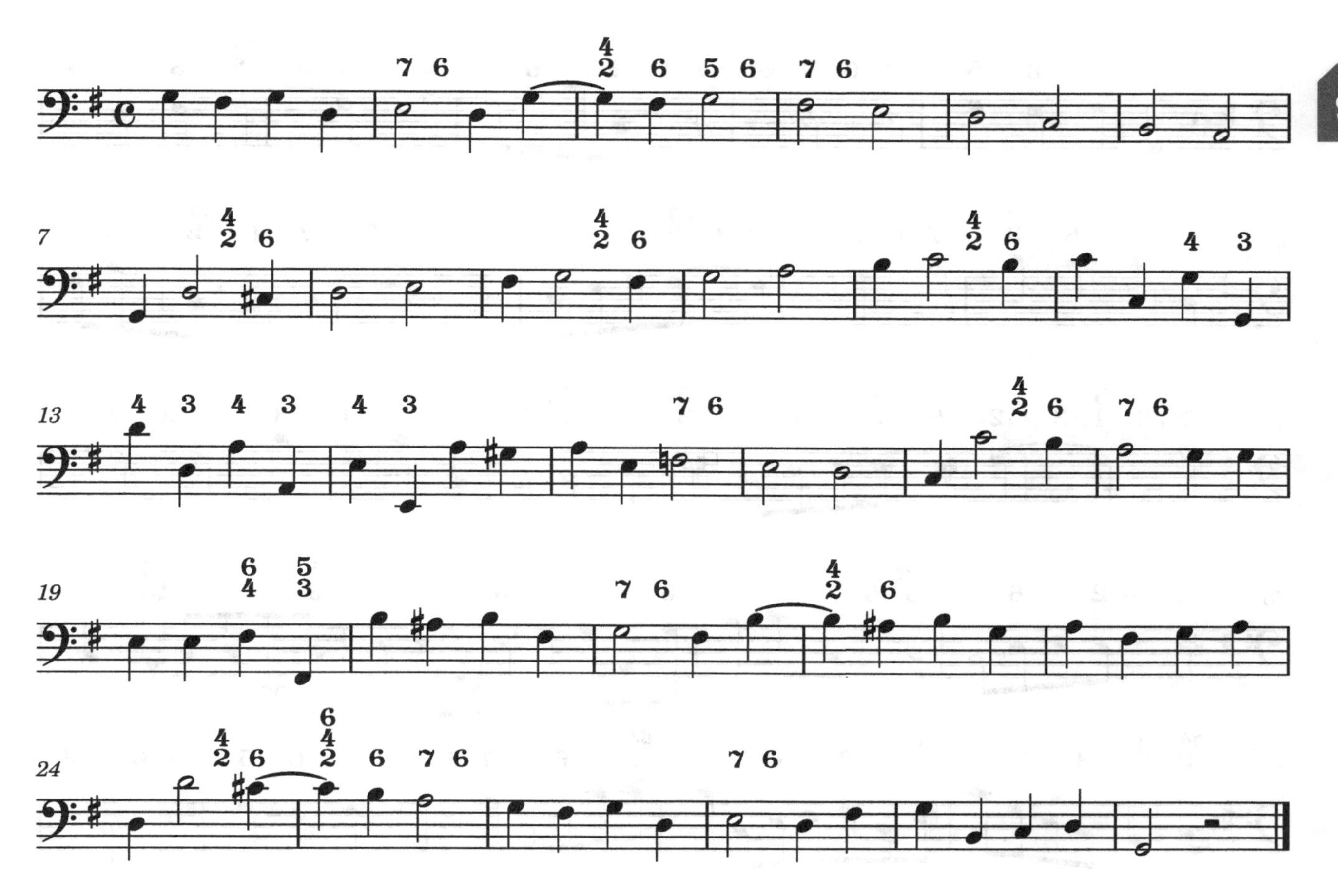

EXAMPLE 5.15 A partimento of Sala with Tied Bass

EXAMPLE 5.16 A partimento of Insanguine with C5 and Cascade

EXAMPLE 5.17 A partimento of Durante with Cascade

EXAMPLE 5.18 A partimento of Insanguine with C5

EXAMPLE 5.19 Fenaroli's partimento Gj 1333

EXAMPLE 5.20 Fenaroli's partimento Gj 1335

EXAMPLE 5.21 Fenaroli's partimento Gj 1359

Examples 5.22–5.25 are by Durante. Along with these partimenti, he wrote out suggested "styles"—that is, fragments of keyboard figurations that will help complete each partimento. If you wish, you can look up the suggested styles on partimenti.org. They will give you a sense of Neapolitan keyboard style. Still, I think it is better if you solve these challenges on your own before getting any help.

EXAMPLE 5.22 A partimento of Durante

Example 5.26–5.29 are from Fenaroli's Book IV (GJ 1346, 1347, 1342, and 1349). They present many diatonic and chromatic motions.

A partimento of Durante appears as Example 5.30. It includes a chromatically inflected Monte Principale.

Example 5.31, from Fenaroli (Gj 13540), features Tied Bass, Cascade, and chromatic motions.

Example 5.32 is from Durante. The main challenges are Domirefa and C5.

Example 5.33 is Fenaroli (GJ 1339). It has some long C5 motions as well as other challenges.

Example 5.34, from Fenaroli (Gj 1336), requires Domirefa, C5, and Tied Bass motions.

Example 5.35 is from Fenaroli's Book IV (Gj 1334). As an extra challenge, you could add diminutions to the bass.

EXAMPLE 5.23 A partimento of Durante

EXAMPLE 5.24 A partimento of Durante

EXAMPLE 5.25 A partimento of Durante

EXAMPLE 5.26 Fenaroli's partimento Gj 1346

EXAMPLE 5.27 Fenaroli's partimento Gj 1347

EXAMPLE 5.27 Continued

EXAMPLE 5.28 Fenaroli's partimento Gj 1342

EXAMPLE 5.29 Fenaroli's partimento Gj 1349

EXAMPLE 5.30 A partimento of Durante with chromatic motions

EXAMPLE 5.31 Fenaroli's partimento Gj 1354 with Tied Bass, Cascade, and chromaticism

EXAMPLE 5.32 A partimento of Durante with Domirefa and C5

EXAMPLE 5.33 Fenaroli's partimento Gj 1339 with C5

EXAMPLE 5.34 Fenaroli's partimento Gj 1336 with Domirefa and Tied Bass

Example 5.36 shows a partimento of Durante that requires the Dolareti motion.

Example 5.37, from Durante, requires the Domirefa motion.

Example 5.38, by Fenaroli (Gj 1332), requires both descending and ascending chromatic motion.

Fenaroli's challenging partimento in B minor (Gj 1357) appears as Example 5.39. The main business is descending chromaticism.

Example 5.40, by Fenaroli (Gj 1357), is also chromatic. Try adding diminutions to the bass if you can.

EXAMPLE 5.35 Fenaroli's partimento Gj 1334

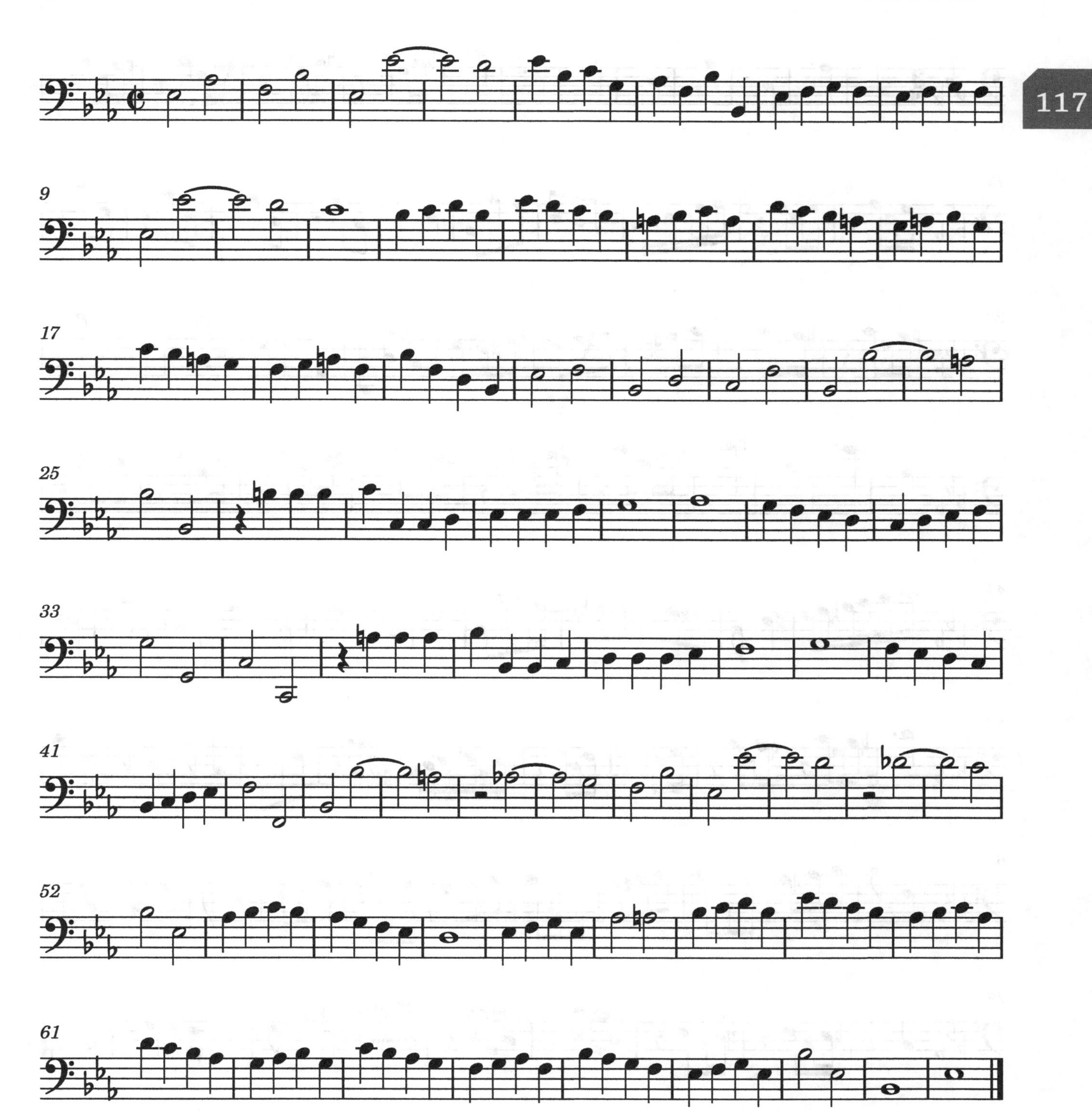

EXAMPLE 5.36 A partimento of Durante

EXAMPLE 5.37 A partimento of Durante

EXAMPLE 5.38 Fenaroli's chromatic partimento Gj 1332

EXAMPLE 5.39 Fenaroli's chromatic partimento Gj 1357

EXAMPLE 5.40 Fenaroli's chromatic partimento Gj 1358

Chapter 6

Partimento Imitation and Fugue

The partimento tradition teaches bass motions by requiring the player to recognize them, realize them with appropriate upper voices, and finally stylize the partimento into a convincing piece of music. Further, partimenti show how bass motions may be shortened or extended, joined with other motions, chromatically mutated to initiate modulations, hidden beneath all manner of diminutions, and seamlessly elided with cadences.

Partimento and Counterpoint

But partimenti also teach counterpoint, and in the most practical, hands-on way ever devised. They do so by presenting little puzzles that can be solved by finding the right combination of themes between bass and upper voices. Sometimes these puzzles, which take the form of points of imitation, are explicitly labeled with terms such *imit* (short for imitation). In advanced partimenti the points of imitation are not always marked; the player must find them by wits alone. Robert Gjerdingen points out that one reliable guide for finding points of imitation is to look for a measure (or group of measures) that is "interesting" followed by one that is "boring," or vice versa. Very often the interesting material will work in one voice, superimposed over the boring material in another, and vice versa.

Because imitation is a crucial element of eighteenth-century music, we consider it good form in partimento playing to include it often in stylizations, whether marked or not. Fortunately, the Neapolitan masters left numerous interesting and fun puzzles to help beginners find their way through partimento imitation.

Counterpoint in Sala

Nicola Sala's fifth partimento, seen in Example 6.1, presents an imitation challenge for the performer. The first measure meets Gjerdingen's description of "interesting" while the second is "boring." While the interesting-boring combination leaps off the page to the experienced partimento player, to a newcomer the cue may not be obvious at all. An additional hint lies in the repeated interesting-boring combinations throughout the piece, although in different tonalities and with small variations. Peter Van Tour, in his edition of these

EXAMPLE 6.1 Sala's fifth partimento

partimenti, explains that the use of the *signum congruentia* (:S:) is a quirk of Sala's, not generally seen in others' partimenti. The signum indicates locations at which imitating voicings should enter. Five instances of the signum appear in this partimento, each signaling that an upper voice should imitate the bass's previous measure.

EXERCISE. Locate each place in Sala's fifth partimento where imitation is to occur. Just look for the signum (:S:). At that point, let the right hand steal whatever the bass played in the previous interesting measure, and play it, one or two octaves higher, against the boring bass. Note that, even in a two-voice texture, the parts outline enough of a harmony to allow you to recognize the familiar pattern that I called "Page One" in *The Pianist's Guide to Historic Improvisation.*

Why is this important? Imitative puzzles in partimenti guide the player in reconstructing passages that the composer had in mind. The process of reconstruction is itself pedagogically valuable. If I can take something apart and rebuild it, I understand it. Further, in working through these imitative puzzles, the player begins to notice subtle cues that hint at the solution. In Sala's fifth partimento, the boring measure in the bass includes a syncopation followed by a descending step. This doesn't mean much to a player trained by modern methods. (Just count and play it, and your job is done.) But to a partimento player, it shouts: "Tied Bass motion! Quick! Find a $^4_2$ sonority in the right hand!" Practicing imitative partimenti trains the player in anticipating solutions.

But notice: not only can we place the interesting measure in the right hand in measure 2, but the boring measure also works in the right hand in measure 1. It turns out that the imitative puzzle was not merely to copy one measure from the bass into the soprano, but to perform a simultaneous switcheroo of two complete measures, as shown in Example 6.2.

In using the material from measures 1–2 as both a bass line and an upper voice, we enter the realm of invertible counterpoint, in which multiple melodies may be combined in any vertical order, appearing in any voice from top to bottom. What is really going on in this partimento is that the player is gaining an intuitive, hands-on, *haptic* sense of how counterpoint works. The implications of this insight are far-reaching.

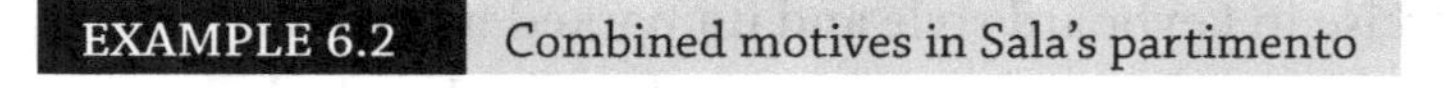
EXAMPLE 6.2 Combined motives in Sala's partimento

Partimento Imitation at the Keyboard

Most modern academic study of counterpoint happens exclusively on paper. Paper is necessary, of course, as most people can't work out and remember long, complex, contrapuntal works in their heads. But the consequence of undertaking counterpoint study *on paper only* is that one gets good at counterpoint—*on paper only*. Crossing the ocean on a luxury cruise ship in no way prepares me for crossing the ocean in a kayak. Creating spontaneous contrapuntal combinations on the keyboard is a completely different kind of skill, requiring different thought processes, habits, and therefore, a different kind of training. The Neapolitan masters understood this, which is why in addition to extensive written work, they created an entire curriculum of partimenti in which were embedded puzzles of invertible counterpoint.

The partimenti in this chapter present challenges of imitation that represent the types of imitation that pop up all over the place in eighteenth-century music. At first, imitations will be at the octave; that is, the imitating voice will use the same pitches, transposed up or down an octave or two. Later we will encounter imitations at other intervals. As you work through these partimenti, your sense of counterpoint will grow, both intellectually and haptically.

EXERCISE. Return to Sala's fifth partimento in Example 6.1 and complete a realization. If you ignore the points of imitation, a simple chordal realization is possible. However, if you pay attention to the imitations, it no longer makes sense to realize the partimento with block chords. You must now think about the upper voice (or voices) as independent lines. Try creating a realization with only one upper voice, such that the soprano touches on all necessary notes to fulfill the imitations and other requirements indicated by the figures. Then go back and try a realization with two upper voices. Even where imitations are not present, incorporate short thematic bits from the interesting measure. You can also invent your own rhythmic motives to place throughout the piece to create thematic unity. If necessary, write out your solutions. But try working without paper as much as possible.

The following partimenti contain points of imitation. Working on these pieces will develop your hands-on sense of contrapuntal combinations, and you will gradually become adept at detecting and solving short points of imitation that are typical of the partimento style.

Fenaroli's twenty-sixth partimento from Book IV (Gj 1356), shown in Example 6.3, is an exercise in keyboard style and unmarked imitations.

The sixteenth-note pattern is a very common keyboard style known as *bariolage*, possibly borrowed from the violin technique of rapidly alternating between two strings to create two voices animated by perpetual rhythmic energy. Bariolage shows up in most keyboard composers of the late eighteenth and early nineteenth centuries, and was a favorite device of Wolfgang Amadeus Mozart (1756–1791). The measures with bariolage, such as 1–2, certainly meet the definition of "interesting" when contrasted with less active measures such as 3–4. Of course, this cue prompts the partimento player to investigate whether imitation is possible in those measures.

EXAMPLE 6.3 Fenaroli's partimento Gj 1356

EXERCISE. Locate cadences, keys, and possible bass motions. Find all instances of imitation. Where no imitation is possible, complete the right hand with bariolage and other patterns from the partimento to maintain thematic unity.

A partimento in E major by Niccolò Zingarelli (1752–1837) appears in Example 6.4.

EXAMPLE 6.4 A partimento of Zingarelli

The indication *prima pos:* over the first measure means first position. That is, the highest note the first chord in the right hand should be E. This prepares for the dissonant seventh on the third beat of the measure. In the second measure *imitazione* is indicated, meaning that an upper voice should imitate the theme from the first measure of the bass. But how long should the imitation last? Is there a way to gauge its length quickly without actually playing the two parts together at the keyboard and waiting until something ugly happens? Yes. A glance at measures 1–2 reveals that the first two beats of each bar are consonant with tonic harmony, and the second two with dominant. This is a reliable clue that the imitation will continue as long as this pattern holds. The seventh bar does not follow the pattern; by that point the imitation must break off, although the player could also decide to abandon it earlier if desired. Note that a slight adjustment is necessary to keep the imitation going on this long. The third beat of measure 3, when placed in imitation above the same location in measure 4, results in an unprepared fourth. At this moment it is best to change the upper voice and not imitate literally. Example 6.5, which includes a free middle voice, clarifies this situation.

The second point of imitation is merely a restatement of the first, but transposed to B major.

EXERCISE. Work out and play the two indicated points of imitation in Zingarelli's E major partimento, using only one upper voice. Then look over the partimento and find other possible points of imitation that may be unmarked. (If the bass reiterates the same intervals as those in the opening measures, that is probably a point of imitation.) Locate all cadences, key areas, and options for bass motions. Create a simple realization that includes the imitations. Try including an additional upper voice. Is it possible for two upper voices to take turns participating in the imitations? Think of the two

EXAMPLE 6.5 Imitation in Zingarelli's partimento

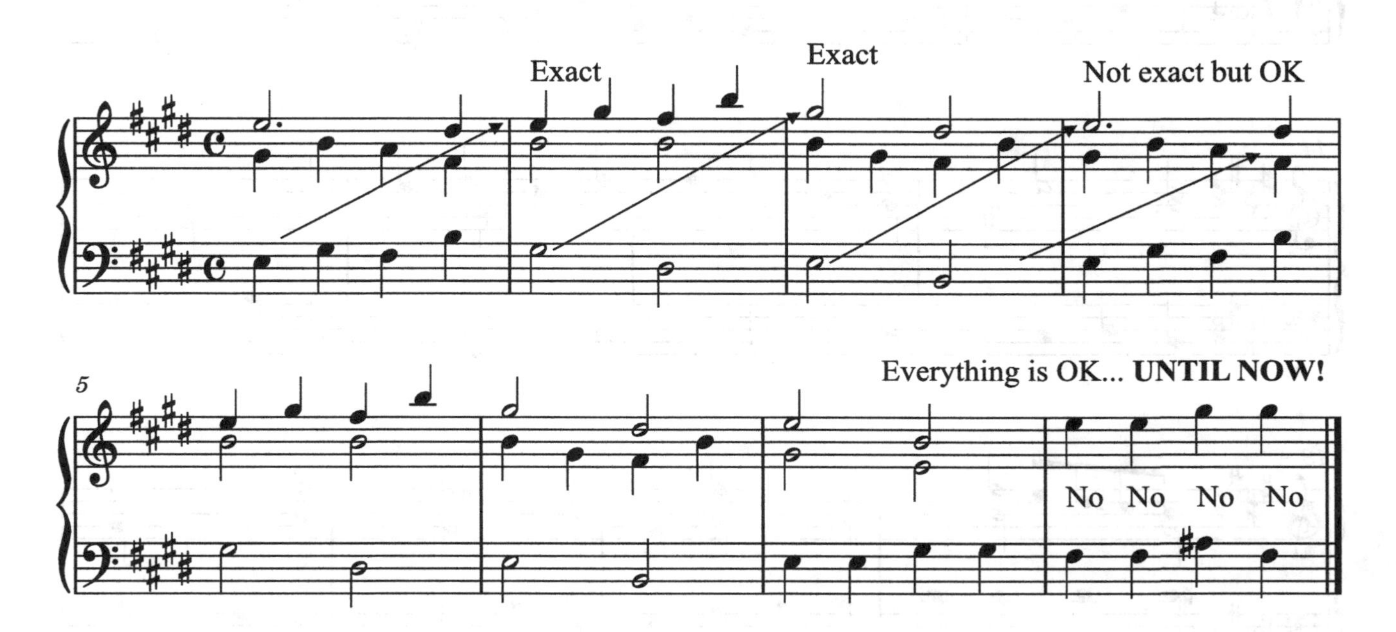

upper voices as soprano and alto. Whenever one gets involved in an imitation, the other should be as boring as possible (that is, moving only as necessary).

As mentioned, the first measure has the figure 7 over beat 3, indicating that one or more upper voices are already present in the first measure—they don't wait until the point of imitation to enter. Example 6.6 provides some guidance.

EXAMPLE 6.6 A realization of Zingarelli

EXAMPLE 6.6 Continued

A partimento in G minor from the *Regole* of Giovanni Paisiello (1740–1816), shown in Example 6.7, is a lesson in imitation and pedal points. Unlike some partimenti that seem musically neutral—flexible enough to be made into many different kinds of pieces but not favoring one over another—this one conveys an introspective pathos that would be fitting in a tragic aria or the soliloquy-like slow movement of a keyboard concerto.

EXAMPLE 6.7 A partimento of Paisiello

EXAMPLE 6.7 Continued

The figures in the first measure include $\frac{3}{8}$, which should alert the player to some very specific requirements for the upper voices. Normally figures are written with the highest numbers at the top, regardless of whether the upper voices are actually in that order. When the figures appear out of order, the intent is usually to direct the exact disposition of the upper voices. In this case, the top voice should take the third and a middle voice should take the octave. Once we observe a single instance of "out-of-order" figures, we should assume that this same procedure might lurk elsewhere in the partimento.

The first five measures require the player to realize two upper voices rather precisely, since the numerous figures leave little choice in the matter. Measures 1–2 feature pitiable double suspensions, and measures 4–5 indicate motion in thirds over a long note in the bass.

The first imitation, at measure 8, requires that the sixteenth note figure from beats 1–2 be placed over the dotted rhythm on beats 3–4. But imitating the at the octave will not work here. You must find a different interval for the upper voice's imitation.

The opening idea returns in the relative major in measure 16; you can use the opening figures over it; likewise with the pedal point that follows. The material in measure 23 suggest more imitation, though it is not marked.

The second marked point of imitation is in measure 37. At this location the dotted rhythm from measure 36 must be made to cooperate somehow with the obvious Tied Bass motion. The long pedal point in measures 44–47, and the measure after that, have out-of-order figures. You have been warned.

EXERCISE. Begin Paisiello's G minor partimento by playing exactly what the figures indicate, and working out the imitations where appropriate. As the movement of the voices becomes clear to you, make the piece more interesting with some tasteful diminutions and ornaments.

Fenaroli's partimento Gj 1362 is shown in Example 6.8.

With experience, one naturally becomes suspicious of the two opening measures of any partimento. Will this be yet another hidden imitation? Indeed so; the first two bars work nicely together. However, we should never assume the imitation spans only the first two measures, but rather try to imagine it continuing until it is impossible. In this case it becomes impossible, as measures 3–4 are identical and therefore do not work together in imitation. Since the imitation can last either two or three measures, one has a few options, one of which is shown in Example 6.9.

The opening two measures do not recur elsewhere, so we can conclude that points of imitation similar to that which began the partimento will not appear later. Measure 8 introduces an idea that combines a descending line with a pedal point. This figure is likely to be unwieldy in imitation, and more probably will serve as an accompaniment to another descending line a third or tenth higher. The aggressive leaping figure in measure 10 also conforms to the interesting-boring scheme, and may admit some kind of imitation.

EXERCISE. Develop a stylization of this partimento, creating points of imitation where possible and using parallel motion over the pedal point idea. As this appears to be a quick, lively piece, keep your solutions fairly sparse so it is playable at a fast tempo.

Insanguine's thirty-second partimento from his "More Difficult" collection, shown in Example 6.10, opens with a theme built around the Monte Principale motion (up a fourth, down a third).

A quick glance reveals that this theme reappears several times, and once (mm. 46–50) with altered intervals such that the theme retains its identifying rhythmic character but now outlines a C5 motion. The recurrences of the theme, and the fact that some of the intervening measures are a bit "boring," suggests that the player is to include this theme in upper voices when possible. Several imitative possibilities are inherent within Monte Principale, and this is why it shows up in partimenti so often.

The C5 version of the theme (mm. 46–50), when placed in an upper voice, fits over the Tied Bass (mm. 38–43). It also works with the Tied Bass over the C5.

EXERCISE. Work on Insanguine's thirty-second partimento. Locate all cadences, key areas, and options for bass motions. Whenever the Monte Principale theme appears, try to imitate it in an upper voice. One possible

EXAMPLE 6.8 Fenaroli's partimento Gj 1362

EXAMPLE 6.9 Imitation in Fenaroli's Gj 1362

solution appears in Example 6.11, in which I sometimes disregarded a few figures and took things in a different direction. I also imitated at intervals other than the octave, which is introduced in detail with the next partimento.

The partimento in B♭ from the *Scuola di contrappunto* of Giacomo Tritto (1733–1824), shown in Example 6.12, presents a new puzzle: imitation at the fourth above. As imitation can occur above or below, to avoid confusion one must specify which; a fourth above B♭ is E♭ and a fourth below is F, so one gets different results depending on the direction chosen. In most cases, when an interval of imitation is indicated, it is meant to occur above. If the interval is not specified, that usually means that it is an octave. But not always.

Tritto's partimento has six marked points of imitation, all at the fourth, indicated by *imitaz*[e] *a 4º* and subsequently *a 4º*. The precise placement in the score of the indication for imitation is, well, not precise. The player must gaze fore and aft to discover the source of the imitative material, how long it is, and where it is to recur.

The first marked imitation involves four quarters followed by a whole note, and then two more sequential iterations to form a pattern. The moving quarters and subsequent whole note resemble the technique I nicknamed "Play & Hold" in *The Pianist's Guide to Historic Improvisation*. This technique allows one voice to move while the other is static, simplifying matters of voice leading. The second, third, and fifth marked imitations are similar.

The fourth imitation involves a bass that is tied over the bar, but appears to rise rather than fall after the tie. Do not be misled; the intervening quarter notes are just diminutions. The "real" resolution happens one bar later and the bass drops one step. The sixth marked imitation is similar.

EXERCISE. Turn Tritto's partimento into music. In addition to the marked imitations at the fourth, stay alert for unmarked imitations at the octave. Where

EXAMPLE 6.10 A partimento of Insanguine

EXAMPLE 6.11 A realization of Insanguine

EXAMPLE 6.11 Continued

EXAMPLE 6.12 A partimento of Tritto

EXAMPLE 6.12 Continued

imitations occur over Tied Bass motions, remember that $\frac{4}{2}$ is called for. If the imitating voice supplies only one of those intervals, you may wish to fill in the other in an additional voice in order to create a full harmonic texture. A possible solution for the first point of imitation appears in Example 6.13.

Insanguine's eighth partimento from his "More Difficult" collection, shown in Example 6.14, employs some familiar bass motions along with points of imitation. Measures 1–2 present a Romanesca thinly disguised with a few

EXAMPLE 6.13 Imitation in Tritto

diminutions. The figures $^{5}_{4}$ over the second beat of measure 1 suggests that each stage of the Romanesca could include a suspension (m. 21 confirms this notion), which would make it the Perfidia variant. A nice Cascade with suspended ninths appears at measure 8.

In measure 12 we encounter the first imitation. While the indication *imit* appears only once, the sequential nature of measures 12–15 suggests that whatever imitation you invent in measure 12 can repeat multiple times. Imitations in easier and moderate partimenti tend to be at the octave, but not so in this case. Insanguine's figures (the 8 and 6 in m. 12) tell us that the upper voice will imitate at the fourth above, that is, beginning on A.

The second point of imitation, marked in measure 28, seems not to be sequential or repeated but rather a one-off. The *imit* calls for an upper voice to steal the last four notes from measure 27 and place them on beat 1 of measure 28. It is possible to take the first two bass notes from measure 28 and place them in an upper voice on beats 3 and 4 of the same measure, completing a four-beat point of imitation.

In measures 17–19 and 29–31 the bass moves in what look like broken triads. We could look at these passages and ask, "Which notes are structural and which are diminutions?" The most likely answer is that third note of each "triad" is the diminution, and the bass motion is Cascade. That solution will sound just fine. But it is also possible to treat these passages as points of imitation. Insanguine's figures hint at this. The last note of the "triad" in measure 17 has a figure indicating an octave, and the rest on the downbeat of 18 has a 3. These figures would result in the first two notes of the "triad" in an upper voice. It is not hard to see where this is going.

Each of these points of imitation is illustrated in Example 6.15.

EXERCISE. Work though Insanguine's eighth partimento, recognizing cadences, modulations, key areas, and bass motions. Figure out the imitations. Develop your own version that incorporates all these devices.

Example 6.16 shows another partimento of Insanguine.

EXAMPLE 6.14 A partimento of Insanguine

EXAMPLE 6.15 Imitation in Insanguine

Three imitations are marked, but more are possible wherever the material from the first two measures recurs. The imitation beginning in measure 23 requires some thought; the solution is not obvious at a glance. Insanguine gives figures for an upper-voice theme that is to repeat over the subsequent Tied Bass motion. On closer inspection, these figures match the opening motive from measure 1. The player must configure this motive to fit with the intervallic requirements of a Tied Bass motion. A suggestion for this passage appears as Example 6.17.

EXERCISE. Work out your own realization for the partimento in Example 6.16.

A partimento of Insanguine is shown in Example 6.18.

This piece is all about imitation, to the exclusion of almost all else. While not quite a strict canon (in which the following voice does everything the leader does, in exact imitation), it is close. Note that the figures never indicate more than one upper part; possibly this partimento is meant to be solved with only

EXAMPLE 6.16 A partimento of Insanguine

EXAMPLE 6.17 A realized passage in Insanguine

a single high voice. The figures appear as hints at moments when the expected imitation at the octave will not work.

EXERCISE. Solve Insanguine's near-canon from Example 6.18. You will need to adjust material where precise imitation does not work. Try it at the keyboard for a while, and resort to paper as necessary. Example 6.19 provides a possible solution.

Partimento Fugue

We now come to partimento fugue. The pedagogical purpose seems to be threefold: to demonstrate how elements of fugue structure fit together, to teach an intuitive sense of counterpoint by solving puzzles mentally and haptically, and to convey keyboard, instrumental, and choral styles that were expected in fugal composition.

Ironically, many partimento fugues are not terribly difficult. In the easiest examples, the player chooses between a narrow range of options and fills in the blanks. Because of this, partimento fugue is a useful step, but not sufficient in itself, when learning to improvise fugue. Because the player is kept close to the printed page, further work will be necessary to break free of the score and invent music that has not been previously worked out in all details. In the meantime, partimento fugue has much to teach us.

The partimento in C minor (Gj 1800) of Leonardo Leo (1694–1744), shown in Example 6.20, is a chromatic fugue.

One would suppose that nothing lumbering across the face of the earth could be more frightening than a *chromatic partimento fugue*. Happily, it is not

EXAMPLE 6.18 A partimento of Insanguine

EXAMPLE 6.19 A realization of Insanguine

EXAMPLE 6.19 Continued

EXAMPLE 6.20 Leo's partimento Gj 1800

so. This piece is already nearly complete and allows the player a very limited range of contributions.

The subject enters first in the soprano, the theme lasting six measures. The player is to add nothing to the written score during this entry (hence the indication *solo*). The second entry, in measure 7, is in the bass voice. The figures above this voice indicate two voices above; the fugue has jumped from one voice to three, as the indication *pieno* (full) confirms. This is typical of the Italian fugal style, where strict accounting of voices was not important. The rich sound of accumulating voices was achieved more by repeated thematic entries rather than the actual presence of separate parts. And by the way, it doesn't matter. In real life, listeners cannot precisely track four voices all the way through a fugue.

The player is responsible to add two voices above the second entry, but the figures don't allow for much choice. This has to be done with a standard Lamento (7-6 chromatic descending motion). Not much new happens over the fourth entry, now in G minor: another Lamento.

The *solo* (actually a duet) in measure 25 takes no accompaniment beyond what is written. This is an episode in two high voices, echoing the chromaticism of the subject without quoting the subject in its entirety.

A new subject enters in measure 40, but breaks off before completing the whole theme. A modulating episode, in which the subject does not appear, lasts through measure 50. We know the subject will not be present because the bass and figures do not support a descending chromatic line. However, it is possible to "fake" the subject in an upper voice during this episode. It will not work if it is strictly chromatic, but a descending stepwise line, using the subject's pattern of repeated notes, will sound a lot like the subject and will probably fool everyone. A full statement in F minor appears in measure 51, followed by a two-voice episode requiring no accompaniment. The final full statement of the subject in the home key arrives in measure 62. After a dramatically evaded cadence in measure 68, business is concluded.

This chromatic partimento fugue requires considerably less from the player than do many ostensibly simpler partimenti. Several passages need nothing at all; others are completely figured and allow only a few options such as inverting the upper voices during the Lamento. The partimento never allows for a complete statement of the subject in an upper voice, and the only chromatic motion one has to employ is the Lamento. (Chromatic lines in upper voices require completely different bass motions, which are not in play here.)

Why write fugues in this way at all? If the shape of the piece is already ordained, why not just write it all out? One might also ask why one should walk to the café when cars are convenient. I will answer just as your mother would: the exercise is good for you. The purpose of partimento is not merely to play the music, but to *participate in its construction*.

EXERCISE. Develop a realization of Leo's chromatic partimento fugue.

EXAMPLE 6.21 Zingarelli's partimento in C major

EXAMPLE 6.21 Continued

Zingarelli's partimento in C major, shown in Example 6.21, is a study in fugal textures. Five instances of subject or answer are marked, but the partimento accommodates more. While the first four bars present the subject, the answer never appears in the bass, so the player must determine its intervals, and in what way it differs from the subject. The solution lies in the fifth bar, where the figures reveal the notes of the answer in the upper voice.

In addition to instances of marked soggetto and risposta, the thematic material also shows up a few more times in this partimento. Its presence in the bass should be easy enough to find. To detect it in an upper voice, look for a Cascade pattern in the bass like measure 7. This pattern will coincide with the third measure of the soggetto or risposta (the bass accompaniments to the first two bars of the soggetto and riposta vary somewhat, so this third measure is a more reliable guide).

EXERCISE. As you work on this partimento, you may wish to copy it out, leaving a blank treble staff above on which to fill in upper voices. You can also carry out your work using only the existing partimento, perhaps marking locations of entries. It is actually possible to play a fugal partimento like this one without writing anything down, but it is quite challenging. All these approaches are valid; you will have to decide what is most helpful. Begin by noting cadences and key areas. Instead of proceeding to bass motions, instead find all the entries of the soggetto and risposta. The intervals between these themes and the bass will largely determine your harmonies, but you may still have some limited harmonic choices even after the themes have been implemented. Of course, when the soggetto appears in the bass, you can apply whatever upper voice solutions seem appropriate (again, the risposta never appears in the bass in this partimento). For any passages remaining that seem not to include thematic material, determine bass motions. If possible, include fragments from the soggetto to create thematic unity. There is no need to retain a consistent number of voices; use two or three whenever you wish. A possible solution is provided in Example 6.22.

After working on this partimento you may notice that, once all the themes have taken their places, the piece is already quite substantial, and it only remains to fill in some corners here and there. Partimenti with many imitations leave the player less freedom, and deliberately so, as their purpose is to demonstrate counterpoint.

Fenaroli's very long partimento fugue in G minor (Gj 1381) is shown in Example 6.23. The subject resembles that of the fugue in D minor, BWV 565, usually attributed to J. S. Bach (although considered spurious by some scholars). Fenaroli's subject is both hyperkinetic and compound—it moves in perpetual eighths for much of its duration, and its pattern of skipping between higher and lower registers suggests two separate voices.

Compound hyperkinetic subjects impose limits on a potential fugue's complexity. Due to the skipping motion between registers, the subject takes up a wide range, crowding other voices and leaving less room for them to maneuver. The implied two-voice texture narrows the possibilities for harmonization, since the harmony is already partially outlined. The fact that one of the two implied voices within the subject is a pedal point further limits the player's

EXAMPLE 6.22 A realization of Zingarelli

EXAMPLE 6.22 Continued

EXAMPLE 6.22 Continued

EXAMPLE 6.23 Fenaroli's partimento Gj 1381

EXAMPLE 6.23 Continued

EXAMPLE 6.23 Continued

options. Having made these observations about the subject, we may surmise that Fenaroli's partimento fugue in G minor will not be terrifying to work out.

Fenaroli provides the subject and answer in complete form in measures 1–7. Accompanying the answer in measure 5 is a countersubject that tracks with the subject in imperfect consonances—mostly parallel tenths. This will be a reliable strategy for the remainder of the fugue, and is really one of the few options for accompanying a compound hyperkinetic subject of this type, anyway. The other foolproof choice is to hold a sustained note on ❺ of the current tonality.

The arpeggio gesture in measure 4 sometimes appears at the end of the subject as a transition to another entry, but is sometimes left off. This one-measure idea serves as the basis for episodes several times, implies a Cascade motion, and is easily imitated in an upper voice.

In measure 46 a figure appears that is derived from a fragment of the subject. This idea may also contribute to episodes; imitating it in upper voices should be simple.

EXERCISE. Work out a solution for Fenaroli's partimento fugue in G minor from Example 6.23. With some determination, you may be able to do it without writing anything. Example 6.24 presents a version using a minimal texture of (mostly) two voices, intended to show what might be done at the keyboard, without working anything out on paper.

Fenaroli's partimento fugue in A♭ (Gj 1452) is shown in Example 6.25. It is from Book IV of his partimenti and is among the most difficult. The subject is a remarkably disjunct series of leaps, ascending by sixths and descending by sevenths. Inverted to smaller intervals, this turns out to be Cascade. In all likelihood this seeming misdirection is part of Fenaroli's teaching strategy to show students that familiar patterns may show up in strange disguises.

EXAMPLE 6.24 A realization of Gj 1381

EXAMPLE 6.24 Continued

EXAMPLE 6.24 Continued

EXAMPLE 6.24 Continued

EXAMPLE 6.24 Continued

EXAMPLE 6.25 Fenaroli's partimento Gj 1452

EXAMPLE 6.25 Continued

The subject as it appears at the beginning of the piece is three measures in length, but later (starting in measures 31 and 36) a longer version shows up, extending the Cascade motion by a few beats. In measure 5 the bass is also a Cascade. At this point the unwritten upper voice will enter with the "upside down" Cascade of the fugue theme. Whenever this "normal" Cascade, consisting of the usual thirds and seconds, appears in the bass, that is a very good indication that the subject will fit in an upper voice.

A long episode of eleven measures begins in measure 20, during which there are no obvious opportunities for placing the subject. Instead, this episode invites you to create points of imitation in several different keys. By now you should be able to figure this out on your own.

When working on possible solutions for this fugue I found that the wide leaps of the subject make it very difficult to manage a third voice, both because the hand is fully occupied managing the subject's large intervals, and because the additional voice has so little room. In order to create a bit of extra space, you may wish to transpose the bass down an octave in certain passages. If you want to try something really difficult, place the subject in the alto voice at some point, such that the right hand must deal with another voice above the subject.

EXAMPLE 6.26 A realization of Gj 1452

EXAMPLE 6.26 Continued

EXAMPLE 6.26 Continued

EXERCISE. Develop a solution for Fenaroli's partimento fugue in A♭. A possible solution appears in Example 6.26. A version like this is not realistic without writing out the parts. While working on this rather minimal solution (mostly in two and three parts), I noticed that one may place the subject in augmentation (that is, note values doubled in duration) in an upper voice beginning on the third beat of measure 9. As this fugue is considered among Fenaroli's most advanced, perhaps this is a deliberate challenge, but I don't know for certain. Upon the advice of a knowledgeable scholar, I constructed a simple stretto

EXAMPLE 6.27 Gj 1452 with augmentation

beginning at measure 30. We will not discuss stretto until Chapter 14, but it will do you no harm to hear what this one sounds like.

My attempt at setting the subject in augmentation appears in Example 6.27, along with some other ideas for the first section of the partimento, such as placing the subject in the alto starting at measure 17.

Learning to work on partimento fugues is a useful step toward becoming a more capable improviser, as the player must walk in the footsteps of the Neapolitan masters. However, playing partimento fugues is still an activity tied to the printed page. Before we can break free and improvise unbound, we must consider still more aspects of music. The following chapter will introduce your next task.

Chapter 7

Bicinium

Beginning with this chapter, we remove the support of written partimento and prepare to improvise without the assistance of the printed page; we are on the way to free improvisation. However, we must first discuss some additional skills that are indispensable for the improviser.

Fugues employ two-voice textures in the exposition and likely elsewhere. A common device, even in music of many voices, is to drop all but two for a time. This thinning of the texture is interesting in itself, but also allows for the dramatic re-entry of the other voices. Pedal points in the bass, to be addressed later, are often matched with two upper voices.

Since these three situations—the entry of the second voice in an exposition, a reduction of voices in an episode, and two voices over a pedal point—are very common in fugues, the improviser will need a repertoire of two-voice patterns available at any moment.

While the term *bicinium* sometimes refers to any two-part counterpoint, in this book I use the word in a narrower sense, to denote a brief transitional passage. Passages in two parts are governed by the principles of species counterpoint. If you have not been trained in this art, I recommend that you acquaint yourself with the basics. Instruction in species counterpoint is widely available in many publications, so I will not repeat all its rules here. The procedures for the preparation and resolution of dissonances and for the treatment of passing and neighbor tones are extremely valuable. To the extent that you adopt them as mental habits, your improvisations will benefit.

While two voices can imply a full chordal texture if either or both use compound melody, they need not do so. Strictly speaking, a two-voice texture does not create triadic harmony. Rather, it is possible to create passages that do not "commit" to a specific chord progression but rather consist of a series of consonances (and perhaps prepared and resolved dissonances). One interesting element of fugue is the manner in which harmonic progressions gradually come into focus; since fugues begin with only one voice, the listener must wait for a complete harmonic picture to appear as each voice enters. This sense of discovery is one of the joys of hearing fugue. Bicinium contributes to this effect by allowing for the creation of passages that hint at full harmonies without actually forming them.

Bicinium follows the customary voice-leading principles of eighteenth-century music. Most important, parallel fifths and octaves are forbidden. Parallel imperfect consonances (thirds, sixths, tenths) are permitted. Oblique and contrary motion are generally safe between consonances. Perfect consonances (unisons, fifths, octaves) are permitted but should be less common than imperfect consonances; bicinium is made mostly of thirds, sixths, tenths, prepared and resolved dissonances, and the diminutions that connect them. Because overly long passages that use the same parallel imperfect consonances don't sound very good, bicinium alternates frequently between different imperfect intervals. In minor keys, voices will usually follow the customary raised or lowered sixth and seventh scale degrees, depending on the direction of the line.

Bicinium Examples

This chapter provides practical strategies for creating bicinium passages. The following examples show passages in two parts. Play them and consider the many patterns and devices available for this technique. Some of the terms in these examples (such as subject, episode, and pedal point) will be addressed more fully in later chapters.

The toccatas of Alessandro Scarlatti employ seemingly endless passages in two voices that are constructed almost entirely of thirds and sixths. A selection is shown in Example 7.1.

The style of Francesco Durante's toccatas resembles that of Scarlatti's, as seen in Example 7.2.

A passage from a Durante toccata appears in Example 7.3. The second measure of the passage almost seems to be made of parallel root-position chords, if each pair of sixteenths were to be "compressed" into a single chord, as if thrown into the garbage masher in *Star Wars*. Such a perception is a result of modern theory, in which we were trained to look for roots. But it is more correct historically to hear no chords and no roots in this passage at all; it is simply a series of intervals between two voices.

Example 7.4 shows a passage from a toccata of Durante. Not surprisingly, several measures are devoted to thirds in parallel motion. Notice that over the trills, the ascending scales begin and end with a note consonant with the bass, showing how the first and last note of a scale passage serve as structural notes while the rest of the scale is heard as diminutions. The passages in parallel thirds

EXAMPLE 7.1 From a toccata of Alessandro Scarlatti

seem to imply a C5 without providing the full harmonies of that motion. This is typical of the "duality" of bicinium: they both are, and are not, harmonic progressions.

Example 7.5 illustrates a passage from a Durante toccata in which mere thirds and sixths are "amplified" into impressive virtuosity by octave displacements and lower neighbors. This is an excellent strategy for making laughably simple intervals sound like real music.

The subject and an episode from the Kleine Fuge in D by George Frideric Handel (1685–1749) appear in Example 7.6. The episode drops to a single voice, quotes a fragment from the subject, then adds a second voice to form a one-measure passage in bicinium. The technique is extremely simple and useful: accompany any theme in thirds.

A passage from J. S. Bach's fugue in A minor, BWV 543, is shown in Example 7.7. While notated in two voices, the repeated note (appearing variously in high, middle, and low register) implies a third voice. This is an example of compound melody, in which one written voice suggests two. For passages in which one voice is static while two others move in parallel motion, I use the

EXAMPLE 7.2 From a toccata of Francesco Durante

EXAMPLE 7.3 From a Durante toccata

EXAMPLE 7.4 A passage from a Durante toccata

made-up term *paralique* (parallel plus oblique). If you follow the strong beats in the lowest voice, you will discover Monte Principale.

Example 7.8 shows the subject and a two-voice episode from the first fugue from *Die wohlklingende Fingersprache* of Johann Mattheson (1681–1764). Note that the episode moves in fifths and sixths (and maybe thirds and octaves, depending upon how you interpret the diminutions). This passage sounds almost like an Ascending 5-6 because it uses the same intervals, but without the complete harmony. The eighth-note figure is derived from the fugue subject.

EXAMPLE 7.5 A selection from a Durante toccata

EXAMPLE 7.6 The subject and an episode from Handel's *Kleine Fuge*

EXAMPLE 7.7 A passage from BWV 543

EXAMPLE 7.8 The subject and an episode from Mattheson

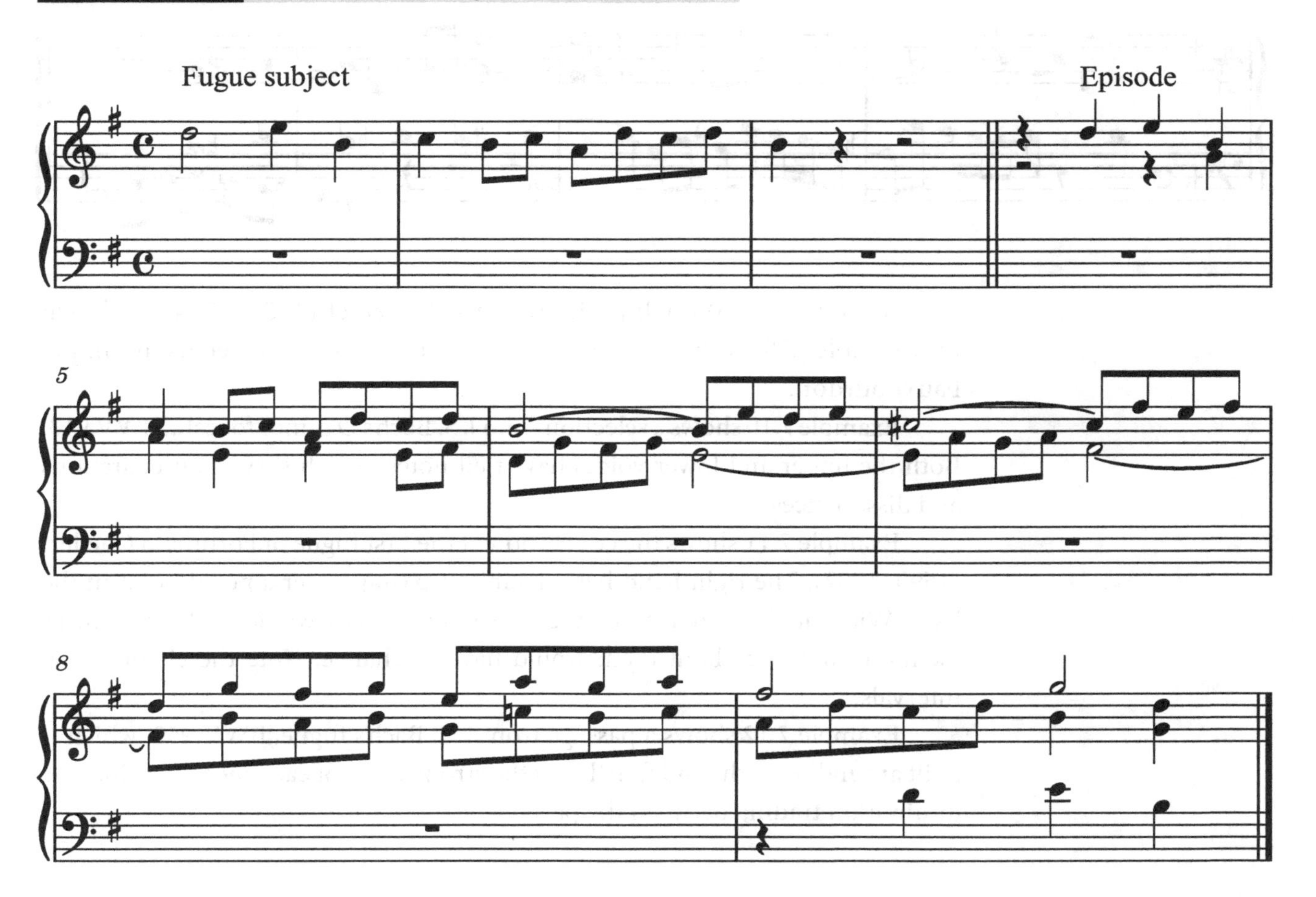

EXAMPLE 7.9 A passage by Pachelbel

EXAMPLE 7.10 A passage from BWV 913

A passage by Wilhelm Hieronymus Pachelbel (1686–1764) is shown in Example 7.9. While written in two voices only, it seems to imply Fauxbourdon.

Example 7.10 shows a selection from J. S. Bach's D minor toccata, BWV 913. Both the upper and lower voices have tied notes, which serve as preparations and dissonances.

Example 7.11 shows the conclusion of the first fugue of Fortunato Chelleri (1690–1757). The right hand has a bicinium passage over a pedal point in the bass. Without the pedal point the two upper voices would still function as bicinium; nothing about them would have to change. Note the chain of 7-6 intervals.

Example 7.12 shows a passage from J. S. Bach's fugue, BWV 950, which is built around sevenths and fourths on the strong beats of each measure. Note the diminution trading between the parts.

EXAMPLE 7.11 The conclusion of a Chelleri fugue

EXAMPLE 7.12 A passage from BWV 950

Example 7.13 shows a selection from Mattheson's fourth fugue from *Die wohlklingende Fingersprache*. The two voices use the same rhythmic figure when resolving dissonances.

In the selection from Durante's *Esercizio overro sonata per organo*, seen in Example 7.14, the lower voice contains the dissonances, and the upper voice gets all the diminutions.

EXAMPLE 7.13 A selection from a Mattheson fugue

EXAMPLE 7.14 A selection from Durante's *Esercizio*

Example 7.15 shows a passage from J. S. Bach's toccata in F♯ minor, BWV 910. Dissonances occur on every beat of the measure and are placed alternately in both voices. The upper voice is a dissonant seventh on the first and third beats, while the lower is a dissonant second (actually a ninth) on the second and fourth beats. Note the resolutions happen very quickly, in a single sixteenth note.

EXAMPLE 7.15 From BWV 910

Certain kinds of bicinium events tend to recur in the keyboard literature of the eighteenth century. Passages based on sequential patterns are very common; they sound good in two voices and are "improv-friendly" because of their predictability. Durante and Scarlatti often used falling and rising patterns of consonances, such as parallel thirds, sixths, tenths, or implied Fauxbourdon.

Dissonance in Bicinium

Almost any bass motion may be outlined with only two voices; C5, Monte Principale, and Cascade are especially common. Most composers employed frequent prepared dissonances when writing in two parts. While any of the dissonances may be used, sevenths and seconds are heard most.

Example 7.16 presents some standard bicinium patterns in structural notes.

If you know these models, it is easy to elaborate them with diminutions. Example 7.17 shows the same bicinium patterns as Example 7.16, but with simple diminutions.

Example 7.18 shows a fugue subject of Padre Martini followed by passages in bicinium based on elements from the theme.

Example 7.19 shows fugue subjects by various composers.

EXERCISE. Study each subject in Example 7.19. For each, develop passages in bicinium that draw from the subject's motivic ideas. Try passages using 7-6, 2-3, C5, and Cascade. Longer bicinium passages may incorporate various techniques, including parallel motion of imperfect consonances and implied bass motions.

EXAMPLE 7.16 Bicinium patterns

EXAMPLE 7.17 Bicinium with diminutions

EXAMPLE 7.18 A Martini fugue subject

EXAMPLE 7.19 Fugue subjects

Chapter 8

Bass Motions in Invertible Counterpoint

This chapter describes some special contrapuntal models that may be memorized and adapted for use in improvisation. The notion of memorizing models may seem to contradict the ideals of spontaneity, but this objection is misguided. An improvising orator does not invent a new language out of nothing, but rather delivers a series of largely prefabricated verbal segments—introductions, arguments, illustrations, exhortations, clever turns of phrase—modified and assembled for the rhetorical purposes of the moment. In the same way, the keyboard improviser has at the ready a large memorized library of contrapuntal schemes.

Chapter 6 introduced the idea of invertible counterpoint in partimento. In invertible counterpoint, themes may be combined in any registral order. The combination of two themes in invertible counterpoint is known as double counterpoint; three themes is triple, and so on. We saw that a few measures of an unfigured bass line may imply, and contain all the necessary ingredients for, a passage in which the bass and upper voices trade thematic materials. In Sala's fifth partimento, the material from the first and second measures works in combination, with either as bass or soprano.

When Sala's first measure serves as the bass, we might describe the motion as Rule of the Octave leading into a cadence. When the second measure serves as bass, we now have a completely different motion: a short segment of Tied Bass. The same combination of materials, when inverted, results in a different bass motion. Example 8.1 demonstrates these combinations.

EXAMPLE 8.1 Inversion of Sala's themes

Combining Bass Motions

This raises many questions. Do all bass motions combine with some upper voice theme, which itself can then be flipped to the bass, resulting in a new motion? Does this new motion match with some other theme, which then can flip and create *yet another* bass motion? Does this process go on forever? Do these combinations result in "prefabricated" options for invertible counterpoint? Can we know these combinations well enough to use them spontaneously in improvisation? Was this art of combinations explicitly taught in the partimento tradition? The answer to all these questions is yes . . . sort of, with many limits and qualifications. Certain motions participate in combinations of double, triple, and even quadruple counterpoint. Others are less useful for such purposes.

Francesco Durante's *Esercizio ovvero Sonate per organo* appears to be a pedagogical piece, as implied by its title, and not only for keyboard training but also for composition and improvisation. The work is notable for its relentless and repetitive employment of certain bass motions and points of imitation, as if to parade their uses before impressionable students. Example 8.2 shows a short selection.

The bass commencing in the second measure, when relieved of its diminutions, is clearly a C5 motion. Two upper voices provide the standard harmonic solution to this motion. The highest voice is syncopated and descends by step. In the fifth measure this syncopated line has moved to the bass, and the C5 line, with its diminutions, now appears as the sole upper voice. This inverted combination, in which both lines have been preserved verbatim, now results in the outline of a Tied Bass motion. This is a perfect example of the way a bass motion may invert with an upper voice and become a different motion.

Note, however, that Durante did not repurpose the middle line from the second and third measures as a bass. This would have resulted in a Tied Bass motion that is not syncopated. In Durante's world, such a thing could not exist; Tied Bass motions, as the name implies, always took place over an offbeat bass line. However, Durante could have kept the middle line from the second and third measures and used it as a middle or top voice in the last two measures. Example 8.3 illustrates this possibility.

EXAMPLE 8.2 A passage from Durante's *Esercizio*

EXAMPLE 8.3 A reworking of Durante

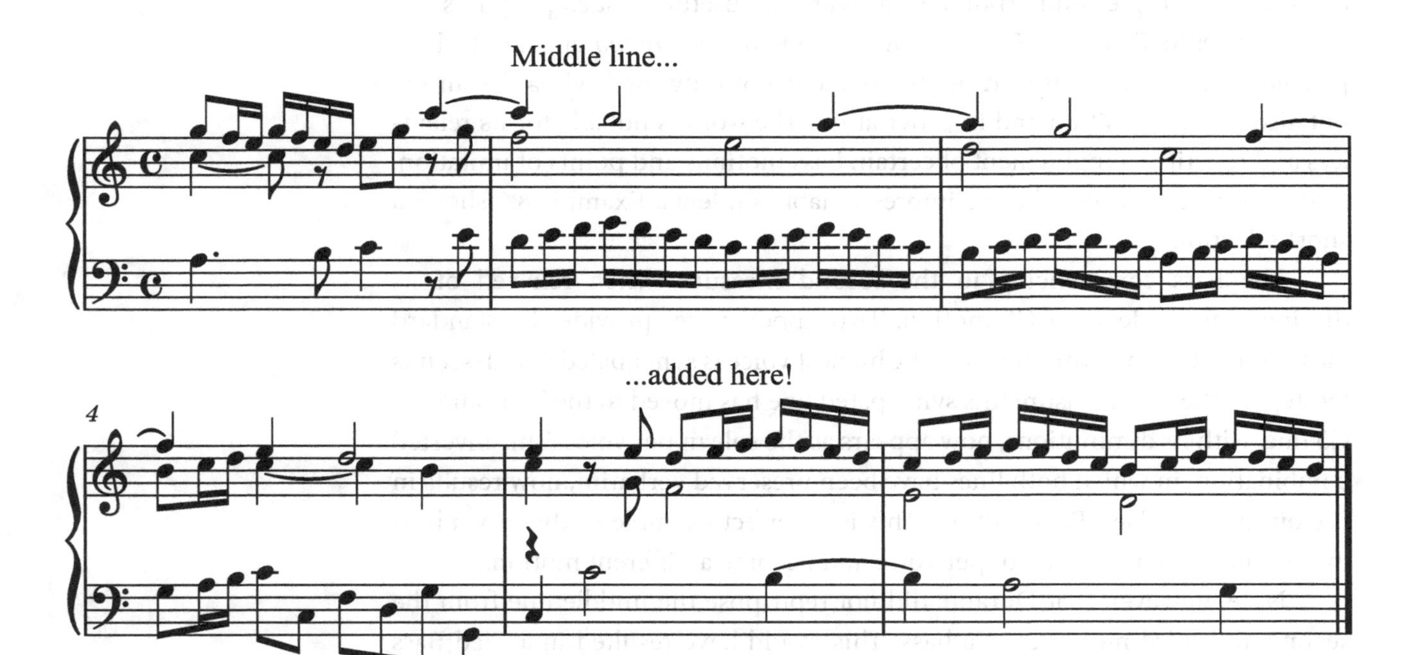

EXAMPLE 8.4 A passage from Durante

From these observations we discover that certain limits apply to the combinations of invertible bass motions.

Another selection from Durante's *Esercizio* appears in Example 8.4.

At A the lowest voice appears to outline a Tied Bass motion. The upper voice provides intervals confirming that this is so: seconds and fourths on strong beats and sixths on weak beats. At B the highest voice begins a syncopated descending stepwise line, exactly like the bass from A but transposed up a fifth. The lowest voice at B copies the material from A exactly, although transposed. The result is an inverted bass motion; the first example is Tied Bass and the second is Cascade.

Again, note the middle voice. It cannot serve as a bass with the other two voices, as unprepared dissonant perfect fourths would result. This is always the case with perfect fifths. As the only interval that changes from consonant to dissonant when inverted, the improviser must watch out for them. They often sabotage the invertibility of lines that would otherwise combine without problems.

A third selection from the *Esercizio* appear in Example 8.5.

Rather obviously, the motion is Ascending 5-6. However, note that the first iteration features soprano scales that descend a seventh. Since a descending seventh is the same as a rising second, the soprano doubles the tenor without creating parallels. Very sneaky. This same descending scale appears in the bass later, resulting in an elaborate but functionally unchanged line of rising steps. In this case, thematic material has moved from the highest voice to the lowest *without changing the bass motion* because the underlying structure interval of a

EXAMPLE 8.5 A passage from Durante

rising second was not altered. Unlike the previous examples of inverted material, this one does not create a new bass motion.

These examples should make the curious improviser wonder exactly which bass motion combinations are available, and how far one can go with the process of combining and inverting. Example 8.6 shows a mildly absurd series of such possibilities. As each motion in the bass is inverted to the top voice, it combines with a new motion in the bass. In this way, the motions morph from Cascade through C5, Tied Bass, 7-6 (which is just a scale), another 7-6, Leaping Romanesca, Monte Romanesca, and a descending chromatic motion.

Examples of Bass Motion Pairings

While it may be enticing to investigate every possible combination of bass motions that could fit together as high and low voices, that project is probably not practical, especially when one considers the endless combinations that open up when two motions move in different rhythmic values. Instead, we should learn certain combinations that were favored in eighteenth-century music and function effectively in improvisation. The following examples present some of the most common pairings of two motions in double counterpoint.

Example 8.7 displays the opening measures of one the Magnificat fugues of Johann Pachelbel (1653–1706).

In Pachelbel's fugue, two Cascades are played, but not quite simultaneously. One might call them "out of phase" by one beat. Vertically, the result is merely a series of thirds and sixths. For those initiated in the secrets of partimento, it is a method for playing a favorite bass motion in imitation against itself.

EXAMPLE 8.6 Bass motion pairings

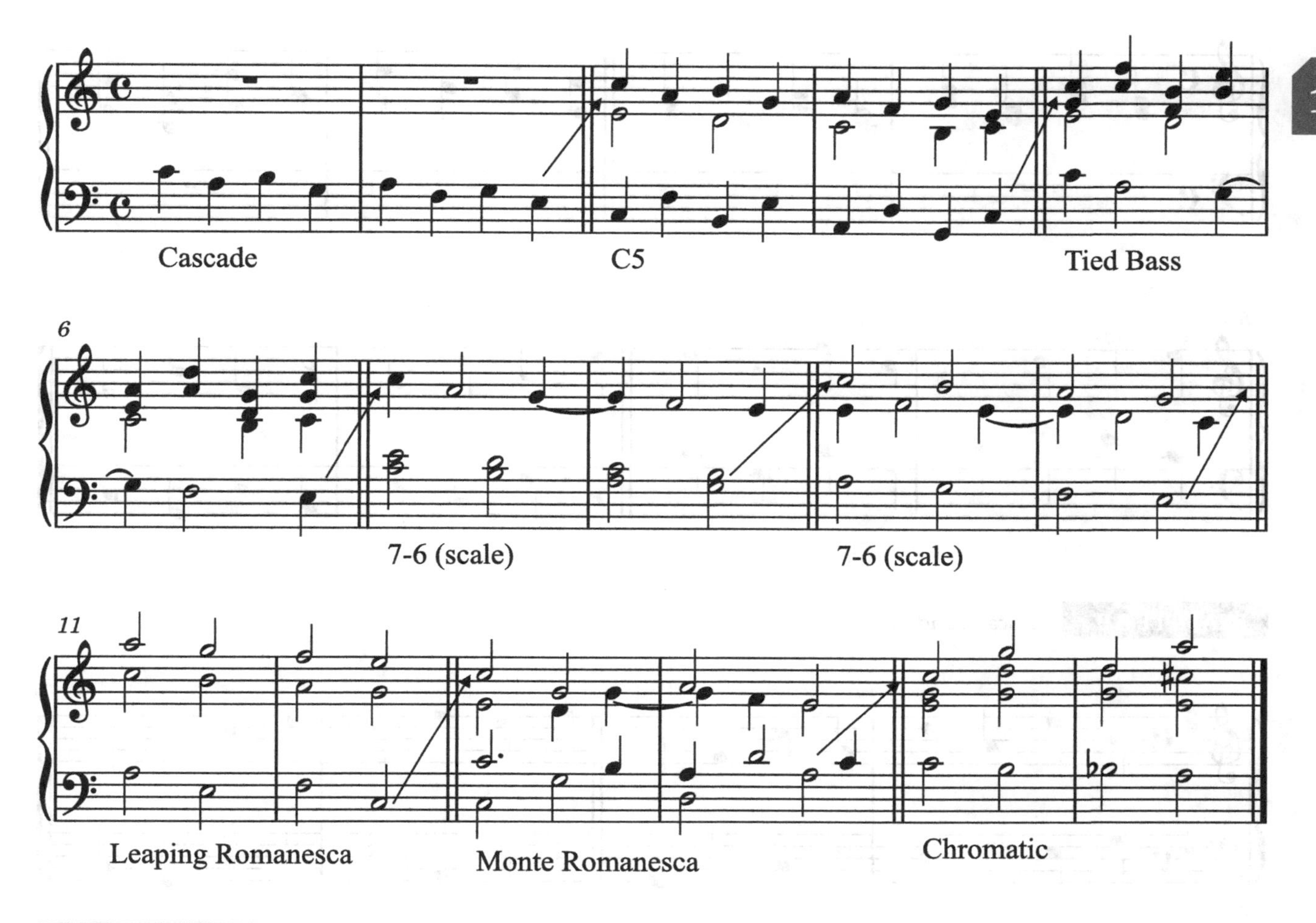

EXAMPLE 8.7 A passage from a Pachelbel fugue

C5 may combine with itself in parallel thirds, sixths, or tenths, and also "out of phase" in contrary motion. All combinations are invertible. These devices appear in Example 8.8.

Cascade combines with C5, as shown in Example 8.9, and results in imperfect consonances alternating with octaves. This is less harmonious than combinations made entirely of imperfect consonances, so this technique will often appear in real music with an additional free voice to fill out the sound.

EXAMPLE 8.8 C5 combining with other motions

EXAMPLE 8.9 Cascade and C5

C5 combines with a descending scale in multiple ways. If the C5 moves at twice the speed of the scale, the result is either alternating thirds and sixths or alternating imperfect consonances and prepared dissonances. The combinations work in inversion. These situations are demonstrated in Example 8.10.

Two descending scales moving at the same speed but offset (or "out of phase") will form a series of sevenths and sixths or seconds and thirds. This pattern is very common by itself in a two-voice texture, and it also combines with several additional bass motions. This pairing is of great help to the improviser. It is so important that it needs a name: Offset Scales. See Example 8.11.

EXERCISE. Play each combination of motions explained previously. Try all possible inversions, and transpose to other tonalities. Add diminutions to make the combinations sound like real music. Once you know the two-voice structures well, add a free voice. The choice of notes in the free voice should be guided by whatever bass motion is currently in effect.

EXAMPLE 8.10 C5 and a descending scale

EXAMPLE 8.11 Offset Scales

Some combinations of three or even four motions are possible. The examples below show these.

Two Cascades will combine with a C5. This set of motions is only partially invertible; the C5 may not serve as a bass due to perfect fifths inverting to dissonant fourths. Example 8.12 shows these combinations in abstract form and as found in a Pachelbel Magnificat fugue.

The Monte Principale motion—up a fourth and down a third—is remarkable for its contrapuntal flexibility. It combines with itself both in and out of phase. Because of its many combinations, it has been a favorite bass

EXAMPLE 8.12 From a Pachelbel fugue

motion and melody in imitative music for centuries. In addition to its contrapuntal potential in two voices, the Monte Principale pattern may participate in triple and even quadruple counterpoint. Three voices employing this motion combine easily, with two moving in parallel tenths and another out of phase. A fourth voice may be added, resulting in quadruple counterpoint. Three of the voices follow the Monte Principale pattern, while the fourth falls a second and rises a third. Such a combination is particularly impressive, as the voices may be placed in any of twenty-four different orders without voice-leading error. Example 8.13 shows several combinations of Monte Principale in two, three, and four voices.

C5, Tied Bass, and a descending scale will work together in triple counterpoint if arranged according to Example 8.14, in which voice leading errors are avoided. In unlimited triple counterpoint, in which all dispositions of the voices are permissible, six possible combinations result. Example 8.14 shows all six, followed by the three motions combined in a measure from a Magnificat fugue of Pachelbel.

In a fugue in G minor by Johann Adam Reincken (1643–1722), a Cascade (elaborated with diminutions) combines with Offset Scales many times. As the elaborated Cascade serves as the second half of the subject, it has good reason to appear often in the piece. The Offset Scales accompany the subject, appearing variously as top, middle, and bass voices. Selections from Reincken appear in Example 8.15.

Two C5s in the upper voices may be combined with a Cascade bass, as shown in Example 8.16.

EXAMPLE 8.13 Monte Principale combinations

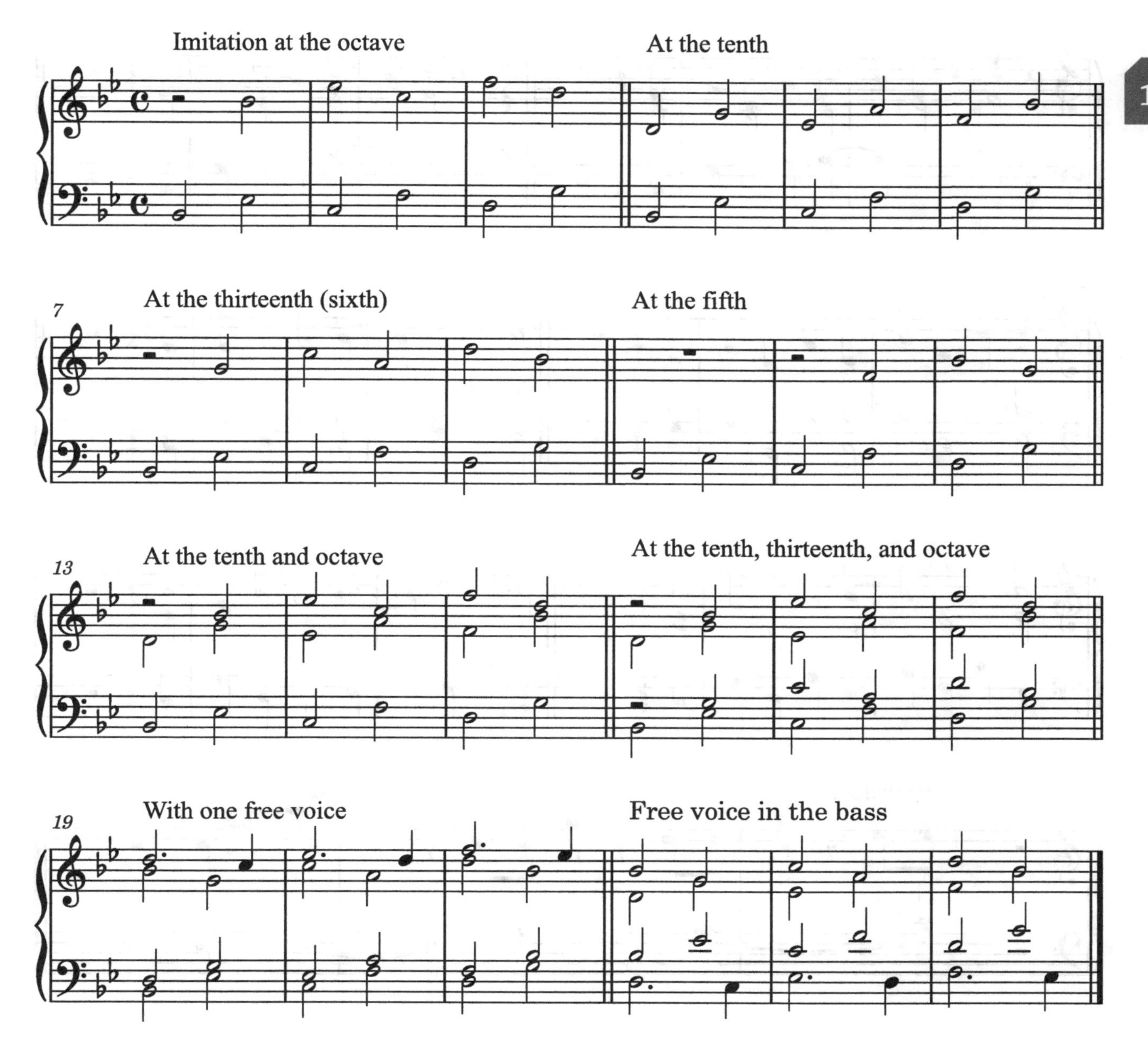

This contrapuntal device will not function in all inversions, as unprepared dissonant fourths will result under certain circumstances. The C5s may move in either parallel thirds, sixths, or tenths, although the tenths will be very difficult for some hands to reach. The Cascade is the best choice for the bass.

EXERCISE. Play each combination in triple and quadruple counterpoint explained previously, trying out all possible inversions and transposing to other tonalities.

EXAMPLE 8.14 C5, Tied Bass, and a scale; a passage from Pachelbel

EXAMPLE 8.15 Passages from Reincken

The Mattei Canon

Some additional standard contrapuntal combinations are worthy of mention. These are for ascending and descending scales in the bass. Of course, scales may be harmonized by Rule of the Octave or Fauxbourdon in either direction. Ascending scales also have solutions such as 5-6, 8-7-6, or 10-9-8. Descending scales have choices such as Stepwise Romanesca, 3-♯4-6, and 7-6.

EXAMPLE 8.17 The Mattei Canon

Stanislao Mattei (1750–1825) offers a special solution for the ascending bass, shown in Example 8.17.

The upper voices move in canon, one voice imitating the other at successively higher pitches, so I call this the Mattei Canon. The Mattei Canon is an adaptation of 8-7-6, with the unusual feature that the dissonance is traded between upper voices rather than appearing always in the same voice. While the upper voices are theoretically invertible, trading them will result in voice-crossing, which is possible on a two-manual harpsichord or organ, but impractical on piano.

Once I learned about the Mattei Canon, I wondered if something similar could work on a descending scale. I made up this solution as a prediction of a technique I expect to find in real music someday. It was fairly easy to work out, so I assume someone far smarter than me found it centuries ago. (Perhaps we should call it the 7-6 Prediction.) As in the Mattei Canon, the upper voices are in imitation, and take turns providing the dissonant seventh. They are invertible but will cross if traded. The 7-6 Prediction is shown in Example 8.18.

EXAMPLE 8.18 The 7-6 Prediction

EXAMPLE 8.19 Cherubini's passage

[Excuse the interruption. This is me speaking to you from the future, a few months after I wrote the previous paragraph. Indeed, I found what I was looking for. Luigi Cherubini, who will show up again in Chapter 9, wrote something very similar to my 7-6 Prediction. In fact, once the diminutions are taken away, it is really the same thing. After Cherubini's death his teaching materials were assembled and published as *Marches d'harmonie (Harmonic Progressions)* in 1851. Among his many solutions for a descending scale was the model shown in Example 8.19. Note that, just like my 7-6 Prediction, the upper voices tie over the bar line to create the dissonance, fall a step to resolve, descend a fifth, and then rise a fourth to prepare the next dissonance. And they do this in strict imitation. Future John out.]

Contrapuntal Models for the Improviser

What is the purpose of studying these combinations? Are they truly practical for the improviser? Apparently so. In a 1774 letter C. P. E. Bach (1714–1788) described his father's manner of listening to others' fugues:

> When he listened to a rich and many-voiced fugue, he could soon say, after the first entries of the subjects, what contrapuntal devices it would be possible to apply, and which of them the composer by rights ought to apply, and on such occasions, when I was standing next to him, and he had voiced his surmises to me, he would joyfully nudge me when his expectations were fulfilled.

How did J. S. Bach predict in advance the techniques of counterpoint that would unfold in a fugue? I believe that he did so partly by recognizing intervals in the themes that conformed to standard models of combination and invertibility. (Of course, Bach would have also noticed other factors such as real and tonal answers, motives suitable for episodes, and the subject's potential for counterpoint with itself in a stretto. More on these topics later.) If an average clod such as myself can hear a melody with rising fourths and falling fifths and predict that it will return later as a bass supporting a C5 motion, Bach could surely do far more. His recognition of the contrapuntal potential of these motions likely enhanced his ability to predict events in fugues upon hearing the first few bars. It seems probable, then, that he drew upon this same insight when improvising.

EXERCISE. Example 8.20 is a preposterously overachieving partimento with several built-in opportunities to try invertible counterpoint. Work through it as usual, but instead of a typical chordal solution, use invertible counterpoint where possible. Example 8.21 provides one solution for this unreasonably convoluted challenge.

EXAMPLE 8.20 A difficult partimento

EXAMPLE 8.21 A solution for the difficult partimento

EXAMPLE 8.21 Continued

Over time you can learn to recognize passages that are suitable for the combinations explained in this chapter. Of course, once you know the combinations, you can invent your own themes for improvisation that are built expressly for such contrapuntal treatment. And of course, techniques such as the Mattei Canon and the 7-6 Prediction are appropriate even for simple partimenti. Substituting them in place of the expected Rule of the Octave would be a very cool thing to do. For now, play through the examples in this chapter. You may wish to return to them later, once you have begun improvising complete fugues.

Chapter 9

Introduction to Improvised Fugue

As we prepare to improvise fugues, we must clarify what we mean by the term, and what kind of music we are trying to make. What is a fugue, after all? What elements must it include? What pitfalls must it avoid? In what models from history do we find guidance?

In the seventeenth and eighteenth centuries, the notion of fugue was broadly inclusive; it is only a mild exaggeration to say that if someone wrote "fuga" on the top of a page, the music on that page was a fugue. However, most readers will have in mind certain works of the celebrated composers of the eighteenth century. This style provides what many think of as the "essentials" of fugue: the expectant drama as music gradually unfolds from a single line; tightly woven thematic unity; the delightful surprise as the familiar subject pops up like a marmot in unexpected tonalities and registers; the relentless determination of a theme enduring the hardships of modulation and contrapuntal devilry, only to emerge victorious at the last cadence. Such things draw us to fugue.

If they are to be considered "legitimate," fugues must include most or all of the following events.

The Exposition

The exposition is the most recognizable element; without one, a fugue isn't a fugue. In this section the subject, which is the main theme, appears first in one voice alone. When that voice completes the subject and continues with other material, the subject appears in a second voice and is called the answer. Subjects and answers continue entering until all voices of the fugue are in play. Material that accompanies a subject is known as the countersubject. Fugues with a fixed countersubject will use the same theme against the subject many times, and in so doing grant the countersubject its own thematic significance. The countersubject combines with the subject in invertible counterpoint.

The Episode

Episodes are bridge-like passages that connect other events within a fugue. The purpose of the episode is to create contrast with the more thematically intense sections by refraining from prominent use of the subject and answer, and to modulate. The episode will often include fragments of the subject, which generates thematic unity and makes the piece sound like itself. Many episodes are harmonically sequential. They vary in length and number, but almost always serve as "spacers" between other events.

The Presentation

In the presentation the subject makes one or more appearances in its full (or nearly full) form. Many fugues are structured around the goal of reaching various tonalities and achieving presentations in each, separated by episodes. The middle portion of a fugue is likely to consist of alternating episodes and presentations. The subject may appear in any voice or combination of voices.

The Pedal Point

An optional section, the pedal point consists of a long note held on ① or ⑤ in the bass, with activity in the upper voices. If no stretto is present, the pedal point may lead to a final presentation or straight into the last cadence.

The Stretto

Historically, the stretto is not an indispensable element of fugue. Some have them; many do not. If a stretto appears, it will be nearer the end of the fugue. In this event, the subject is arranged to overlap itself, such that one appearance is "interrupted" by another before the first is done. The word means "narrow," as if a group of subjects crowded into a tight spot and piled on top of each other. Stretto is a strategy for dialing up thematic density to the maximum.

Final Cadence

Obviously, fugues must conclude with a final cadence. Frequently the subject appears once in a prominent manner as the piece ends.

The *Fugue d'école* Tradition

We may gain further insight into fugue improvisation by considering the history of those who devoted themselves to this art with an intensity perhaps unmatched anywhere in the world. In the nineteenth century the Paris Conservatoire developed a tradition of the *fugue d'école* (academic fugue), which was stringent and extensive in its requirements; the Paris curriculum was exacting about what did, and did not, belong in a fugue.

Treatises are available from the early days of this tradition to the dawn of the twentieth century. Luigi Cherubini's *Cours de contrepoint et de fugue* (Course in Counterpoint and Fugue) was published in 1835, although he had become director of the school over a decade earlier, and contributed fugue subjects to the Conservatoire's fugue-writing contest beginning in 1818. André Gedalge (1856–1926) wrote *Traité de la fugue* (Treatise on Fugue), which appeared in 1901. A comparison of these two books reveals the trajectory of the *fugue d'école* across much of the nineteenth century.

The requirements for the *fugue d'école* grew in scope, prescriptiveness, and difficulty during this time. Representative of this tendency is the fact that Cherubini's treatise discusses episodes for two pages. Gedalge covers the same topic in forty. Similarly, Cherubini's explanation of the stretto (the section of the fugue where the subject is set in counterpoint against itself) fills barely one page of text, while Gedalge requires twenty-eight pages. Gedalge does much more than merely explain the stretto in greater detail than Cherubini; rather, Gedalge's exhaustive treatment reflects its metamorphosis, through the nineteenth century, into the dramatic pinnacle of the fugue and the showcase of the composer's best moves.

From its beginning the tradition emphasized that fugue study exists for the sake of developing general compositional prowess, and not merely to generate stacks of student fugues, most of which would never be heard. The faculty understood that the rigors of this dense and highly regulated writing style would prepare composers for anything. They were also aware that they were turning an art form into an academic exercise that, even if written correctly according to all the rules, might bore the audience. After mentioning a variety of possible contrapuntal combinations, Cherubini advised his students to exercise restraint:

> We may employ all these combinations, and even various others, in a fugue merely intended for study; but, in one which is to be given to the public, we must make a choice, and not introduce them all: without this precaution, the fugue would be too long, and consequently become tiresome.

The study of academic fugue culminated in the annual Concours de Conservatoire (Conservatory Contests), which were essentially final exams. Instead of grades issued confidentially, students were ranked with publicly announced prizes or soul-crushing absence thereof. The fugue *concours* was utterly terrifying by modern standards. Students arrived early in the morning to be seated in cubicles with pen and paper—no keyboard, no lifelines, no mercy. Given a subject, they had eighteen hours to compose a four-voice fugue in open score, not merely avoiding voice-leading errors but discovering and exploiting the inherent contrapuntal possibilities of the subject.

Where, in the *fugue d'école* curriculum, was improvisation? The *concours* exalts the silent, solitary, pen-and-paper act of composition while seemingly diminishing the noisy, public, hands-on-keys performativity of improvisation. Neither Cherubini's nor Gedalge's treatise mentions it even once. The study of fugue, beginning in counterpoint classes and culminating in the annual *concours*, was exclusively an act of written composition.

In the same school but a world away, the organists of the Paris Conservatoire kept improvisation alive. Traditions of organ playing developed within the liturgical services of the church, in which improvisation is arguably the most important practical skill. The organist's tasks ranged from lofty to mundane. Within a single service the player might be expected to provide an erudite contrapuntal setting of a religious tune; moments later, one might be required to fake a few bars of superficially reverent music as the aging priest waddles more slowly than expected to his post up front.

Because of this history, improvisation was central rather than peripheral to organ study. The first professor of organ at the Conservatoire was François Benoist (1794–1878). He won the Grand Prix de Rome for composition in 1815 and was appointed to the faculty in 1819. He taught generations of students for over fifty years, including César Franck (1822–1890), Charles-Valentin Alkan (1813–1888), and Camille Saint-Saëns (1835–1921)—names well known to pianists as well as organists. Benoist taught improvisation only, to the exclusion of repertoire, for decades.

Were Benoist's students creating, spontaneously and in real time, fugues of the same rigor that took the composition students eighteen hours of imprisoned agony? Apparently not. Benoist allowed certain accommodations for the improvised fugue. Four voices were expected in the exposition, but thereafter the density of vocal parts could vary freely. Subject entries were in outer voices only. While a stretto was customary, the requirement to use a fixed countersubject was waived.

This last compromise is notable, as the fixed countersubject must function in invertible counterpoint with the subject. Creation of this invertible relationship in improvised fugue is exceptionally difficult, even for the most experienced performers. The subject, given on the spot, must be quickly memorized, and its contrapuntal potential analyzed. The countersubject must then be invented very quickly, and must contain no errors, or the wheels will come off the fugue. The countersubject must then be committed to memory, as well. In the midst of the fugue, the subject and countersubject must be recalled and placed in appropriate contrapuntal relationship in a variety of tonalities. All this must be achieved while the player is also concerned with episodes, modulations, and many other details. The waiver of the fixed countersubject requirement was a crucial decision in improvisation pedagogy because fugue became accessible to more performers.

Where were the pianists? Were they improvising fugues along with the organists? It seems that they were not.

Pierre-Joseph-Guillaume Zimmerman (1785–1853) was appointed to the Conservatoire faculty in 1816. As dedicated to composition as to piano, he studied with Cherubini and won first prizes in both piano and harmony. His piano students included Alkan, Franck, and Antoine François Marmontel (1816–1898).

He stands out even in an age when so many musicians could do so many things so well. The notion, accepted today, that keyboard virtuosity and compositional fluency are irreconcilable pursuits that belong in separate academic departments, was unthinkable to Zimmerman. His *Encyclopédie du pianiste compositeur* (Encyclopedia of the pianist-composer), published in 1840 as a set of three volumes, lays out his vision for the ideal musician of his time.

The first explains piano fundamentals for the absolute beginner: this is a treble clef, this is a quarter note, these are black and white keys. The second volume contains a series of exercises typical of the French school, with emphasis on brutal routines of "finger independence," that narrow and lonely pathway to virtuosity that may have worked on light piano actions of the early nineteenth century, but since the arrival of the modern piano has inflamed the tendons of millions of diligent but hapless students. The third volume addresses the entire world of composition, with lessons on species counterpoint, fugue, orchestration, and reading open score.

Zimmerman's *Encyclopédie* illustrates the scope of the aspiring pianist-composer's labors. One must master every aspect of music. The book also stands as an idealized picture of the concert artist of the mid-nineteenth century: if one learned everything in this book, one could write and orchestrate piano concertos, and then turn around and perform them brilliantly, like Chopin, Franz Liszt (1811–1886), or Henri Herz (1803–1888).

I doubt that the book actually served in this way, however. While Zimmerman probably used many of the piano exercises with students at the Conservatoire, the fact that the *Encyclopédie* starts with beginner lessons suggests that it was not intended exclusively for professionals. The cursory treatment of profoundly complex topics (like writing fugues) and the lack of practical exercises in those areas suggests that it may have been for dilettantes who wanted to learn something *about* music without actually learning music. The instruction in counterpoint and fugue is just detailed enough that, after careful study, the reader could sound smart at parties. The marketing of a professional-sounding book to amateurs was typical of nineteenth-century piano methods.

Amateurs liked them because they could brush up against professional-level musicianship vicariously, and authors liked them because amateurs outnumbered professionals by several orders of magnitude, a disparity favorably reflected in sales figures.

Despite Zimmerman's attention to counterpoint and fugue in the *Encyclopédie*, he offers no instruction in improvisation; in fact, he never mentions it. In a book purporting to serve as a reference for every aspect of a pianist-composer's work, this omission is significant and certainly a sign of changing times. By the time the book appeared in 1840, a pianist-composer could be considered a complete master without improvising.

The Conservatoire's first piano professor of great international fame was Henri Herz, a virtuoso, composer of études and charming concert pieces, publisher of method books, piano manufacturing tycoon, and instigator of scandalous affairs. He was also the inventor of the Dactylion, a hideous contraption marketed as a finger-strengthening miracle device. Joining the faculty in 1842, Herz reinforced technical virtuosity as the cornerstone of the conservatory piano program. In making virtuoso technique the highest ideal, Herz joined Zimmerman in marginalizing improvisation and contributing to its demise among pianists.

In *Henri Herz's New and Complete Pianoforte School* of 1844, the author dissuades his readers from attempting public improvisation at all:

> Whatever may be the idea of the glory attached to improvisation when this glory is without alloy and free from charlatanism, the author would still advise his pupils to refrain from engaging in it, except in private, or before such intimate friends as shall have previously consented to pardon the imperfections attendant on instantaneous and unpremeditated performance. As to improvisation in public, to those who look upon it in a high point of view, and comprehend the conditions it imposes, it is the most dangerous ordeal to which a pianist can expose himself, provided he abandons himself entirely to the sway of his imagination. If we are aware of our real interest, we should not think of elevating ourselves to so high a standard; for many ambitious though talented pianists have, by one hazardous effort, descended below mediocrity. Even Hummel, the first and unrivalled improvisatore of the present day, has sometimes failed to sustain his usual degree of excellence.

Herz was himself an improviser; as was still common (although in decline) among concert virtuosi of his day, he occasionally asked for themes from the audience upon which to extemporize variations. Why he saw this skill as unfit to pass on to his students, one can only speculate. Perhaps he hoped they would occupy themselves with his own compositions; he was a relentless self-promoter. In advising his students to indulge in improvisation only in the presence of forgiving friends who have agreed in advance to overlook its wretchedness, Herz nails shut its coffin as a form of public music making. Curiously, he holds up Hummel's occasional fumbles as a cautionary tale, but I wonder if perhaps he is haunted by a memory of his own onstage disaster. Whatever the reason for his disinterest in teaching the subject, his decision to train pianists as virtuosos who cannot improvise affirmed a precedent that remains to this day.

The picture that emerges, then, is of three branches of the Conservatoire treating fugue in three different ways. The counterpoint faculty continued to teach written fugue according to the strict requirements of *fugue d'école*, reaching a peak of achievement (and perhaps anxiety) in the annual Concours du Conservatoire. The organists improvised fugue, allowing themselves some relaxation of rules (under Benoist) given the difficulties of spontaneous creation. The pianists ignored fugue entirely, devoting themselves to exercises and virtuosity at the keyboard.

The organists, however, were not content to improvise a simplified form of *fugue d'école*. The standards of organ improvisation steadily increased during the nineteenth century and into the twentieth. In 1926, Marcel Dupré (1886–1971) took charge of the class and instituted a level of improvisation equal to that of the written *fugue d'école*. His student Marie-Claire Alain (1926–2013) described the standards of fugue improvisation in Dupré's class in a 1993 interview:

Q. Was fugue taught in organ class before completion of the class in counterpoint and fugue? Was it concurrent?

A. Fugue was not taught in organ class. Students were supposed to know what the fugue was before being accepted to the class.

Q. Was *fugue d'école* a written exercise only? Or were the essentials of *fugue d'école* discussed and expected in organ class fugue improvisation?

A. The *fugue d'école* was a must. It was not discussed. All you had to do was to exercise yourself to make it all the way through without hesitating too much.

Q. Was any part of the fugue, that is, the countersubject, prepared by students in advance?

A. We were given the theme of the fugue at the beginning of the lesson, then allowed a few minutes of preparation in which we had to find: the answer, the *stretto veritable* (in order to check the mutations in the answer) and make our own countersubject in invertible counterpoint. The countersubject had to be memorized. We were never allowed to write it down, even for ourselves.

Q. Was the study of fugue broken into sections (example, several weeks spent on exposition, then on episodes, then stretto)?

A. From the very beginning we had to improvise the whole fugue, trying very hard not to stop or to get lost.

Q. Which sections presented the most difficulty for students improvising fugue?

A. That depended upon the people. Some students found the stretto the more difficult because you had to follow both voices of the canon. Personally, I had not much trouble with canonic problems. My main problem was the relative key, in which we had to use the subject in the tenor and the countersubject in the bass, then the answer in the alto and the contrasubject in the soprano. Try it . . . you'll understand!

Q. Was the stretto section the part of the fugue with the least requirements? Were three stretti mandatory? Was the subject in the last stretto an exact duplicate of that in the first stretto? Could the stretto be comprised of only the head of the subject?

A. The exposition of the stretto allowed only one note: the head of the subject, at an always shorter distance from the entry before. But the *stretto veritable* always had to be complete, and the last canon, that had to be very close (one or two beats of distance), had also to be complete in the two voices where it was exposed.

Q. What missing element would be most likely to be forgiven in an examination (i.e., a missing countersubject in one entry of the soprano or alto in the exposition)?

A. No missing element was forgiven. You had to do it. If you lost your countersubject, you lost the competition.

Q. At what point in improvisation was it permissible to have more than the specified number of voices (i.e., a four-voice fugue expanding to a chordal structure or five or six voices)?

A. The fugue was always with four voices. No chord structures were permitted. Sometimes we had a pedal point toward the end with four voices above it. But no one ever tried to improvise with five voices . . . too difficult! Dupré also allowed episodes with three voices, but never less (no recitative, no two-voice episodes).

Q. Were treatises on fugue discussed in organ class (i.e., the DuBois or Gedalge)?

A. We had no treatises. We were already trained.

Q. Was the Dupré *Cours complèt de fugue* used as text in counterpoint and fugue? Was it used or referenced in organ class? Were earlier tests studied, compared, or mentioned?

A. No study, no comparison, only exercising.

Q. Were any written *fugue d'écoles* [*sic*] ever performed in organ class?

A. No written fugues were ever performed. We were supposed to know about musical analysis. Remember, we had already several years in harmony, counterpoint, and fugue.

The severity of *fugue d'école* training is evident from Alain's interview. Notable, however, is that she mentions that students had to try "very hard not to stop or to get lost." Elsewhere she states that students aspired to "make it all the way through without hesitating too much." These remarks suggest that not all improvisations were polished masterpieces, even in the exclusive class of Dupré. (From that, take whatever comfort you can.)

Alain also reveals that the *fugue d'école* was actually quite scripted, and had to proceed with a set of established events in precise order. The order of key areas was given, and within each, the placement of subjects and answers was assigned to specific voices. In a sense, the *fugue d'école* was already composed in its broad outlines. The students' task was to invent, in their heads with just a few minutes' notice, suitable counterpointing material that would function with the given subject. They then placed these contrapuntal solutions in the correct locations as required by the *fugue d'école* outline.

During a century and a half of fugue study at the Conservatoire de Paris, the standards of written composition were extraordinarily high, while improvisation at the organ gradually advanced to a similar level. Meanwhile, among pianists, improvisation was largely discarded, establishing the tradition of the classically trained pianist who cannot make music without the printed page—a tradition which (ahem) "flourishes" to this day.

Improvising According to the *Fugue d'école* Tradition

As improvisers, what practical measures can we take from the history of fugue in Paris? All teachers—Cherubini, Benoist, Gedalge, Dupré, and others—were unanimous in their assessment that *fugue d'école* was an abstract exercise, suitable for study but not public performance. To reiterate Cherubini's view, if one dutifully strings together all the required elements, one will bore the audience. The four-voice, open-score format did not help; this manner of scoring places emphasis on contrapuntal combinations, but leaves the individual voices neutral and unassociated with any specific instrument. The resulting music lacks the idiomatic interest of vocal, keyboard, or instrumental writing; it refrains from indulging in cool things keyboards can do, or cool things strings can do, or cool things voices can do. Consequently, it isn't all that cool. Cherubini was right.

Dupré's recorded improvisations from the 1970s reveal that even the undisputed master of strict *fugue d'école* took a more liberal approach when extemporizing in public. He does not insist on a fixed countersubject and does not follow the prescribed form. Small voice-leading imperfections, barely audible but technically "wrong," appear occasionally in inner voices. He does not create stretti according to *fugue d'école* standards, but rather invents passages of stretto-like thematic density to serve in the same place—a clever solution we will revisit later. Aspiring improvisers should take encouragement from the fact that one of the greatest and most rigorous extemporizers found it necessary to *approximate* some aspects of fugue when playing for the public.

The Paris tradition created a pathway for understanding the elements of fugue and assembling them deftly. If we follow Benoist and Dupré and allow for some simplifications, and simultaneously pay attention to the idiomatic possibilities of keyboard instruments, nothing prevents us from adapting the guidance of *fugue d'école* for our purposes of study, enjoyment, and even public performance of improvised fugue.

As we proceed with improvised fugue, the resultant music will take shape more or less like the plan shown below. The plan is derived from the *fugue d'école* but simplified for use in improvisation. The bass motions chosen for the episodes are arbitrary; any other could be substituted.

Exposition: 3 or 4 voices entering in ascending or descending order
Episode 1: C5 (or other bass motion) with thematic fragment; modulate to related key
Presentation 1: Subject in one of the outer voices
Episode 2: 7-6 (or other bass motion) with thematic fragment; modulate to related key
Presentation 2: Subject in one of the outer voices
Episode 3: 5-6 (or other bass motion) with thematic fragment; modulate to dominant
Presentation 3: Subject in one of the outer voices
Pedal point on ⑤: Thematic fragments in upper voices
Presentation 4: Full statement of subject in the tonic
Final Cadence

The plan is flexible; it can accommodate any subject, and some of the key areas are interchangeable. This plan, and others similar to it, will inform our work in the chapters that follow. As confidence and familiarity with all the sections grows, we will gradually fill in plans like this and create complete improvised fugues.

Two accommodations must be explained further: lack of a fixed countersubject, and the optional stretto. It is important to recognize that improvised music has limits; it can never match the refinement and complexity of a composition worked out on paper over an extended period. For this reason, the player must be shrewd about what is, and what is not, "improvisable." Necessarily, improvised fugues will be somewhat simple, at least to start. When I look over music literature, I always think about what passages are "improvisable"—what techniques I could steal and use in concert—and what could never be devised except on paper outside of real performance time.

One area in which we simplify improvised fugues is the countersubject, as permitted by Benoist. To reiterate, the countersubject is the material that goes against the subject. When the first entry concludes and the answer enters, the first voice must continue with something. If that "something" is used consistently throughout the remainder of the fugue and works with the subject in invertible counterpoint, it is a countersubject. If, however, the material accompanying the answer does not take on this important role, and may be different whenever the subject or answer is accompanied, the fugue has no fixed countersubject.

Because composed countersubjects are normally designed to work in invertible counterpoint with the subject, it is not reasonable to expect an improviser to design such a relationship in mere moments while sitting at the instrument before expectant listeners. (Although if both subject and countersubject were conveniently made of some of our favorite invertible bass motions, maybe . . . just maybe.) Many composed fugues do not use countersubjects. I take this as permission from history to show a little mercy to the reader, and move forward on fugue improvisation without insisting on the use of fixed countersubjects immediately.

The stretto, in which the subject overlaps itself in various combinations, is probably out of reach for those beginning to improvise fugue. A subsequent chapter will present a method of creating passages, either with actual stretto or with the dramatic effect of stretto but without the degree of difficulty imposed by *fugue d'école*. At first, however, stretto will be left out entirely. Again, many fugues from the literature do not include stretto. From the point of view of history, stretto is not indispensable.

In the next chapter we will begin to learn the process of staring down a subject and figuring out how to turn it into a simple fugue.

Chapter 10

Improvising a First Fugue on Handel

If you have carefully studied and mastered all the preceding concepts in this book, you are ready to improvise your first fugue.

Exposition

Let us begin with an exposition using a simple and memorable subject derived from Handel's first easy fugue, seen in Example 10.1.

EXERCISE. Memorize the subject by scale degrees and intervals, not just by actual notes, because you will need to recall it many times in various keys in each hand. Observe where each note lies within the measure, and the important fact that it begins on a downbeat. The subject fits within the first five scale degrees, so you will not have to worry about chromatic alterations to ❻ and ❼ when the subject appears in minor. Play the subject from memory in several keys, and with each hand.

Descending Expositions

The exposition will begin with the subject entering alone in the highest voice, and then the answer will appear below it in a second voice. When the answer enters, the first voice must then do something to accompany the answer, which is the first time within the fugue where you must make up music on the spot. The easiest way is to use your bicinium skills from Chapter 7, placing thirds and sixths against the notes of the answer. This accompaniment serves as a temporary countersubject, but at this time we are not worrying about using a fixed countersubject, so you will not need to recall these accompaniments and reproduce them later.

EXAMPLE 10.1 Handel's fugue subject

EXERCISE. Play the subject in the right hand. Simultaneously with its last note, bring in the answer in the left hand, in the dominant key. As the answer proceeds, accompany each of its notes with a third or sixth in the right hand. (For now, be patient and accompany even the first note, the dotted half, with another dotted half in the right hand.) You may use all thirds, all sixths, or both intervals alternating, either in a neat pattern or with no particular pattern. Now start over, beginning the subject in the left hand, answering in the right, and improvising in the left. Try this in many different keys. In minor keys your invented accompaniment may have to contend with raised ❼ and possibly ❻ as well as potential augmented seconds. Practice this exercise until it seems easy in every key, both major and minor. Example 10.2 shows some possible solutions to this exercise.

You may notice that, when the answer appears below the subject, the interval of a sixth does not sound quite right. The sixth, unto itself, is not dissonant, but we still have a problem: the sixth weakens the answer, because our ears will tend to fill in a forbidden $^6_4$. In such cases the player should add a short transition to the end of the subject in order to provide a third or octave at the moment of the subject's entrance. (As we will see later, Handel's actual subject does just that. For now, we will practice making up our own transitions.) Note that your transition must be one measure in duration so that the answer enters on the correct beat. Example 10.3 and all subsequent examples in this chapter include transitions where necessary. When the answer appears above the subject, the interval is a third, which is not problematic.

Once you are fluent in placing thirds and sixths with each note of the answer, you can begin to expand your approach by adding fifths and octaves as long as they follow general principles of good voice-leading. In two voices, perfect intervals should be preceded and followed by imperfect, and approached by contrary or oblique motion. They should also be less common than thirds and sixths. You may add passing and neighbor tones, as well. The dotted half note of the answer is a good place for this, since nothing is happening for three beats and some activity would be interesting. If you are a very cautious person, you can simply add a neighbor. You have time to play the consonant note, add a neighbor, and return to your first note.

Another idea is to flip between consonances in the accompanying voice while the answer holds a long note. This is ideal when you wish to create distance between the voices when, say, the lower voice is about to ascend and you suddenly realize that the upper voice is too close.

EXAMPLE 10.2 Handel's subject imitation

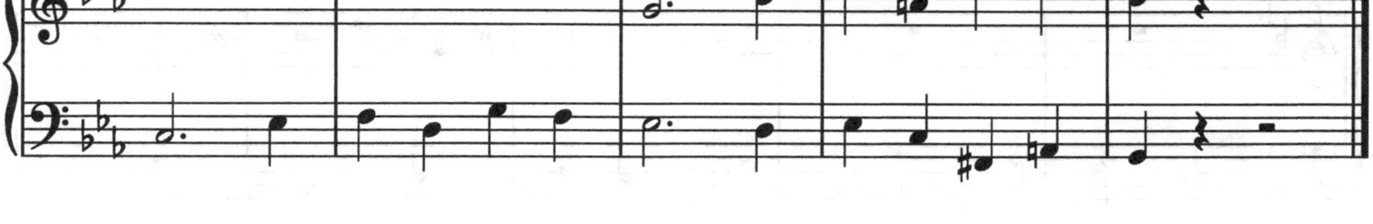

If the answer moves between two notes, the accompaniment may remain on the same pitch if that pitch is consonant with both notes in the answer. Example 10.3 illustrates all these points.

EXERCISE. Improvise more accompaniments to the fugal answer using the new techniques discussed previously. Take turns starting the subject in right and left hands, and transpose to many major and minor keys.

When the third voice enters, everything changes, because now instead of bicinium we have complete chords. (Two voices often allude to full harmonies, but that is an illusion. In two voices all you really have is a series of intervals.) If the third voice enters in the bass, obviously the subject will serve as a bass line.

EXAMPLE 10.3 Various combinations of Handel's subject

From partimento you already know how to apply Rule of the Octave to a bass. We will use that technique here.

EXERCISE. Play the subject in the left hand in the tonic key. Using the principles of Rule of the Octave, provide two voices in the right hand to complete the appropriate harmonies. Mind your voice-leading. Try this in various positions of the upper voices and in many different major and minor keys. Example 10.4 provides guidance.

Fugue answers normally imitate at the fifth; in practice this often creates alternating tonic and dominant keys. As mentioned, it may be necessary to

EXAMPLE 10.4 Harmonizing Handel with RO

add a short transition to arrive in the right key for the next entrance. After the second entrance, for instance, the harmony might temporarily reside the dominant key. In some cases, in order to get ready for the third entrance, a transition of at least one measure must be improvised. The transition, sometimes called a coda, can be very simple. If possible, touch upon ❹ of the tonic key (lowered ❼ of the dominant) and move the voices into a position appropriate for the moment when the third voice enters. In minor keys, the leading tone must also be adjusted. Mind the spacing between voices; the two upper voices will need to remain close together to be played by the right hand, and distant enough from the bass to avoid conflict. The transition may be longer than one measure if desired. Example 10.5 shows how this may be done.

EXERCISE. Using the techniques previously discussed, improvise in three voices, placing each entrance in successively lower voices to create descending expositions. Create a coda after the answer if you wish. Play in many different keys. Keep working on this exercise until it is easy.

Once you can improvise a three-voice descending exposition, playing in four voices is only a small adjustment. The fourth entrance will be lower still, and in the dominant key. You may wish to improvise a transition to prepare for the fourth entrance. Perhaps you will wonder how to keep track of four independent voices while improvising. In reality, it is not difficult because you can switch freely between textures of three and four voices. In eighteenth-century keyboard music, after the third entrance many composers casually disregard a precise accounting of the number of present voices, anyway. The listener tends to notice the *entrance* of each part more than its subsequent *presence*. Each voice has

EXAMPLE 10.5 A coda before the third entrance

its moment of glory when it first appears, but thereafter blends into the crowd. Example 10.6 shows a descending exposition in four voices in a minor key.

EXERCISE. Improvise descending expositions on the Handel subject in four voices.

Ascending Expositions

Expositions with ascending entrances differ from those that descend in one important way. In descending expositions, each subsequent entrance will place the subject or answer in the role of the bass, but ascending expositions will not. Therefore, in descending expositions we always know what the bass line is (since it will always be the subject or answer). Therefore, we can predict the appropriate bass motions, and consequently what harmonies are available for the upper voices. In ascending expositions, the entrance is always in a new upper voice and is therefore *never* the bass, and thus provides less specific guidance on harmony. Because of these factors, *expositions with descending entrances are easier to improvise.*

EXAMPLE 10.6 A descending exposition in four voices

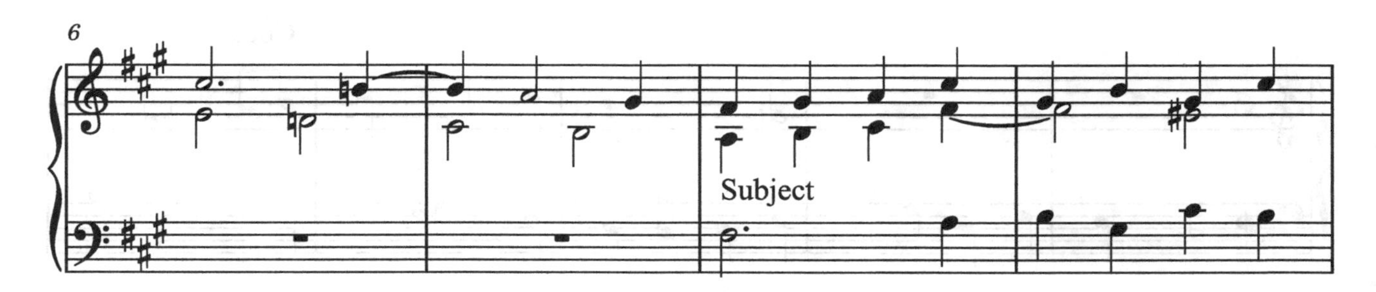

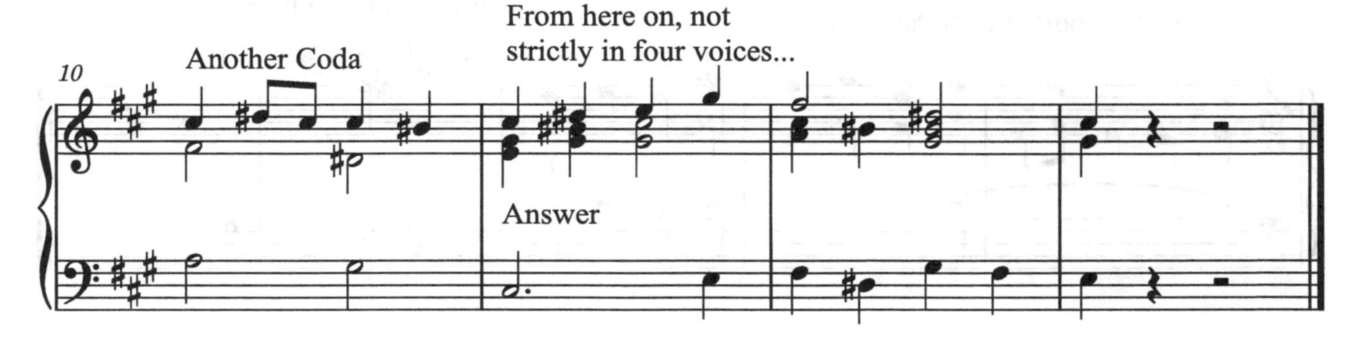

To create an exposition with ascending fugal entrances, one must consider how the bass should accompany each new subject or answer. In situations like this, the study of partimento is a tremendous advantage because it accustoms the player to this kind of thinking, hearing, and predicting.

The Handel subject may take multiple bass accompaniments, but it fits ideally over a Page One. Indeed, it was designed this way, as the original composition shows. Even in two voices, the voice-leading suggests the possibility of a Page One, placing ① in the bass against ❹ and ❷ in the second measure of the subject, followed by ⑦ in the bass against ❺ and ❹, followed by a resolution to ① and ❸. Example 10.7 shows measures 16–18 from Handel's original.

EXERCISE. Improvise an exposition on the Handel subject with the entrances in ascending order. Add codas before entrances as necessary. Because of the tendency of the upper voices in eighteenth-century music

EXAMPLE 10.7 The beginning of Handel's fugue

EXAMPLE 10.8 An ascending exposition

to space closely together and maintain some distance from the bass, you may have to play multiple voices in the right hand with the subject in the highest voice. When doing so, keep the inner voices or voices conservative and boring, moving as little as possible, especially since you might only have one or two fingers available. Try ascending expositions in both three and four voices, noting that in three voices the exposition concludes in the tonic, whereas in four it concludes in the dominant. Example 10.8 shows some possible solutions.

Staggered Expositions

Of course, the exposition need not ascend nor descend exclusively; voices may enter in any order. Voices that enter in the middle of a texture pose the same challenge as those that enter as top voices: because they are not the bass, one must determine what an appropriate bass accompaniment should be. Often the right hand will play the inner voice. If the subject has fast notes or a wide range, most of the right hand's resources will go to managing the subject, leaving perhaps one or two fingers on the outside of the hand to create a top voice. For practical reasons, then, the top voice should not be ambitious. If harmonic circumstances allow, the top voice could be something as simple as a few long notes that move by step, if moving is necessary at all. Alternatively, one may try out a top voice in parallel thirds or sixths with the subject, assuming one has the technique to do so. (While parallel imperfect consonances are certainly an important part of eighteenth-century music, in overabundance they can be tiresome. Be judicious.) If the bass moves in long note values or is otherwise easy, the middle voice could possibly go to the left hand.

EXERCISE. Improvise expositions in three voices with the middle voice entering last. Try some in the order soprano-bass-alto and then bass-soprano-alto. Remember to establish adequate distance between the highest and lowest voices so that there is room for a third. Improvise transitions between entries as needed. Practice in several major and minor keys. You can also create expositions with the middle voice entering first. In three voices there are six possible orders of vocal entries. If your keyboard technique is equal to the task, try expositions in four voices, which allows for twenty-four possible orders of vocal entries. Example 10.9 provides guidance.

The Handel subject was designed to match with a Page One bass, as mentioned. However, other basses are possible. Example 10.10 shows a few (along with a middle voice to help make sense of the harmony), but you should try inventing your own, as well.

EXERCISE. Using your new basses, improvise ascending expositions. Try using a different bass for the entrance of each upper voice.

Episodes

Episodes are the sections of a fugue that refrain from full presentations of the subject. Because fugues are characterized by thematic density, episodes provide a break in which the music seems to open up and think about something else for a minute before returning to the obsession of the subject yet again. Episodes also serve to modulate to new tonalities to prepare for subsequent subject presentations. They may consist of entirely free material (that is, thematically unrelated to anything else in the fugue) but typically they derive from elements of the subject or other musical ideas that have appeared along the way. An episode that uses a motivic fragment from the subject (but not the whole thing) retains a connection to the main theme of the piece while also creating space away from it. This is the perfect balance you need. Episodes are often sequential, which makes modulation predictable and easy.

EXAMPLE 10.9 Staggered expositions

In 1753 Friedrich Wilhelm Marpurg (1818–1895) wrote in his *Abhandlung von der Fuge (Treatise on Fugue)*, "Where should the composer look for musical ideas from which episodes might be formed? In the theme and in the counterpart with which the theme is combined. If the nature of the theme is such that it does not yield suitable elements, one should invent simple, agreeable melodic progressions for episodes which are well adapted to the character and to the melodic and rhythmic movement of the theme." Developing episodes from thematic ideas found elsewhere in the piece contributes to a sense of musical unity.

Fortunately, Handel's subject provides a good idea for a subject: the second measure. These four notes can be copied and pasted into a longer pattern, with each "pasted" measure transposed down a step, as seen in Example 10.11.

EXAMPLE 10.10 Harmonic ideas for Handel's subject

EXAMPLE 10.11 A sequential pattern based on the subject

The partimento tradition will help us develop this idea into various episodes. First, consider the line, not as a melody, but as if it were a partimento bass. What motion is suggested? If we take the strong beats as structural and the weak beats as diminutions, a pattern of down a third up a step emerges, which is the good old Cascade. Using this motion and its upper voice harmonizations, it is easy to improvise a sequential episode and prepare a modulation to a new tonality.

But what if the pattern appears in an upper voice? Fortunately, we already know from invertible partimento that Cascade, when inverted to an upper voice, fits over the Tied Bass motion. With this knowledge you will be able to create multiple episodes from the same thematic fragment. Some

EXAMPLE 10.12 Ideas for episodes

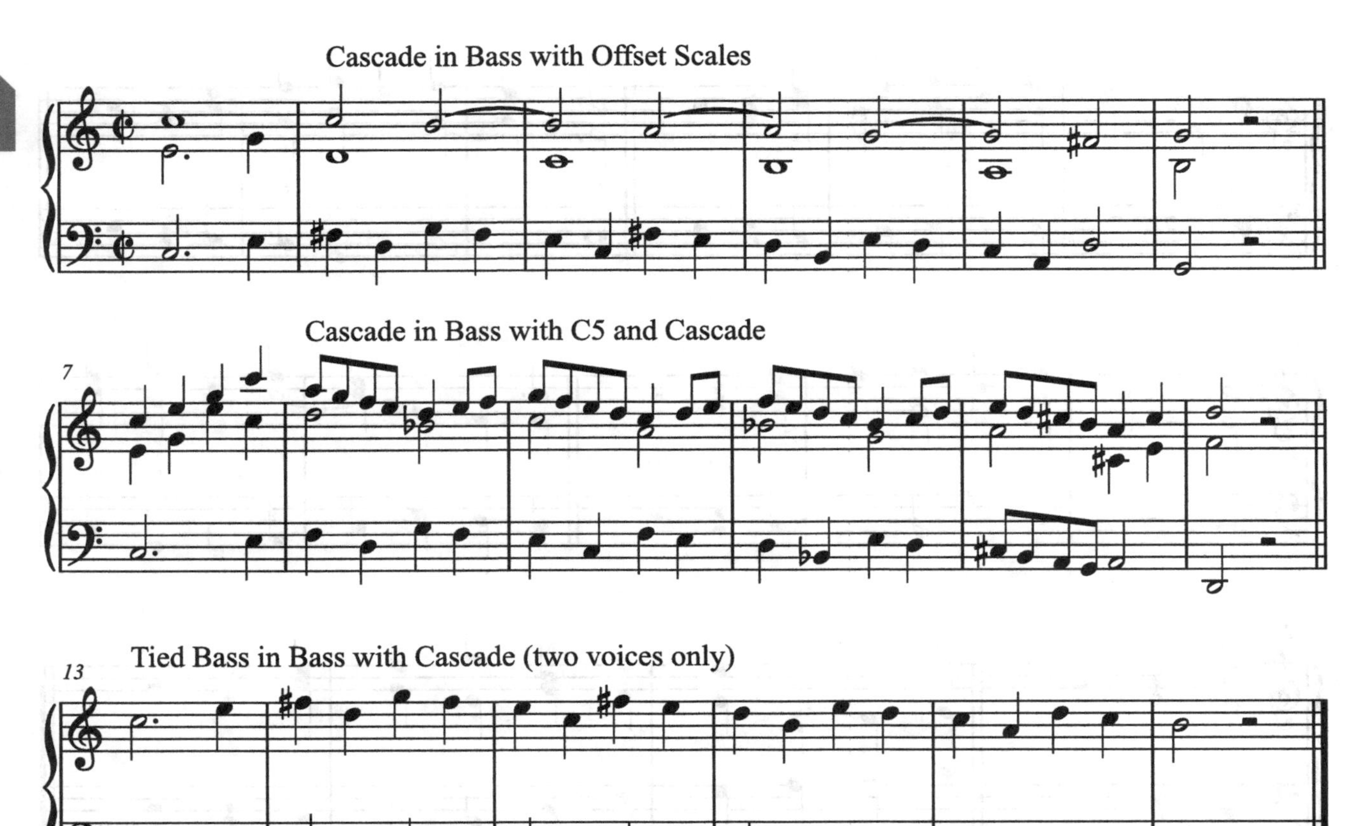

possibilities are shown in Example 10.12, all of which modulate; one of them is in two voices.

Marpurg states that "[t]he episodes need not be formed by all voices. One or two voices may be suspended [i.e., left out] one after another, or simultaneously, so that the theme may re-enter all the more clearly and emphatically, especially if it appears in an inner voice." This is good advice. If you like, you can reduce to two voices for your episodes, and develop them according to the principles of bicinium.

Episodes are often built on sequential passages. For example, the improviser may simply decide that an upcoming episode will be a nice long C5, with some recognizable motive somewhere in the mix. Any bass motion or sequential pattern will work as the basis for an episode, as will Rule of the Octave. However, there is no requirement that episodes be constructed in this way; it just happens to be an effective strategy. If a musical passage maintains the style and texture of the fugue, departs from a full subject presentation, modulates as needed, and generally sounds like it fits, then it is a good episode.

EXERCISE. Improvise modulating episodes using the fragment from Handel's subject as a bass, and then as an upper voice. Try creating episodes in three voices, then in two. Choose a major or minor key, and in each episode modulate according to one of the plans below. (Note that while Roman numerals are not as useful as bass motions in improvising, they are quite helpful in describing large-scale key areas!)

I to ii
I to vi
I to V
i to III
i to v
i to VII

Presentations

After the exposition and first episode, the fugue subject returns in a presentation. Normally the entire subject appears, although it is possible to shorten or otherwise modify the subject for musical purposes. Even if the entire subject is not presented, the listener should hear enough of it to get the impression that the subject made a prominent appearance.

Each presentation features the fugue subject at least once. It may appear in any voice, but following Benoist and placing it in the outer voices will help avoid difficulties. Inner voice presentations are far more daunting, both physically and mentally. The fugue will be more interesting if the subject does not always appear in the same voice in all the presentations. The process of harmonization is the same as for the exposition: if the subject is in the lowest voice, it serves as a bass and the upper voices must harmonize accordingly. If the subject appears in an upper voice, a suitable bass must be found. If one wishes to follow the example of the *fugue d'école*, both subject and answer will appear in each presentation. Upon completion of the subject, the presentation must, in turn, connect seamlessly with another episode.

EXERCISE. Practice presentations in the outer voices, and in many keys. Accompanying voices should be kept very simple. Then practice connecting a presentation to an episode, and then connect that episode with another presentation. Your goal is to improvise at least three presentations in three different keys, connected by two episodes. Example 10.13 shows how this could be done.

EXAMPLE 10.13 Connecting presentations and episodes

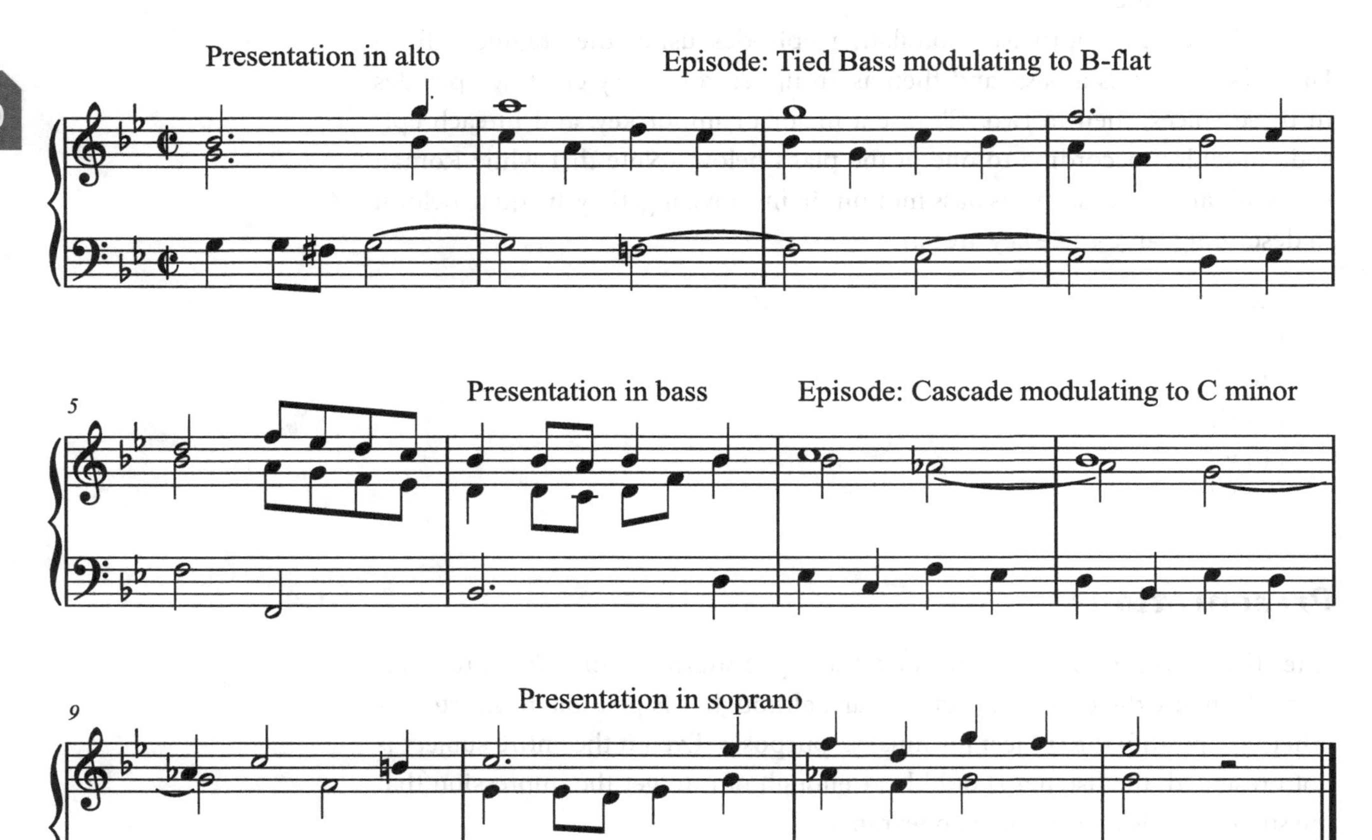

Pedal Points

After a few alternating episodes and presentations, the fugue must return to the home key for a final presentation. The pedal point can help heighten the drama of the return to the tonic. The pedal point is a sustained low bass note over which a drama of consonance and dissonance plays out in the upper voices. The organ is ideal for this technique, since the bass note is managed with a foot, leaving both hands free for the upper voices. On the piano and harpsichord this is obviously impossible, so pedal points are necessarily less ambitious on these instruments. (Pianos with sostenuto pedals do allow for the capture of a bass note or octave, which will then sustain after the key is released; I use this method very often in concert. The effect can be impressive.)

Pedal points may occur on ⑤ or ①. When placed ⑤ it will sound like, and function as, a giant extended dominant chord, and musical tension will tend to rise over the course of the pedal point.

EXERCISE. Play a pedal point on ⑤ in the left hand. In the right hand, spin out an idea using a rising or falling sequence over the pedal point to heighten the tension. If you can prepare and resolve dissonances, the result will be dramatic. When the time seems right, resolve the bass to the tonic and play the subject one more time in a decisive and authoritative manner. Add a strong cadence by way of conclusion. Try this is in major and minor, in several different keys. Example 10.14 provides guidance.

EXAMPLE 10.14 Ideas for fugue endings

A Complete Fugue

We now have everything we need to improvise a simple but complete fugue on the Handel subject.

EXERCISE. Improvise complete fugues according to the plans that follow. This exercise will be very difficult for almost everyone except improvisers with extensive prior experience. Do not be easily dismayed, and give yourself a long time to work on it. Do not worry if, after trying for a while, your expositions (and perhaps other parts of the fugue) start to sound too similar each time you play. Right now, your task is to persist and to take note of small problems that seem simple but trip you up in practice. Find solutions for these problems. If necessary, set a metronome to a slow, comfortable tempo while you improvise. Very often improvisers crash and burn merely because they try to play too fast. Refrain from any elaboration beyond thematic fragments that lend unity to your piece; keep it simple and direct the voices to their destinations with a minimum of fanfare. When you are confident in the fugue plans, scramble the order of the tonalities of the presentations and episodes and do them again. Example 10.15 shows one possible solution for the first plan, and Example 10.16 shows one for the second.

Major Key Fugue:
Descending exposition in three voices
Episode modulating to ii
Presentation in ii (soprano voice)
Episode modulating to vi
Presentation in vi (bass voice)
Episode modulating to V
Presentation in V (soprano voice)
Pedal on ⑤ with subject spun out in upper voices
Final presentation (any voice) in I with cadence

Minor Key Fugue:
Ascending exposition in three voices
Episode modulating to III
Presentation in III (soprano voice)
Episode modulating to VII
Presentation in VII (bass voice)
Episode modulating to v
Presentation in v (soprano voice)
Pedal on ⑤ with subject spun out in upper voices
Final presentation (any voice) in i with cadence

These fugue plans are somewhat arbitrary, as no unshakeable historical precedent exists for a specific number of episodes and presentations, or for the order of neighboring tonalities. There are no "required" tonalities you

EXAMPLE 10.15 A solution for the first fugue plan

EXAMPLE 10.16 A solution for the second fugue plan

absolutely must visit, although the dominant might be offended if you don't stop by for a polite cup of tea. Given this arbitrariness and freedom, you can make your own fugue plans, laying out the specifications for the exposition, episodes, presentations, and conclusion as you wish.

Certain other fugue subjects will fit easily into these plans. The subjects shown in Example 10.17 should not be too troublesome; they are short and

EXAMPLE 10.17 Fugue subjects

memorable, begin and end on sensible beats, and require harmonic treatment that should be familiar to you.

EXERCISE. For each fugue subject in Example 10.17, determine what harmony it would suggest if serving as a bass line, and what possible harmonies would match if serving as an upper voice. Further, you must consider how it will function in both major and minor. Is it possible to bring in the second and third entries immediately at the conclusion of the subject, or do the last notes of the subject not play nicely in the sandbox with subsequent entries (in which case a coda will be necessary)? For each subject, find some musical idea that could be fashioned into an episode. Even a very simple rhythm from the subject (such as a quarter note followed by two eighths) can work. Can anything in the subject be copied and pasted into a sequence? If the subject has no salient motives for episodes, perhaps make an interesting coda between the second and third entrances, and borrow a motive from this coda. Using the subjects from Example 10.17, improvise fugues on the plans shown previously.

EXERCISE. You can improvise on your own subjects if you keep them simple and short. Create subjects that are only a few measures long, use primarily steps or familiar bass motions, and are memorable. Be sure they begin and end on logical beats. Don't start on weird scale degrees; many easier subjects often begin on ❶ and end on ❸. Combine an original subject with your own plan for the exposition, episodes, presentations, and conclusion. Improvise complete fugues.

Chapter 11

Exposition

Chapter 10 presented an introductory approach to creating simple but complete fugues on a theme of Handel. This chapter will explore in greater detail the possibilities and problems specific to expositions.

The Subject

Because the entire fugue proceeds from the subject, the performer must devote considerable attention to the characteristics of this theme. Crucially, the subject must be memorable, as it will need to be recalled many times in multiple voices and keys. Stepwise subjects are easy to memorize because one must simply remember the inflection points at which they change direction. Fugues with leaps can be difficult to recall once they begin modulating; therefore, the improviser should take careful note of any disjunct intervals.

The harmonic implications are important as well. The subject will serve sometimes as an upper voice and other times as a bass. When preparing to improvise, the player must quickly determine one or more harmonic solutions for the subject as both upper voice and bass, and also how these solutions will be adapted to the opposite mode (that is, if the subject is major, how will it function in minor, and vice versa?). The study of partimento bass motions is helpful in this task, as it accustoms the performer to predict these combinations.

Padre Martini distinguishes between three types of fugue subject based on length. In his *Esemplare, o sia Saggio Fondamentale Pratico di Contrapunto Fugato* (Exemplary or wise practical foundations of fugal counterpoint) of 1774, he categorizes themes as *attacco, soggetto*, or *andamento*—that is, short, medium, or long. The attacco is just a few notes and is more like a motive than an actual theme. Gedalge cautions that "[w]ith too short a subject the entrances and modulations are too frequent; it creates weakness and destroys the feeling of tonality." On the other hand, the attacco is likely to be memorable and easy to transpose. The soggetto is a subject of average length. The andamento is a longer

EXAMPLE 11.1 Martini's andamento

subject consisting of two parts, a head and a tail. The two parts should have different qualities; the head is concise and makes a strong statement, while the tail may flow for a while with sequential material (the meaning of "andamento" is movement or running). Despite its length, the andamento might still be memorable if the head has a clear, distinctive character and the pattern of the tail is logical. Example 11.1 shows Martini's idea of the andamento.

Note that the head of Martini's andamento is a Monte Principale motion. The tail, while not sequential, is nevertheless constructed of three descending scale fragments, which makes memorization somewhat easier.

The subject from J. S. Bach's organ fugue in D major, BWV 532, is also an andamento. The head is merely the first three notes of the scale running up and down, while the tail is a sequence that lends itself to several different harmonizations. This subject also contains a built-in silence that has potential for dramatic effect. See Example 11.2.

Gedalge recommends careful consideration of the subject's rhythms: "The subject must not include a great number of different or dissimilar rhythms; two or three are sufficient. They should be of the same style . . . one should be careful when writing subjects which include alternating binary and ternary rhythms." Some fugues juxtapose such rhythms as a gesture of virtuosity. These are best avoided at early stages of improvisation, as they will probably lead to polyrhythmic textures when combined with multiple voices.

Limiting the range of a subject to one octave is a good idea. A subject with an enormous range can be impractical in keyboard music. Gedalge goes further, stating that a "fugue subject must not exceed the interval of a minor seventh between its lowest and highest notes; it is even preferable to confine it

EXAMPLE 11.2 The subject of BWV 532

to the sixth so that the answer may be written well within the compass of the voices." In practice, however, the range of one octave is a reasonable guideline.

The subject's tonality, like all its qualities, will affect the whole fugue. The easiest subjects will remain in the principal key of the piece and avoid modulation. Gedalge teaches that "[a] fugue subject should confine itself entirely to one of the two modes, major or minor. Any subject which presents a combination of the two modes should be rejected entirely." The implied harmonic rhythm of the subject should not be too fast; otherwise the improviser will be obligated to deal with rapid harmonic rhythm throughout the fugue and may be overwhelmed.

Real and Tonal Answers

Many subjects do not remain entirely in the principal key, but modulate. Most often, they gravitate toward the dominant. When Chapter 10 used the theme by Handel, the subject was not actually given in its full form; the last measure was not included. Look at Example 11.3 and note the difference between the subject as adapted for Chapter 10 and Handel's original.

The last measure was left off so that we could temporarily avoid discussing a common and potentially vexing problem with fugue subjects: real and tonal answers. I remember these from theory class, but because the question was abstract and without painful consequences in my life, I paid very little attention. I didn't understand because I didn't *have to*. When I began trying to improvise fugues, suddenly the matter became very important—indeed, the source of some painful consequences. Because I *had to* understand the issue, I finally did.

A real answer is when the second entry of the subject, known as the answer, preserves the intervals of the first subject *exactly*, although transposed, usually to a fifth higher or fourth lower. A real answer is copied, transposed, and pasted verbatim. That is why it is real. A tonal answer is a second entry of a subject in which one or more intervals has been modified in order to solve a tonal problem. That is why it is tonal.

Look at Example 11.4, which shows the exposition of Handel's fugue exactly as he wrote it.

Handel has altered one interval in the answer on the third beat of measure 6 where the interval of a third has been changed to a second. Imagine if he had used an exact replica of the first subject: the tonality would have been forced into D major at the end of the answer, which is not acceptable within the exposition's

EXAMPLE 11.3 Handel's complete subject

EXAMPLE 11.4 Handel's exposition

little world of tonic (C) and dominant (G). By changing one interval, the answer points back to C major and paves the way for the third entrance. Example 11.5 shows how a real answer would result in a train wreck in the Handel fugue.

The first portion of Example 11.6 shows a short theme in C major which begins on ❺ and concludes on ❸, a very common trajectory for a fugue subject.

If we answer this subject a fifth above or fourth below (that is, in the dominant), the first note of the answer would be D, which would be a nasty jolt against the concluding E of the first voice. We could solve this tonal problem by extending the first voice with an extra measure (a coda) that navigates to somewhere consonant with D. However, we do not want to be forced to use codas all the time; the obligation to create constant safety bumpers between entries has been ruled unacceptable over the course of music history. If we modify the answer's first note to C instead of D, the problem vanishes and the answer may appear at the moment of the subject's conclusion, as shown in the latter portion of Example 11.6. A tonal problem has been solved with a tonal answer.

In Example 11.6, only the first note of the tonal answer required adjustment; after that the answer could proceed without messing with any other

EXAMPLE 11.5 Problems with real answers

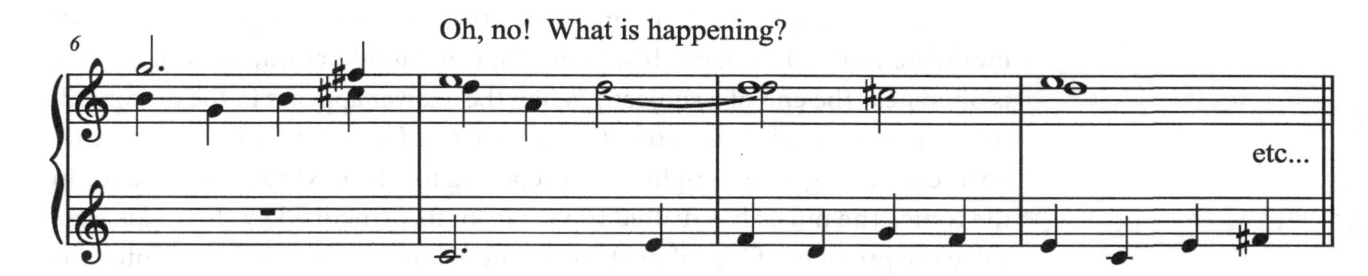

EXAMPLE 11.6 A sample fugue subject

notes. If the subject began by descending instead of ascending, it would have been necessary to contract rather than expand an interval. Very often, this is precisely how tonal answers are managed.

Tonal answers are usually the result of a prominent ➎ in the subject that, when transposed to a dominant answer, would create ➎ in the dominant, which is problematic ➋ in the tonic. Intervals are adjusted so that the troublesome note becomes ➍ in the dominant and ➊ in the tonic.

EXAMPLE 11.7 A subject with a tonal answer

Another way to think of tonal answers is to consider fugue subjects that modulate to the dominant, like Handel's. (This modulation, when it occurs, is often near the end of a subject.) When the answer appears in the dominant, this modulation takes us to the *dominant of the dominant*, a place we have no business visiting, as we ought to be preparing for the next subject entrance in the tonic. The music has drifted too far from its principal key. Tonal answers solve the problem of "tonal drift" by changing one or more selected intervals to direct the tonality back toward the tonic. Example 11.7 shows a subject with a tonal answer. The entire first measure of the answer has been shifted down a step.

Likewise, where several notes near the end of the subject are all in the dominant, the entire corresponding passage in the answer may be transposed down a step, which will put it safely back in the tonic, where it belongs.

Gedalge summarizes tonal answers by stating that any portion of the subject that is in the tonic, when appearing in the answer, will be in the dominant. Any portion of the subject that is in the dominant, when appearing in the answer, will be in the tonic. *The portion of the subject that is in the dominant will be altered when it shows up in the answer—often by lowering it a step.*

By "in the tonic" and "in the dominant" we mean any portion of the subject that strongly evokes one of those two tonalities. A portion of a subject that arpeggiates the tonic triad is clearly "in the tonic." A portion that contains raised ❹ (the leading tone of the dominant) is "in the dominant." ❺ that is early or late in subject, and is emphasized, is "in the dominant" and is calls for a tonal answer.

Finding tonal answers may seem impossible without extensive preparation. Can one really solve this problem when improvising? Fortunately, most tonal answers only involve lowering by a step a prominent ❺ that appears early or late in the subject. The reason early and late notes are important is because the answer, which is in the dominant, is sandwiched between subject statements that are in the tonic. The answer must connect on both ends with the tonality of the tonic. This is why many tonal answers only require lowering an early or late ❺.

EXAMPLE 11.8 Subjects and answers from Pachelbel

Example 11.8 shows three sets of subjects and tonal answers from Pachelbel's Magnificat fugues. Note carefully the intervals in each answer that have been adapted.

EXERCISE. Find tonal answers for the subjects in Example 11.9. Look for prominent ❺ both early and late in the subject, and any group of notes that is clearly in the dominant. Find answers for each subject both above and below the subject. Remember, anything in the subject that is in the tonic will appear in the dominant in the answer. Anything in the subject that is in the dominant will appear in the tonic in the answer.

Subdominant Answers

When a subject begins on ❺ and skips down to ❸, the tonal answer may collapse the interval between ❺ and ❸ into a step. What if the subject starts on ❺ but has no intervals available to adjust? If a subject steps down the pentachord (❺-❹-❸-❷-❶), there are no intervals available to collapse. Three solutions are possible. One may extend the subject with a coda that prepares for a real answer in the dominant, one may collapse a step into a repeated note (this is sometimes

EXAMPLE 11.9 Subjects in need of tonal answers

done, but it may sound weird), or one may toss the entire tonic-dominant relationship out the window and place the answer in the subdominant instead. This third solution appears quite often with descending stepwise subjects that begin on ❺, such as the famous fugue in D minor, BWV 565, attributed to J. S. Bach. See Example 11.10.

EXAMPLE 11.10 The subdominant answer in BWV 565

By placing the answer in the subdominant, the answer may begin on the tonic's ❶, (which is the subdominant's ❺) making for a seamless transition from subject to answer.

Order of Entries

The order in which voices enter in an exposition has implications. As mentioned previously, fugue expositions in descending order are easiest, as each entry will always be the lowest sounding voice and thus function like a bass. Ascending order provides the additional challenge of determining a bass to go with the entry, but is still something that a dedicated improviser can master. Expositions in "staggered order" (anything other than ascending or descending) are more difficult, especially if a third or fourth voice must be improvised in the middle, sandwiched between other voices that entered previously. One may create a staggered order that is slightly less difficult by starting with an inner voice and adding the outer voices later. By exposing the inner voice (or voices) first, the improviser can cleverly avoid the obligation to play the subject or answer between other voices.

Improvised Countersubjects

The written *fugue d'école* tradition required a fixed countersubject, meaning that students had to contrive an additional theme that combined with the subject in invertible counterpoint. Even the improvised *fugue d'école* eventually adopted this practice during the reign of Marcel Dupré. Recalling the interview from Chapter 9, Marie-Claire Alain states that students "were given the theme of the fugue at the beginning of the lesson, then allowed a few minutes of preparation in which we had to . . . make our own countersubject in invertible counterpoint. The countersubject had to be memorized. We were never allowed to write it down, even for ourselves."

This requirement was rather extreme. On the other hand, to be admitted to Dupré's class at all, one had to be a musician of extraordinary skill. Alain and her fellow students were elite keyboard improvisers. Should aspiring fugue improvisers today expect to create fixed countersubjects on the spot, without writing anything down and with only a few minutes to think?

At first, no. It is better to follow the earlier tradition of François Benoist, and skip the fixed countersubject until later, if ever. According to Gedalge, this was a recognized practice. He states that " 'simple fugue' was the name given to a fugue in which the countersubject was replaced by various noninvertible counterpoints." For purposes of improvisation, these "various noninvertible counterpoints" will serve as our countersubjects. They will be freely created lines that accompany the subject, in which the player does not need to worry about invertibility.

The first location where a countersubject must be improvised is in the exposition at the entrance of the answer. At this moment, the voice with the

EXAMPLE 11.11 An improvised countersubject

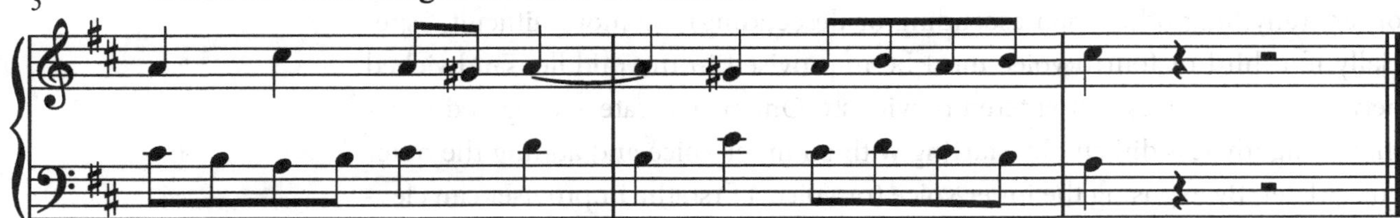

subject will continue, and its ongoing, newly invented line will accompany the answer. Example 11.11 illustrates this idea.

The resulting two-voice structure is rather exposed and fragile; there are no chords into which one can inconspicuously blend. Therefore, the improviser will be wise to devote considerable attention to methods of improvising countersubjects. This is done according to the principles of bicinium.

On the rhythmic construction of the countersubject, Gedalge advises that the "principal beats in a measure must be sounded by either the subject or the countersubject. The countersubject should not simultaneously with the subject sound notes of the same value. When there are rests in the subject, the countersubject should fill them in, and reciprocally, rests or notes of long values should be used in the countersubject when the subject moves rapidly." (Of course, Gedalge is referring to a fixed countersubject, but his recommendations apply equally to the type of countersubject—"various noninvertible counterpoints"—we are using instead.) The point of these instructions is that answer and countersubject together should make a seamless texture, with both parts contributing rhythmic activity but neither overpowering the other. Gedalge's prohibition against any identical note values is perhaps too strict for improvised fugue; a few matching rhythms are perfectly acceptable.

On harmonic aspects of the passage, Gedalge advises that the "harmonies induced by the countersubject should be as rich and varied as possible. Prepared dissonances should be used whenever feasible. Frequent changes of harmony within the measure should be avoided, and all notes whose harmonization is unnecessary should be treated as passing or neighboring notes, that is, as nonharmonic."

In order to obtain "rich and varied" harmonies and to treat many notes as nonharmonic, you will need to determine the implied structural notes of the answer, and those which are diminutions.

The exercises in Chapter 7 introduced the idea of accompanying the answer very simply, with thirds and sixths. This will work, but may seem bland. One can always add some neighbor and passing tones to the countersubject, especially when the subject moves in long note values. When the subject is made of fast notes, the improviser should determine which of them may be considered diminutions, and use longer, structural notes in the corresponding parts of the countersubject.

Concerning the prepared dissonances Gedalge suggests, the most effective in a two-part texture are 7-6, 2-3, and 4-3. 9-8 often sounds weak in two voices. In scanning the subject for possible locations for dissonances, your experience with partimento bass motions will be helpful; the thought process is the same. For example, a line that descends by step in syncopated notes, when in the lower voice, will support 2-3 suspensions, similar to a Tied Bass motion. The same line in an upper voice suggests 7-6. A single instance of an upper voice tied note that resolves down by step might be suitable for a 4-3. Tied notes that do not resolve down cannot be used for dissonances. Keep in mind, though, that diminutions may be inserted between a dissonance and its resolution (most often by filling in weaker beats).

Beyond these generalizations, it is difficult to say much more about improvised countersubjects because most of the decisions are context-specific. The best way to study the matter further is to go to the keyboard and play.

EXERCISE. Example 11.12 provides three fugue subjects. Examine each subject in turn and decide what kind of answer you wish to create: real, real with a coda, or tonal. Once you have an answer, consider what the countersubject could do against it. Which notes are structural, and which are diminutions? Will the answer support any dissonances as either a higher or lower voice? Does the

EXAMPLE 11.12 Fugue subjects

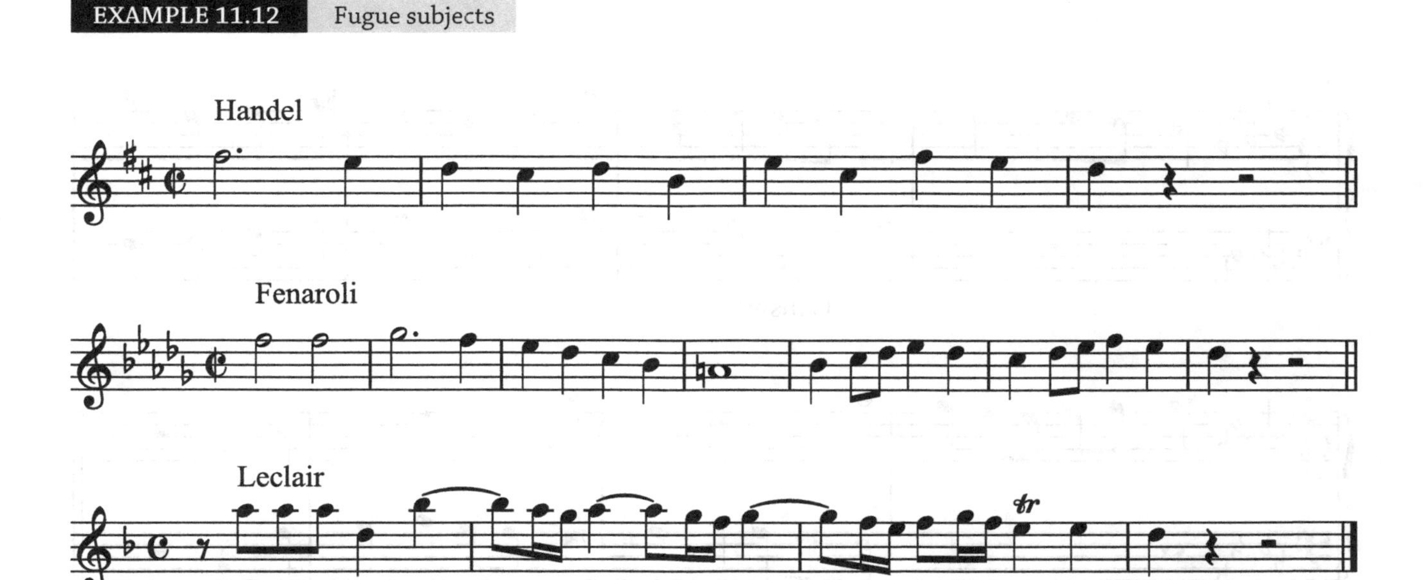

countersubject need to use any accidentals? Play the answer in one hand and improvise a variety of countersubjects in the other. Then reverse the ranges of answer and countersubject. Finally, improvise complete expositions on each subject. Example 11.13 provides possible answers and countersubjects for this exercise.

EXAMPLE 11.13 Answers and countersubjects

EXAMPLE 11.13 Continued

Second Codas

Many expositions include a short coda after the completion of the first subject and answer. This optional coda is in two voices and thus follows the procedures of bicinium. Not infrequently, the coda may be sequential. Its musical purpose is to grant a brief respite from the thematic density of the fugal entries, delaying the third entrance and making it more dramatic. A typical coda is one or two measures, although longer ones of five or six measures are certainly possible.

In comparison with a very short coda after the first subject entry, Gedalge states that a second coda "can be more developed, and can consist, according to the movement of the fugue, of two or three measures."

The majority of fugues from J. S. Bach's *Well-Tempered Clavier* have codas after the first subject and answer, usually of one or two measures. The thematic material for the coda may derive from the subject or countersubject, or may be freely invented. Sequential patterns are effective for this purpose. Example 11.14 shows some codas from Bach.

EXERCISE. Returning to the subjects in Example 11.12, create codas that follow after the first subject and answer, using thematic fragments from the subject. Improvise complete expositions on each subject, and include an answer, countersubject, coda, and at least one more subject entry. Example 11.15 provides a possible solution for the first subject.

Chromatic Subjects

When improvising fugues in the style of the eighteenth century, one will not use subjects that are completely chromatic in the sense of being atonal. However, Baroque harmony certainly has a place for chromaticism. As

EXAMPLE 11.14 Codas from Bach

EXAMPLE 11.14 Continued

EXAMPLE 11.15 An exposition with a real answer and codas

EXAMPLE 11.16 Chromatic subjects with simple countersubjects

always, the improviser must ask how such passages will be treated when in the bass and when in an upper voice, and in major and minor. Yet again, partimento thinking comes to the rescue. Descending chromatic bass lines may take any of several solutions presented in Chapter 4, of which Lamento is the most common. Ascending chromatic bass lines often support Monte motions. In an upper voice, descending chromatic lines are often supported by a chromatic variant of Cascade. Rising chromatic melodies have multiple possible solutions.

In two-voice contexts, however, the full harmony of these bass motions is not present. Many of these chromatic lines may be accompanied by thirds, sixths, and diminutions. Example 11.16 provides a few instances of chromatic subjects with simple countersubjects.

It is not necessary to memorize, and have at the ready, every imaginable solution for chromatic subjects. As long as you know one or two ways to manage chromatic material in subjects and answers, you can try simple chromatic fugues. A fugue with a chromatic subject need not be relentlessly chromatic from beginning to end; in fact, the piece may sound better if long episodes grant respite from chromatic passages. The chromatic material will be all the more dramatic upon reappearance. Chromatic subjects in major keys are less common because the favored chromatic motions such as Lamento are strongly associated with minor tonalities.

Chromatic subjects can take real, tonal, or subdominant answers. I advise real answers at first, employing a coda to prepare, if necessary. It is very easy to lose track of your harmony when transposing a chromatic subject! Tonal answers that must collapse one or more intervals in the answer will often result in some of the subject's semitones being transformed into repeated notes in the answer.

Subjects Ending on ❶ in Descending Expositions

Look at the subject from Fenaroli in Example 11.17.

In a descending exposition, the subject will conclude on ❶ on the downbeat of the fifth measure. If a real answer starts at that same moment in a lower voice, an unprepared dissonant fourth will result. On the other hand, in an ascending exposition, this same moment would result in a perfect fifth, which is no problem at all. To avoid this problem in descending expositions, you may improvise an extra measure (a coda) before the entrance of the answer, as explained previously. In descending expositions, if the subject concludes on ❶ before the measure ends, it is possible to tie a concluding ❶ over the bar and thus create a prepared dissonance over the answer's entrance, eliminating the need to add an extra measure. In the case of the theme by Cherubini, shown in Example 11.18, the subject may remain on ❶ and tie over the answer's lower appearance, resolving thereafter. Whether this works or not depends on the rhythmic placement of the subject's beginning and end. The conclusion on ❶ on the last beat of the measure allows for a convenient tie over the bar line.

EXERCISE. Improvise a descending exposition on Cherubini's subject, shown in Example 11.18.

Improvising More Expositions

Gedalge advises against cadences that halt the flow of a fugue: "Continuity of writing will be assured only if we completely abstain from the use of perfect cadences; the slightest stop in a work of this kind gives a feeling of a definite conclusion, at which, in the school fugue, we must arrive only at certain well chosen points." We need not follow Gedalge scrupulously on this matter,

EXAMPLE 11.17 A subject of Fenaroli

EXAMPLE 11.18 A subject of Cherubini

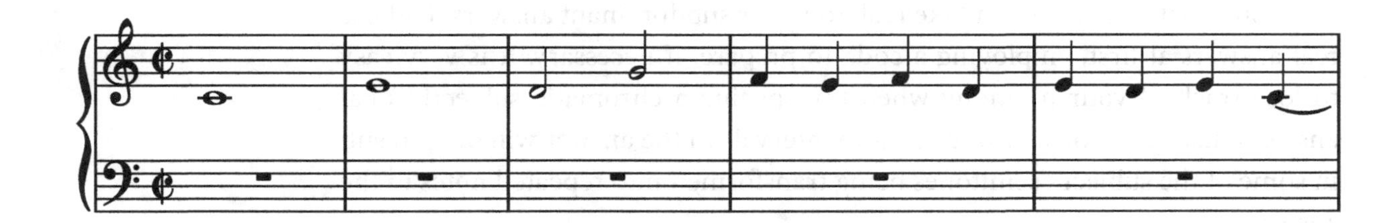

although his point is valid. You should not worry if you need to plant cadences here and there throughout your fugues. Doing so helps organize your harmonic thoughts. However, as you improvise expositions on the subjects that follow, try to avoid too many cadences or other choices that seem to disrupt the seamless progress of your music.

EXERCISE. Improvise expositions on the subjects in Example 11.19. Determine whether you should use real, tonal, or subdominant answers. Use ascending, descending, and staggered entrances. Transpose the subjects to various keys, including the opposite mode (major to minor and vice versa).

EXAMPLE 11.19 Fugue subjects

Chapter 12

Episode

Remember that the episode has three main functions: to serve as a bridge between the exposition and first presentation (and between all subsequent presentations), to modulate to new tonalities, and to provide respite from full subject presentations by using short motives or completely free material. Gedalge says that the episode is built on sequences or other predictable harmonic patterns, and both he and Cherubini recommend that it be made from thematic fragments from the exposition. This is good advice, although the episodes of a great many fugues do not follow it. If we take history as a guide, an episode can be almost anything, as long as it fulfills its purposes.

Memorable Motives

If the subject provides one or more short, memorable thematic fragments, the improviser's work is much easier. If, however, the subject is not especially memorable and contains no interesting rhythmic ideas, the performer may be required to invent some motives for use in episodes.

The fugue in A minor of Charles Burney (1726–1814) contains an episode that conforms to the recommendations of Cherubini and Gedalge. The subject and one episode appear in Example 12.1.

Burney's subject concludes in a rising arpeggio with a memorable rhythmic inflection. This fragment bounces between the voices while also providing the necessary intervals to create a Tied Bass motion, resulting in a textbook episode—almost: it does not modulate. At this point the fugue has already reached its final tonality.

Similarly, the subject of Johann Mattheson's first fugue from *Die wohlklingende Fingersprache* contains a motive of four eighth notes that outline the interval of a fourth, and this motive serves as the basis for an episode. The subject and episode are shown in Example 12.2

EXAMPLE 12.1 A subject and episode of Burney

EXAMPLE 12.2 A subject and episode of Mattheson

In this case, the episode is reduced to two voices, a common compositional strategy (and useful improvisational technique). The two voices trade the motive as the strong beats of each measure land on intervals of fifths and sixths, implying an Ascending 5-6 motion. Near the end of the episode, both voices take the motive simultaneously in parallel sixths, increasing thematic density as the next presentation approaches. This episode also carries out a modulation, seen in the change from C♯ to C♮, as it sets up a subject presentation in G major.

Chelleri's Episodes

The subject of Fortunato Chelleri's fugue in G major contains promising fragments, but for the first episode, the composer draws instead upon a motive from the countersubject. The subject and answer entries and first episode are shown in Example 12.3.

The episode begins with a point of imitation on the countersubject fragment, after which the structural notes in the bass outline the Monte Principale

EXAMPLE 12.3 Subject, answer, and episode of Chelleri

motion while carrying out a modulation from G major to E minor in preparation for the next presentation.

The second episode will surprise those who are accustomed to the fugal style of Bach. Here Chelleri seems to abandon contrapuntal texture and instead dive into something more like virtuosic Classical keyboard style. For Italian fugues of this era, however, it is not unusual. The episode has no thematic relationship to subject or countersubject, and indeed has nothing like a real theme at all; it's just chords and arpeggios. It does carry out its duty to modulate, though; the previous presentation was in E minor and the next is in B minor. This episode bridges the tonalities admirably. Example 12.4 shows Chelleri's second episode.

EXAMPLE 12.4 Chelleri's second episode

EXAMPLE 12.5 Chelleri's third episode

Chelleri's third episode is a standard Cascade passage, with a virtuosic bass and standard voice leading of seconds and thirds (Offset Scales) in the upper voices. This passage could appear almost anywhere in Italian music of the time, such as a toccata of Alessandro Scarlatti or a sonata of Francesco Durante. Even though it is generic music, it sounds quite good. The improviser should have many such passages ready and waiting at all times. Before the episode concludes, a short fragment, similar to the opening gesture of the subject, appears in imitation, as if to hint at the next presentation. The third episode is shown in Example 12.5.

The fourth episode, shown in Example 12.6, combines elements of the second and third episodes.

The "classical" arpeggios come first, followed by the Cascade with virtuosic bass, and lastly a point of imitation. The imitation is a Monte Principale.

"Requirements" for Episodes

Cherubini and Gedalge state that episodes must be thematically related to something in the exposition, must modulate to a new key, and must be sequential or some other "regular" progression. As we note from the examples in this chapter, episodes may not do all these things. In fact, they may do none of them. The only thing one can reliably say about an episode is that it takes a break from full presentations of the subject. Still, the teachers from the *fugue d'école* tradition knew whereof they spoke. Following their recommendations will make constructing episodes simpler and more musically coherent.

EXAMPLE 12.6 Chelleri's fourth episode

EXAMPLE 12.7 A subject of Fenaroli

Creating Episodes

We now proceed to create episodes by drawing out fragments from various subjects, superimposing those fragments onto harmonic progressions, and carrying out modulations.

Example 12.7 shows a subject (previously encountered) by Fenaroli.

EXERCISE. Play Fenaroli's subject and consider what portion might serve as an interesting, memorable fragment for an episode. (Note that "memorable" means that the listener must recognize it such that the episode bears thematic resemblance to the exposition, but it also means that the improviser must be able to commit it to memory very quickly for later recall and deployment in the piece.) Really, any part of this subject will work. Let's start with the first two measures so that we may take advantage of the stepwise ascent. I would probably play these notes staccato so that they have some character; they will contrast with the following eighth notes, which are likely to be legato. Choose a bass motion that includes stepwise ascent, create a polyphonic texture that incorporates the staccato quarters, and make an episode that modulations from A major to E major. Example 12.8 shows possible solutions.

When choosing thematic fragments or motives for episodes, one must consider to what extent the fragment reminds the listener of other elements in the fugue, such as the subject. As long as the fragment prompts some recognition in the listener, it is thematically significant. This is another reason I would play Fenaroli's subject with staccato quarters: they are much more recognizable than regular boring quarters. Since this is the case, is it possible to change the direction from ascending to descending and still achieve this sense of thematic relationship?

EXERCISE. Using the staccato notes from Fenaroli's subject in a stepwise descent, construct an episode on a bass motion that modulates from E major to F♯ minor. Example 12.9 provides a possible solution.

The third measure of Fenaroli's subject is also promising as the basis of an episode. The eighths fill the entire measure and outline the interval of a third. This motive could serve in countless ways.

EXAMPLE 12.8 A possible episode on Fenaroli's subject

EXAMPLE 12.9 A modulating episode on Fenaroli's subject

EXAMPLE 12.10 An episode on Fenaroli's subject

EXERCISE. Create an episode based on the third measure of the subject and modulate from F♯ minor to B minor. Example 12.10 provides one idea.

Improvising Complete Fugues with Thematic Episodes

EXERCISE. Improvise a complete fugue in A major on Fenaroli's subject. Note that the subject concludes on ①. Remember that in descending entries, this means that the answer cannot appear on the same beat, as this would result in an unprepared dissonance of a fourth. You will need a coda of at least one measure to prepare for the answer. Create your piece according to the following plan.

Exposition: Three voices, descending entries
Episode 1: Modulate from A major to E major
Presentation 1: Subject in soprano
Episode 2: Modulate from E major to F♯ minor
Presentation 2: Subject in bass

Episode 3: Modulate from F♯ minor to B minor
Presentation 3: Subject in soprano
Episode 4: Modulate from B minor to A major
Presentation 4: Subject in bass

Final Cadence

Example 12.11 shows a possible solution.

EXERCISE. Transpose Fenaroli's subject to a minor key, create your own plan for an exposition, episodes, and presentations, and improvise a fugue.

The subject from the fugue in C major by Johann Ernst Eberlin (1702–1762) appears in Example 12.12.

This subject has interesting rhythmic features that are ideal for episodes. Thematic fragments from this subject can be fashioned into sequential passages in many ways, two of which appear in Example 12.13.

Episodes on Inverted Subjects

Some may wonder if it is possible to improvise episodes based on inversions of subject fragments. While the beginning improviser may lose track of so many moving parts, with time and experience, one acquires such skills. On the way to this goal, you should not worry if you need to work out some episodes in advance, almost to the point of composing them. If you need to write them out, do so, but the best procedure is to try out possibilities on the keyboard, writing nothing down, and committing to memory your favorite solutions. Just keep in mind that inverting fragments from the subject can yield useful motives for episodes.

EXERCISE. Improvise a fugue on the Eberlin subject using the following plan. You may find it necessary first to practice several episodes separately, using fragments from the subject, including inverted material.

Exposition: Three voices in ascending order. The subject concludes on ③, which makes a tonal answer easy.
Episode 1: Modulate from C major to A minor
Presentation 1: Subject in bass
Episode 2: Modulate from A minor to D minor
Presentation 2: Subject in soprano
Episode 3: Modulate from D minor to G major
Presentation 3: Subject in bass
Episode 4: Modulate to C major
Presentation 4: Subject in soprano

EXAMPLE 12.11 A fugue on Fenaroli's subject

EXAMPLE 12.11 Continued

EXAMPLE 12.12 A fugue subject of Eberlin

EXAMPLE 12.13 Possible episodes on Eberlin's subject

EXAMPLE 12.14 Inverting Eberlin's subject

Final Cadence

While we are on the topic of invertibility, the Eberlin subject may be inverted in its entirety. Two ways to do so are shown in Example 12.14.

EXERCISE. Improvise a fugue on one of the inverted subjects from Example 12.14 according to your own plan for the exposition, episodes, and presentations. Improvising on inverted themes is excellent practice because it teaches you how to predict the ways in which harmonic and contrapuntal circumstances are changed when the tune is turned upside down.

Additional Subjects for Improvisation

A subject by August Klengel (1783–1852) appears in Example 12.15.

The subject's important characteristics are its perpetual rhythm, repeated notes, simple implied harmonic landscape, and "running start" anacrusis (which is then echoed throughout the rest of the subject).

EXERCISE. Improvise a fugue on Klengel's subject, following the same procedures you have used previously. Create your own plan for the outline of the piece.

Example 12.16 shows a subject by Frederick Arthur Gore Ouseley (1825–1889).

Remember the interesting and boring measures from partimento imitations? Ouseley's subject looks like that. And sure enough, the first and third measures work in imitation, but only with the third measure as the upper voice, because the starting interval of a fifth may not be inverted to a dissonant fourth. The fragments from these measures could be combined in many other ways to create episodes, two of which appear in Example 12.17.

EXERCISE. Work out some interesting episodes using Ouseley's subject, and then improvise a fugue according to your own plan.

A subject from one of Johann Pachelbel's Magnificat fugues appears in Example 12.18.

Like Ouseley's subject, Pachelbel's is made of two parts. The first is an insistent drumbeat and the second is a stepwise ascent of a sixth. Both are easy to remember and flexible for use in episodes. The drumbeat rhythm will be very effective if passed among different voices like a conversation. The stepwise ascent is a useful fragment, as well. Example 12.19 illustrates two possibilities for using these materials in episodes.

EXERCISE. Develop some episodes based on Pachelbel's subject, and then improvise a fugue.

EXAMPLE 12.15 A subject of Klengel

EXAMPLE 12.16 A subject of Ouseley

EXAMPLE 12.17 Possible episodes on Ouseley's subject

EXAMPLE 12.18 A subject of Pachelbel

EXAMPLE 12.19 Episodes on Pachelbel's subject

In this book, the examples of episodes are short for two reasons: in order to demonstrate clearly their three purposes, and to make them easily comprehensible. However, episodes can be quite long if one wishes to depart from the subject for a substantial period. No rules govern the construction of such episodes, except that they must be musically compatible with the rest of the fugue. As you gain confidence and begin to consider ways to improvise larger works, expansion of episodes is an excellent strategy.

Chapter 13

Presentation

A presentation is an appearance of the fugue subject, sometimes accompanied by an answer. Presentations alternate with episodes, which together comprise the middle section of a fugue, at times called the development. Presentations are like islands, and episodes are bridges that connect them. The subject (and perhaps answer) may appear in any voice or pair of voices. Each presentation takes place in a different key, which will normally be one of the five neighboring keys of the principal tonality. An important function of episodes is to modulate to these neighboring keys so that presentations may occur.

The neighboring keys are all those within one accidental of the principal key. There are five: the relative major or minor of the principal key (which shares its signature) and the major and minor keys with one more and one fewer sharp or flat than the principal key. Or you can think of it this way: in any major key, the neighboring keys will be those beginning on each note of the scale except ⑦. In a minor key, the neighboring keys are all those except ②.

Gedalge's Order of Tonalities

Gedalge prescribes a specific order in which the tonalities of the presentations must be arranged. In major fugues, the order is vi, iii, IV, ii, and V. In minor fugues the order is III, VII, iv, VI, and v. His instructions follow:

> The *fugue d'école* modulates in the following order. The episodes must therefore be planned to modulate to, or permit the entrance of the subject at the keys indicated. In major, the first modulation is made to the sixth degree (minor) of the principal key, in which the subject is heard followed by the answer, which leads the fugue to the key of the third degree (minor). By means of an episode, modulation next is made to the fourth degree (major) where only the subject is heard, as the answer would bring the fugue back to the principal key. In a short episode, or with no transitional passage, if possible, modulation is next made to the key of the second degree (minor)

> in which a single entry, either of subject or answer, is made. A new episode, more developed than the others, follows. During it, the subject may be heard at the key of the dominant. . . . In minor, the number of episodes . . . is the same as in major. The order of modulations is different. The first episode leads to the subject in the key of the third degree (major), where the answer brings about modulation to the unaltered seventh degree (major). From there, modulation is made to the fourth degree (minor), and the answer is heard at the sixth degree (major). Finally, an episode [appears] in which the subject is heard in the key of the dominant.

Note that in Gedalge's terminology, the episode and the presentation are elided; he considers the subject's appearance to be at the conclusion of the episode, not separate from it. Note also the extreme prescriptiveness of the *fugue d'école* tradition, where the precise order of events is determined in detail.

His order is completely arbitrary and he states as much: "Obviously, the fugues of Bach, Handel, Mozart, or Mendelssohn will not yield exact examples of these arrangements; not one of their fugues abides by these rules. However, guideposts are necessary to the beginner, and, although no special value attaches to the proportions and modulations given, they are useful in organizing the work." I will attest to the wisdom of this approach; when first improvising fugue, I found Gedalge's method of using a "modulation map" of great assistance in keeping my limited supply of wits about me. As he says, there is nothing special about the order he gives, except that saving the dominant key until nearer the end makes sense, as it sets up a return to the tonic. His plan will be easier to understand if translated from a paragraph to a list.

Major Fugue:
Exposition (I)
Episode 1 (I–vi)
Presentation 1 (vi)
Episode 2 (vi–iii)
Presentation 2 (iii)
Episode 3 (iii–IV)
Presentation 3 (IV)
Episode 4 (IV–ii)
Presentation 4 (ii)
Episode 5 (ii–V)
Presentation 5 (V)

Minor Fugue:
Exposition (i)
Episode 1 (i–III)
Presentation 1 (III)
Episode 2 (III–VII)

Presentation 2 (iii)
Episode 3 (VII–iv)
Presentation 3 (iv)
Episode 4 (iv–VI)
Presentation 4 (VI)
Episode 5 (VI–v)
Presentation 5 (v)

Note that Gedalge's plan does not mention a final presentation in the tonic. This is because the final portion of the *fugue d'école* was reserved for the pedal point and stretto, which would include the subject in the principal key. Gedalge's "modulation map" is easily adapted for fugues without pedal points or stretti simply by adding a final episode and presentation in the tonic.

Characteristics of the Presentation

The presentation, as mentioned, consists of a statement of the subject in its entirety, or at least enough of it to convey a sense of being fully present, not merely suggested by shorter motives or fragments. The answer may also appear in another voice. Normally the presentation would not continue with yet another subject and answer in additional voices, as this would re-enact an exposition, but obviously it is possible to do so if that is the desired effect.

Subjects and answers may appear in any of the voices, although over the course of the fugue they must vary their locations, not always carried by the same voice. I have noticed that it is easy to fall into a pattern of continuing to place the subject in the same voice (usually soprano or bass) in every presentation. (Occasionally in the middle of a concert I have caught myself doing this.) We have already noted the difficulties inherent in placing subjects in inner voices; this is why François Benoist permitted his improvisation students to present them in outer voices only. As long as the presentations alternate between soprano and bass, this approach can result in a satisfactory fugue. It is certainly a good strategy.

The improviser must choose an appropriate keyboard texture for the voices that accompany the subject. Because seamless continuity is a core aesthetic of fugue, accompanying textures in presentations should maintain a style that matches the rest of the piece. By the point at which the exposition is complete, you should have generated enough material to have established a sense of style. Ultimately, everything in fugue flows from the subject, even the accompaniments of the presentations.

Improvising Presentations

EXERCISE. Study the subjects in Example 13.1 and determine possible solutions for each as a bass and as a soprano in the context of a presentation rather than an exposition. Improvise presentations in various major and minor keys, placing

EXAMPLE 13.1 Fugue subjects

EXAMPLE 13.1 Continued

the subject in an outer voice. Examine the subjects further to determine correct answers, then improvise major and minor presentations with various combinations of subject and answer in the outer voices along with free material in other voices. If possible, try presentations with the subject or answer in an inner voice.

Gedalge is clear that his plan for modulating between episodes and presentations is arbitrary, and that real fugues don't conform to such tidy organizational charts. Nevertheless, having such a plan is a brilliant approach, as it provides a viable overall structure, allowing the improviser to concentrate on immediate matters of voice-leading and keyboard style. The performer will also get plenty of practice developing episodes that modulate between many different tonalities. A fugue improvised according to the Gedalge plan (assuming the playing is competent and expressive) will sound very good, despite its seemingly scripted, predetermined nature.

Plans for Improvising

EXERCISE. Create your own plans for organizing episodes and presentations. No historic precedent requires that every fugue visit all the neighboring tonalities, and no prescribed order of keys exists. If you wish to design a shorter plan that only visits three or four keys, do so. You may find it helpful to write out your plan and indicate, for each presentation, the voice of the subject's appearance, and whether an answer follows.

EXERCISE. Using your own plans for episodes and presentations, improvise complete fugues on the subjects from Example 13.1. The expositions should have three entries so that the first episode commences in the tonic. Your last presentation should be in the tonic. Conclude with a strong cadence.

Chapter 14

Stretto

Stretto means "narrow." In music, a stretto is a "narrow place" where motives get crowded in proximity, even closer than in an exposition. Just as an episode lowers thematic density, a stretto raises it.

The stretto is perhaps the most artificial, prescriptive, and difficult aspect of the *fugue d'école* tradition; the teachers of the Paris Conservatoire made it into a severe test of contrapuntal skill and gave it a prominence that it rarely had in the literature. In real music the stretto occasionally stands out as the climactic section of a fugue; at the Conservatoire, it was that way every time.

Characteristics of the Stretto

Gedalge defines a stretto as an event in which the subject is presented but is answered in another voice before the first statement is complete, resulting in an overlap. The stretto is distinguished from the exposition by this quality of interruption and simultaneity. According to Gedalge, a complete ideal stretto section will have three instances of overlap, at successively closer time intervals, so that the subjects are interrupted by answers earlier each time. Again, this formulation rarely occurs in music outside the *fugue d'école* tradition.

Stretti could be made of the subject, answer, countersubject, or any other significant thematic material that appears in the exposition. Imitation may be at the octave, fifth, or any other interval. The *fugue d'école* tradition developed an exhaustive array of contrapuntal techniques that could be employed in a stretto, and the teachers cautioned students not to use every available device within one piece, as it would grow tiresome. However, students were required to learn them all.

Creating the Stretto

Gedalge explains the process by which such intricate imitations are created: "Now, if we compare subject and answer, it will be seen that the latter can be made to enter at various distances from the head of the subject, and that its entrance need not interrupt the subject. By trial and error, we can find the places, starting from the last measure, where the answer will go. By this process of investigation, beat by beat, and measure by measure, we can arrive at a number of combinations that form canonical strettos."

In other words, themes to be combined in a stretto must be set against one another starting on different beats to see what works. This process will be drawn out much further if the themes are tried out in inversion, and at various intervals in addition to the octave. Example 14.1 illustrates this process with the subject of Chelleri's first fugue, which turns out not to be so great for stretto.

EXAMPLE 14.1 Seeking a stretto on Chelleri

(One could try the combinations with the subject in the soprano as well, but the results would be similar.)

Example 14.2 shows the same process with a more promising theme, the subject from the 1858 Prix de Rome contest, written by Henri Reber (1807–1880). After many attempts, one discovers that imitation at the fifth will work.

Clearly, the stretto as conceived by Gedalge is impractical for many improvisers. Testing subjects at different time and melodic intervals is painstaking, and no technique exists to streamline this process for real-time improvisation. Even Marcel Dupré's students, among the finest in the world, hoped to "make it all the way through without hesitating too much . . . trying very hard not to stop or to get lost," as Maire-Claire Alain admitted in the Chapter 12 interview.

Nevertheless, today's improvisers need not despair. Stretto can be improvised, if we do not insist on following all of Gedalge's demanding specifications. By relying on a few pragmatic strategies, we can work toward improvisations that are within reach of avid improvisers yet still convey the sense of culminating drama and thematic density that is the core aesthetic of the stretto.

EXAMPLE 14.2 Stretto on a subject of Reber

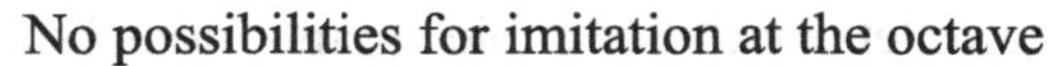

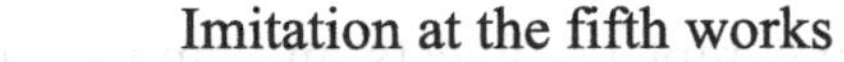

15 And it still works when inverted

EXAMPLE 14.3 A stretto in Bach

The first strategy is to disregard the requirement to construct three separate stretti, each with ever-earlier interruptions. (This is an artifice of the *fugue d'école* teachers and is rare in actual fugues.) A perfectly convincing stretto can be made with regularly recurring imitations, that is, with the interruptions not getting any closer. Example 14.3 shows the stretto of the G minor fugue from the first book of *The Well-Tempered Clavier*. The entries don't get closer each time.

This stretto does not consist of three complete subject statements; the first includes an altered note (the last one, on beat 3 of measure 2), the second is complete, and the third breaks off, continuing with similar motives but the not subject itself. From this example we can derive a second strategy: stretti can be made from incomplete or altered subjects, and indeed subject fragments. All we really need is the subject head, the first few notes that cause the listener to recognize the subject. From this fragment excellent stretti may proceed.

A third strategy is to set imitation at the octave rather than other intervals. While many stretti in the literature imitate at the octave anyway (such as the Bach example discussed previously), momentarily leaving aside any thought of additional intervals will simplify the task considerably.

We can play simple stretti by combining these strategies: deploying imitations at regular time intervals, using incomplete subjects, and limiting imitation to the octave only.

Strategies for Developing the Stretto

Example 14.4 shows a subject by Sala.

The first four bars are easy to memorize: ❶-❼-❻-❺. It is also easy to perceive that this four-note fragment could imitate itself after two measures, as

EXAMPLE 14.4 A subject of Sala

EXAMPLE 14.5 Stretto for a stepwise descending theme

that would place the voices a third apart. In fact, since the fragment descends, new entries could begin at the same pitch level. Upon the third entry, a triad is formed, and so the voices can no longer continue to descend stepwise together, as parallel fifths would result. If the lower voices are modified, the pattern may be transformed into Fauxbourdon. A very simple (but legitimate and satisfactory) stretto is born! If the four-note fragment imitates at the octave below, a new configuration results. At the octave above, the voices will move in tenths. A third entry will be difficult to reach for most keyboard players. All these situations are illustrated in Example 14.5.

EXERCISE. Improvise simple stretti on the Sala fragment. Find as many solutions as you can. Transpose.

The subject of the A minor fugue from Book I of *The Well-Tempered Clavier* is shown in Example 14.6.

EXAMPLE 14.6 The subject of a Bach fugue

EXAMPLE 14.7 Possible stretto on Bach

Though it is a long subject and would be difficult to overlap in stretto in its entirety, fortunately it has a smaller fragment that is suitable for the purpose: the head of the subject. The first measure (including the downbeat of the second), when reduced to its structural notes, begins on ❶, rises by a third, then rises another third. Imitation at the octave below or above can begin at the half measure, resulting in parallel thirds or sixths. If any subsequent voices were to enter, the first two would need to find something constructive to do, as they could not continue with the subject. Example 14.7 shows these combinations.

EXERCISE. Improvise simple stretti on the Bach fragment in as many combinations as you can. Transpose.

A subject by Martini appears in Example 14.8.

This subject, when reduced to its essentials, rises by step. Just as with the Sala fragment, this stepwise theme will imitate at the octave when it has moved up a third. Therefore, the imitation may begin in the second measure. However, this time we are lucky; the entire subject may be completed without voice-leading error. Maybe a third voice could even get into the picture. When subjects work surprisingly well in stretto, it is often because they were designed that way; the composer planned to construct a stretto all along, and stacked the deck to make it easier. (In this case, however, the fugue by Martini has no stretto and does not take advantage of this convenient quality of the subject. Go figure.) Martini's subject in one possible stretto appears in Example 14.9.

EXERCISE. Improvise stretti on the Martini subject. Try starting an imitation at the unison so the voices move in thirds. At the octave above they will move in sixths. If a third voice were to participate, where would it enter?

A fourth strategy, in addition to the three discussed already, is to add a free voice. If the imitative portion of the stretto consists of two voices, a third may

EXAMPLE 14.8 A subject of Martini

EXAMPLE 14.9 A stretto on Martini

fill out the harmony in a satisfying manner. This free voice could be a bass or an upper voice.

A fifth strategy is to find a motive in the subject that outlines a specific interval, and then superimpose that motive on bass motions that include the same interval in two different voices. For example, if a subject contains a motive that, after diminutions are removed, outlines a descending step, that motive can be placed in imitation between the two upper voices of a C5 motion, because the upper voices in a C5 move by descending step. For this strategy to work, the motive must be identifiable as part of the subject. It is best if the motive is the head of the subject and has enough notes and rhythmic activity to be clearly recognized. Less important portions of the subject are more suitable for episodes. When the subject head is present, it simply sounds more significant, as if is it conjuring or evoking the presence of the entire subject. While this strategy is not all that different from how one might construct an episode, it can be effective in stretti, as well. Example 14.10 shows a subject from Dietrich Buxtehude (1637–1707) and how the head of the subject may be incorporated as part of a C5.

EXAMPLE 14.10 A subject of Buxtehude

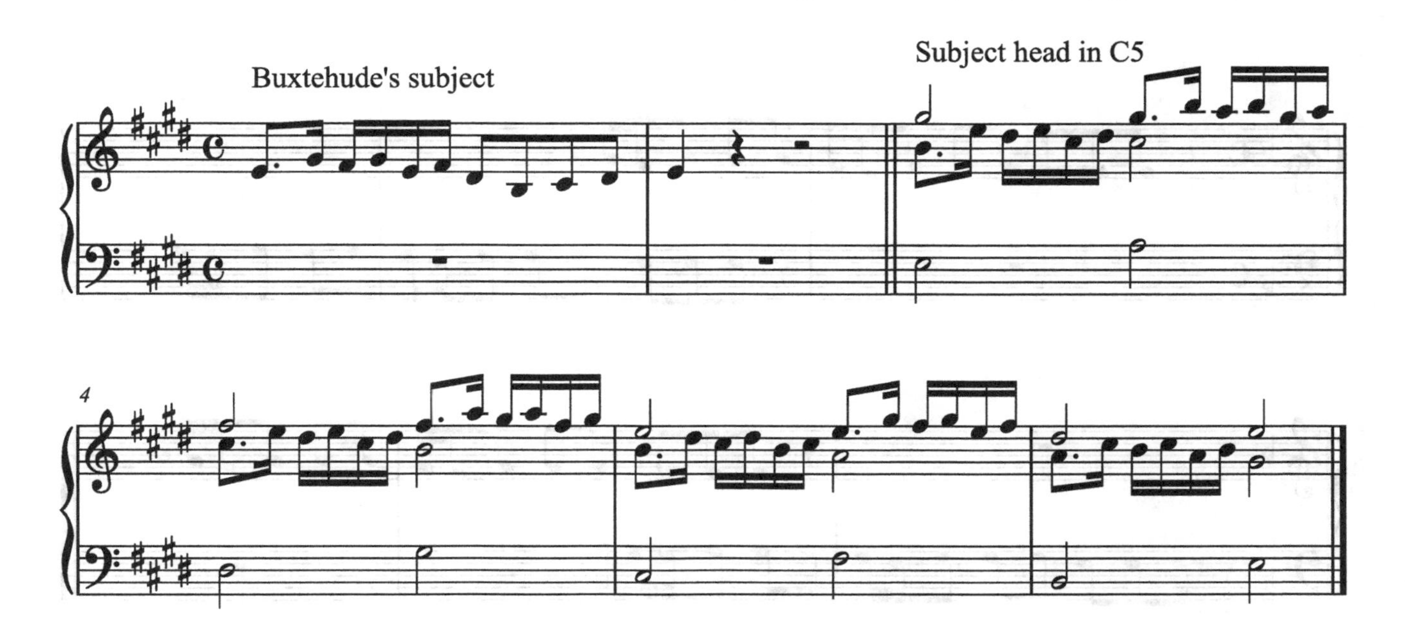

A sixth strategy is to use the inherent imitative characteristics of certain interval patterns, if you are lucky enough to have a subject thus constructed. The subject by Sala in Example 14.4 descends by a step each measure and is easy to imitate at the octave above or below simply by waiting two measures. In fact, any subject built on repeated intervals will allow imitation at some point, as long as the motion occurs in regular "stages," whether a full measure or a consistent number of beats. Predicting imitation for a subject with uneven stages far more difficult; it will probably be necessary to check it one beat at a time, as Gedalge recommended.

Example 14.11 shows subjects built on regular intervallic stages and imitation at the octave above and below for each. Combinations of this kind are similar to those studied in Chapter 8.

EXAMPLE 14.11 Subject with imitations

Imitation at the Fourth and Fifth

We have said previously that in the stretto, imitation at anything other than the octave should be considered optional (actually, the whole stretto is optional, but never mind). But for those who wish to invest a bit more study and effort, imitation at other intervals (especially the fourth and fifth) can be rewarding, and sometimes surprisingly easy. As we saw in Example 14.2, sometimes imitation will work at some other interval more readily than at the octave. It turns out that the octave is not necessarily the easiest interval for imitation. And anyway, we have already been imitating at the fifth during expositions for some time. While imitation at any interval is possible, those at the fourth and fifth are nearly as common as those at the octave. Therefore, in this chapter we will explore imitation at the fourth and fifth.

Subjects must be examined to discover what kind of stretto is possible. This is what Marie-Claire Alain was talking about in the interview from Chapter 9. According to Alain, in the organ class at the Conservatoire students had to do so simply by sitting and thinking for a few minutes—no paper allowed. Some subjects are completely unsuited for any kind of stretto at all, and in such cases the stretto is created with fragments, an altered subject, or omitted altogether.

Is it possible to predict ways in which fugue subjects will work in stretto without checking them beat by beat? Yes, but only if the subject moves at repeated intervals in regular stages.

Subjects that descend stepwise in regular stages may imitate at the fifth at one stage, and at the octave or the fourth at two stages.

Subjects that ascend by step in regular stages may imitate at the fourth at one stage, and at the octave or the fifth at two stages.

Subjects that descend by thirds in regular stages may imitate at the octave or the fourth at one stage. They may not imitate at the fifth.

Subject that ascend by thirds in regular stages may imitate at the octave or the fifth at one stage. They may not imitate at the fourth.

Cascade-based subjects that move in regular stages may imitate at the octave at four stages, at the fifth at two stages, and at the fourth at one stage.

C5-based subjects that move in regular stages may imitate at the octave or fifth at three stages.

Monte Principale–based subjects that move in regular stages may imitate at the octave above at one stage, the octave below at four stages, the fourth above at three stages, and at the fifth at four stages. The reason one must specify above or below is that some Monte Principale imitations involve fifths which may not invert to dissonant fourths.

Leaping Romanesca–based subjects that move in regular stages may imitate at the octave at two stages, at the fourth at one stage, and at the fifth above or below at three stages.

Chromatic subjects that move in regular stages in either direction may imitate at the minor third or major sixth. See Example 14.12.

EXAMPLE 14.12 Imitation at various intervals and stages

EXAMPLE 14.12 Continued

You will rarely find subjects so conveniently fashioned. But when creating your own subjects, you can use these principles and design them to facilitate imitation if you wish.

The subjects in Example 14.13 are built on intervals at regular stages. They will allow for imitation at various intervals and stages.

EXERCISE. Find the possible stretti for each of the subjects from Example 14.13. Some will allow for the entire subject to be set in imitation with itself, and others will require modification or use of fragments. Include an extra free voice to fill out the harmony as necessary. Example 14.14 provides possible solutions for two of the subjects. Note that imitating voices are shown as lower than the subjects in Example 14.14, but these stretti would work inverted, as well.

Further Stretto Practice

A variety of subjects from real music appear in the following examples, and each is accompanied by an exercise. These are to help you practice making stretti out of subjects. They will not be as convenient as the artificial subjects (with regular stages) from Example 14.13. Explore possibilities for stretto at the octave, fourth, and fifth.

Example 14.15 shows a subject by Sala. This one should prompt you to remember the partimento technique of boring and interesting measures.

EXERCISE. Experiment with the Sala subject and discover its possibilities for stretto. Can it imitate both above and below? Where does the imitation start? Does it have more than one possible starting point?

Example 14.16 shows a good old subject of Fenaroli that we have seen before.

EXERCISE. Explore the stretto possibilities of the Fenaroli subject. How far can the imitation proceed before hitting an unprepared dissonance? Can it imitate above and below?

Example 14.17 shows a subject of Handel that gets a running start with repeated notes.

EXERCISE. At what point could imitation begin? Can you find a starting point for imitation that will allow most of the subject to participate? Can it imitate above and below?

Example 14.18 shows a subject by Giuseppe Sarti (1729–1802). Even though the rhythmic divisions differ in each measure, the structural intervals move in regular stages.

EXERCISE. Reducing Sarti's subject only to pitches on the first and third beats of each measure, what do you find? At what point could imitation start? How far could it proceed?

EXAMPLE 14.13 Subjects for imitation

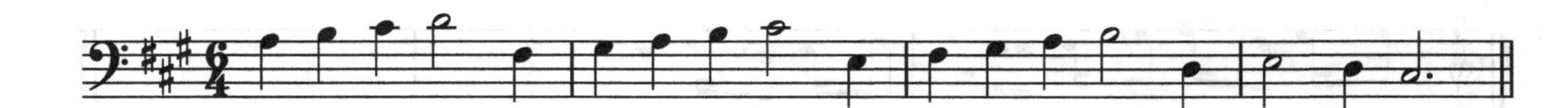

EXAMPLE 14.14 Possible stretto solutions

EXAMPLE 14.15 A subject of Sala

EXAMPLE 14.16 A subject of Fenaroli

EXAMPLE 14.17 A subject of Handel

EXAMPLE 14.18 A subject of Sarti

Example 14.19 shows a subject of J. S. Bach. At a glance it appears to rise by step, which seems promising for stretto. But look closely. Does this subject work in imitation at the octave?

Example 14.20 shows a subject of Mendelssohn. Find the intervals and locations of imitation, try it above and below, and discover where the imitation must break off.

Example 14.21 shows another subject of Fenaroli.

EXAMPLE 14.19 A subject of Bach

EXAMPLE 14.20 A subject of Mendelssohn

EXAMPLE 14.21 A subject of Fenaroli

EXAMPLE 14.22 An anonymous subject

EXAMPLE 14.23 A subject of Albrechtsberger

EXAMPLE 14.24 A subject of Eberlin

EXERCISE. Find the possibilities and limitations for stretto in Fenaroli's subject. Do any voice-leading errors show up in one inversion but not the other?

Example 14.22 shows an anonymous subject. It is partly outlined by rising fourths and falling thirds, the Monte Principale motion, which has excellent imitative qualities. But something about the subject is problematic.

EXERCISE. Can you identify the problem with the subject above and discover a point of imitation that will allow at least some imitation? How far can the imitation go? Can it imitate above and below?

Example 14.23 shows a subject of Johann Albrechtsberger (1736–1809).

EXERCISE. How would you create a stretto on Albrechtsberger's subject?

Example 14.24 shows a subject by Eberlin that, for the first two measures, rises by step in regular stages.

EXERCISE. Find a point of imitation for the Eberlin subject. Try imitations above and below. How far can imitation proceed? At the fourth, where is the point of imitation, and how far does the imitation go? Now try imitating at the fifth, beginning on G. Where does the imitation begin, and how far can it proceed?

This is interesting. Imitation at the octave only allows for one measure of overlap before hitting an unprepared dissonance, but imitation at the fourth or fifth *allows the entire subject to participate.* Imitation at the fourth begins on beat three of the first measure, and imitation at the fifth begins after one full measure. The Eberlin subject almost seems perfectly designed for this purpose. If one predicted that the composer of this subject would create a stretto with imitation at the fourth and fifth, starting at the locations mentioned, one would be correct. Example 14.25 shows first my own stretto on this subject, which I

EXAMPLE 14.25 Speculative and actual stretti on Eberlin

made without looking at Eberlin's; thereafter the composer's own stretto follows in the same example. Both stretti create imitation at the fourth and fifth. This does not imply any particular like-mindedness between myself and Eberlin, but shows that potential for stretto is inherent within a subject.

We return again to the familiar subject of Sala, as seen in Example 14.26. It descends by step in regular stages. We already discovered that imitation at the

EXAMPLE 14.26 A subject of Sala

octave takes place after two measures. Imitation at the fourth is also possible at two measures, and imitation at the fifth may begin after one measure.

EXERCISE. Create a stretto on the Sala subject, imitating at the fourth and then at the fifth.

Yet one more Sala subject is shown in Example 14.27. This one rises by step in regular stages.

EXERCISE. Discover the imitative possibilities of this subject at the octave, fourth, and fifth, and improvise stretti.

Remember that ascending stepwise subjects may be imitated at the octave or fourth after two stages, and at the fifth after one stage; descending stepwise subjects may be imitated at the octave or fourth after two stages, and at the fifth after one stage. This means that, for stepwise subjects moving in regular stages, *imitation at the octave offers the least overlap*, as it always takes two stages. Depending on the direction of the subject, either the fourth or the fifth will be able to imitate after one stage. While not all subjects move in regular stepwise stages, many do, and those will allow for easy construction of stretti if the improviser understands their hidden potential. When inventing your own subjects, the knowledge of the imitative properties of regular stepwise stages will allow you to "stack the deck" for easy stretto at the fourth or fifth.

Another subject of Albrechtsberger, shown here in Example 14.28, almost looks stepwise to the eye, but on closer inspection turns out to be a Cascade.

EXERCISE. Check Albrechtsberger's subject for imitative possibilities at the fourth and fifth, and create a stretto.

EXAMPLE 14.27 A subject of Sala

EXAMPLE 14.28 A subject of Albrechtsberger

EXAMPLE 14.29 A subject of Cherubini

Example 14.29 shows a chromatic theme by Cherubini, which was the *concours* subject for the Paris Conservatoire in 1840. It has a chromatic head and a diatonic tail.

EXERCISE. Figure out whether Cherubini's subject has any stretto possibilities at the octave, fourth, or fifth.

Practicality of Improvising Stretto

Is this level of contrapuntal sophistication practical for the improviser? Without some preparation, most players will be unable to find these solutions in real time. I have seen rules for an organ improvisation competition that allows *one entire day* of contemplation after a subject is given; surely a dedicated improviser could find a stretto for the Cherubini subject in that amount of time (or much less).

But it is not always necessary. Remember, Gedalge teaches that a stretto can be made from merely the head of a subject, not the whole thing, if a subject proves to be unwieldy. If an improviser adopts this approach, could one create a stretto without twenty-four hours of anxious calculation? The subject head is merely a chromatic line. Keeping in mind that descending chromatic imitations will need to line up as minor thirds, imitation at the fifth after half a measure will work beautifully.

EXERCISE. Work out a stretto on the Cherubini subject at the fifth. If you are ambitious, improvise a complete fugue on the Cherubini subject. Example 14.30 demonstrates a few attempts at stretto.

Location of the Stretto

The *fugue d'école* teachers viewed the stretto as the dramatic high point of fugue, the moment of maximum thematic density and most complex counterpoint. This does not represent the real situation of all fugues in the literature, many of which have no stretto at all. But it's a cool idea. Setting up the stretto as the pinnacle will help the improviser create a fugue of musical interest and structural integrity.

Gedalge suggests that "the stretto section may be joined to the first part of the fugue in these ways: a) By linking the first stretto directly to the last episode. b) By making an averted or broken cadence, with a pause marked by a pedal point between the stretto and the episode. c) By placing a pedal point on the

EXAMPLE 14.30 Stretti on Cherubini

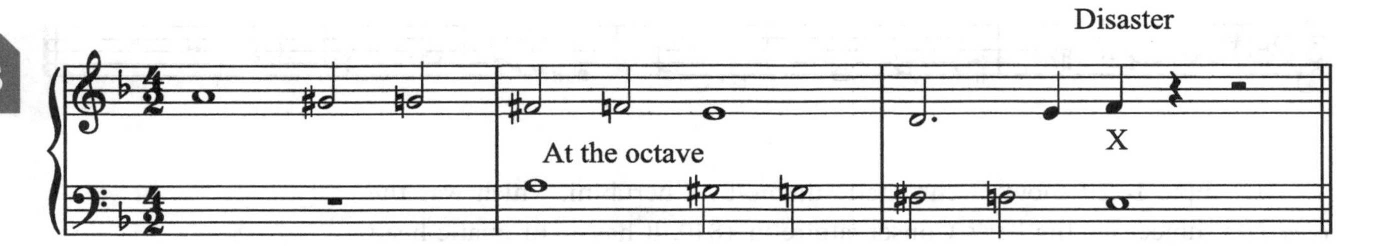

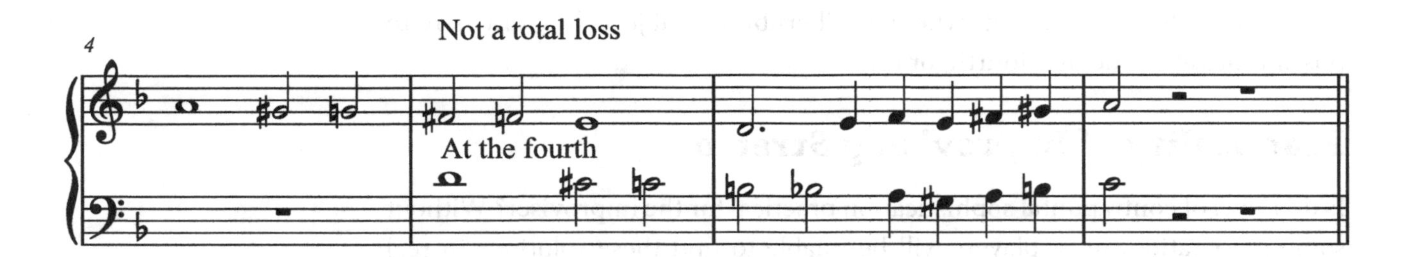

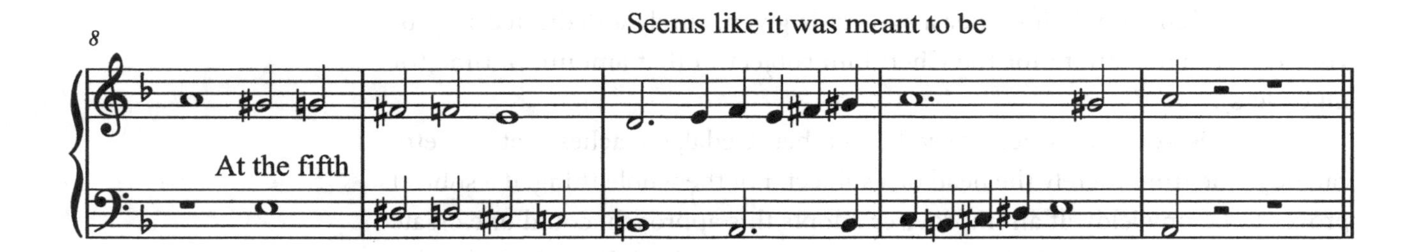

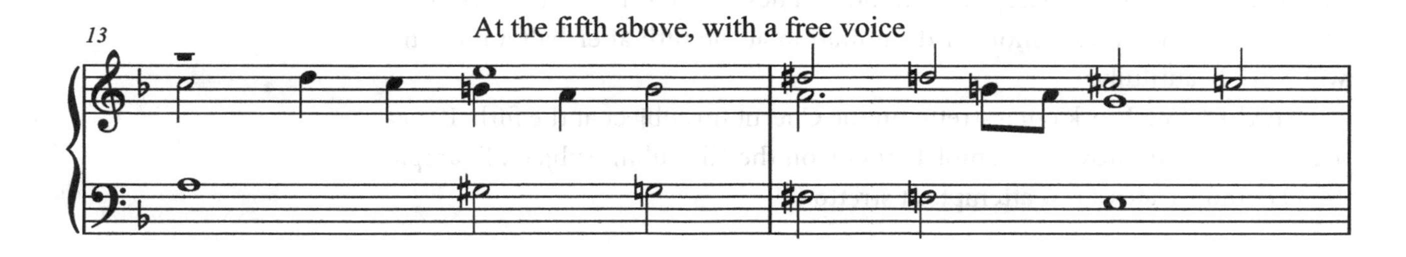

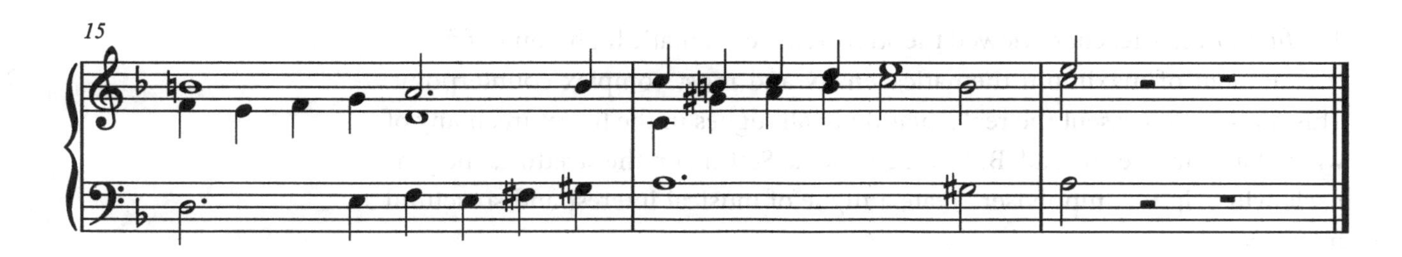

dominant before the stretto section, linking it directly or separating it from the stretto section by a hold."

Gedalge's first method is subtle: the stretto begins without any special fanfare, proceeding seamlessly from the previous episodic section. (Remember that Gedalge includes presentations within episodes; he means that the stretto can flow out of an episode or a presentation.) His second and third methods, however, are both intended to highlight the beginning of the stretto as much as possible, either by stopping the music completely for a moment or by sounding a pedal point immediately before the stretto commences.

J. S. Bach used similar techniques at times. Example 14.31 shows the stretto section from the A minor fugue from the first book of *The Well-Tempered Clavier.*

Indeed, the music is brought to a screeching halt at a fermata before resuming and making its way to pedal point on the dominant (the fact that the E in the bass is interrupted by rests does not change its function as a pedal). While this piece is too complex for most improvisers to use as a model, nevertheless it demonstrates how a stretto may serve as the dramatic summation of a fugue.

Similarly, Mattheson's fughetta from *Die wohlklingende Fingersprache* begins its stretto after a break at a half cadence, as shown in Example 14.32.

Mattheson's subject begins by ascending stepwise in regular stages. As we might expect, the first imitation is at the fifth after two stages (one measure).

EXAMPLE 14.31 Stretto in Bach

EXAMPLE 14.32 Stretto in Mattheson

EXAMPLE 14.33 Stretto in Delandres

Adolphe Delandres (1840–1911) wrote a fugue for the Paris *concours* and won first prize in 1858. His stretto is shown in Example 14.33.

Delandres's stretto begins with a complete pause after a half cadence. The stretto begins with a subject statement followed by imitation at the fifth. Delandres's piece sets the stretto apart clearly, which accomplishes the goal of making it sound like a distinct and important moment in the fugue. This method is one more option for the improviser. Note that Delandres uses a tonal answer for the imitation.

EXERCISE. Revisit several subjects from this chapter. Find fragments suitable for episodes. Work on improvising episodes that lead into stretti. Use various techniques of connecting the episodes and stretti: seamless elision, complete stop on a half cadence or cadence evasion (such as a deceptive move to a diminished chord), unaccompanied subject entry, subject entry accompanied by a pedal point on tonic or dominant, or any combination thereof. (We will consider the pedal point in greater detail in the next chapter.) Then create stretti with two voices imitating at the octave, fourth, or fifth, with or without free voices to fill in the harmony. Two voices over a pedal point is probably enough to keep you busy! On the piano, you may wish to catch the pedal point in the sostenuto pedal (if you have one) as this will free up both hands. (In my opinion this capability alone is sufficient justification for the existence of the sostenuto pedal.) Devote considerable time to this exercise.

Chapter 15

Pedal Point, Cadenza, Ending

A pedal point is a musical device in which a single pitch sounds continuously while activity, including harmonic movement, occurs in other voices. The same term also denotes the section of a musical composition in which the pedal point technique is used. Theoretically, the held pitch may be located in any voice, but is by far most commonly heard in the bass. For our purposes in this book, it always sounds the tonic or dominant note in the bass. We will consider methods of improvising pedal points, and strategies for incorporating such sections into larger plans for complete fugues.

Gedalge's Rules for Pedal Points

Gedalge stipulates rules for beginning and concluding pedal points: "The harmonic rules governing the pedal point are the same in fugue as in harmony: it can only begin and end on a consonance; it must enter as a consonant part of a harmony, and can only be quitted as if it were a consonance." That is, the note chosen to serve as the pedal point (always ① or ⑤ in the lowest sounding voice) must be consonant with the rest of the harmony at the moment it begins, and at the moment it ends. However, after the pedal point has begun, the upper voices may go about various harmonies that do not include the pedal note. Gedalge explains: "As soon as it is heard, the pedal point becomes a note foreign to the harmonies of all the other parts, and, in consequence, can form any number of prepared dissonances with them."

The Pedal Point's Effect

The musical effect of the pedal point is simultaneous stability and instability. The pedal, sounding either of the two most stable pitches, represents stability.

The changing harmonies of the upper voices, at times quite dissonant, represent instability. The result is a heightened sense of musical significance, of momentousness. Many decades later, the song "The Wall" by progressive rock band Kansas captured this aesthetic: "The moment is a masterpiece; the weight of indecision's in the air." This lyric is sung over a pedal point on B while the upper harmonies alternate between B major 7 and C♯ major.

Gedalge, though unaware of the music of Kansas, describes this same feeling in different terms: "One of the great advantages of placing the pedal point on the tonic or dominant is that this enables the composer, while affirming the principal key of the fugue, to sound at the same time various neighboring keys. It therefore binds tighter the threads of the fugue and revives interest."

Location of the Pedal Point

Gedalge further states that pedal points do not have a specific required location within the structure of the fugue. A pedal may serve "as preparation for the first entries of the stretto section if it be placed immediately before the first stretto. . . . In this situation, it is almost always heard in the dominant. The pedal point on the tonic, however, is always reserved for the conclusion of the fugue."

In other words, a pedal point on the dominant may sound during the stretto, in which case the pedal point and stretto are present simultaneously as a single event. Gedalge's point regarding tonic pedal points is broadly true for fugues in the literature; once a pedal sounds on the tonic, the final cadence is probably not far away. (This should not be confused with an opening tonic pedal point, used frequently at the beginning of preludes and toccatas.)

According to Gedalge, the pedal point is not a required section, and when included, its uses and locations vary: "As the pedal point is the part of the fugue in which great liberty is permitted, it is impossible to formulate strict rules for it. The ways of treating it depend on the ingenuity of the composer. It should, however, be said that all the kinds of episodes hitherto studied, as well as strettos, may be used with a pedal point."

This freedom notwithstanding, it is advisable to place the pedal point near the end of the fugue due to its aesthetic of drama and summation. Gedalge states that the listener must endeavor "somehow, to feel its approach. Although this is impossible to define, it does pave the way, when properly handled, for the end of the fugue if on the dominant; if on the tonic, it sets forth the conclusion itself."

Examples of Pedal Points and Endings

Before commencing exercises, we will consider techniques of pedal point from various composed fugues. At the same time, it will be necessary to discuss endings, as pedal points so often prepare for, or directly participate in, the conclusion of fugues.

When he uses pedal points, Eberlin prefers short ones on the dominant that lead directly to the final cadence. Example 15.1 shows pedal points from Eberlin fugues.

The pedal points of Buxtehude are longer and more elaborate. Example 15.2 shows the pedal point from a fugue in D major in which a Tied Bass motion, and then a 5-6, play out over a tonic pedal.

Buxtehude's F♯ minor fugue has extended passages in parallel tenths over a tonic pedal, as seen in Example 15.3.

EXAMPLE 15.1 Pedal points from Eberlin

EXAMPLE 15.2 Pedal point in Buxtehude

EXAMPLE 15.3 Pedal point in Buxtehude

Buxtehude's fugue in E minor has a sequential stepwise descending Fauxbourdon passage over a tonic pedal, as shown in Example 15.4.

The F major fugue has both dominant and tonic pedal points, shown in Example 15.5.

Buxtehude's fugue in B♭ places Fauxbourdon over a tonic pedal, as seen in Example 15.6.

EXAMPLE 15.4 Pedal point in Buxtehude

EXAMPLE 15.5 Pedal point in Buxtehude

The pedal point from the fugue in Martini's fifth *Sonata d'intavolatura*, shown in Example 15.7, places a four-measure dominant pedal point before a stretto. Note that the left hand must play the pedal tone and assist with inner voices, as this is harpsichord music.

EXAMPLE 15.6 Pedal point in Buxtehude

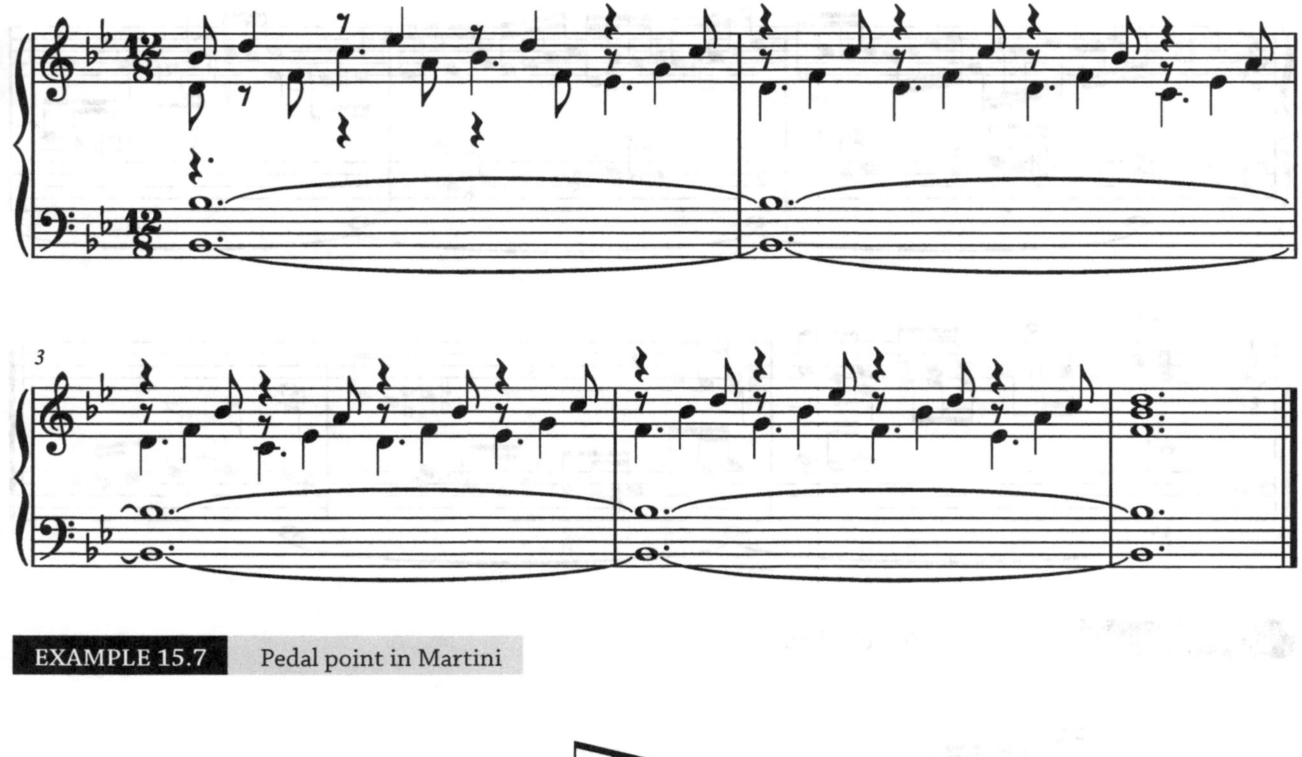

EXAMPLE 15.7 Pedal point in Martini

Example 15.8 shows the pedal point from a fugue in A major of Nicola Porpora (1686–1768). The pedal point makes no subject reference at all, consisting only of standard Alberti-like keyboard figurations.

The first Contrapunctus from J. S. Bach's *Die Kunst der Fuge* ends with shifting harmonic gestures over a tonic pedal point, and is shown in Example 15.9. The voice-crossings may seem confusing when notated for keyboard, but

EXAMPLE 15.8 Pedal point in Porpora

EXAMPLE 15.9 Pedal point in *Die Kunst der Fuge*

EXAMPLE 15.10 Pedal point in *Die Kunst der Fuge*

EXAMPLE 15.11 Pedal point in Krebs

Bach's original was in open scoring, where voice-crossings in upper voices are not a problem.

The end of the fourth Contrapunctus appears in Example 15.10. Note the chromatic nature of ❷ and ❻, which change between flat and natural, thus showing the range of harmonies possible over a pedal point. Even though no single voice moves in constant eighths, continuous rhythmic movement is achieved by placing activity in at least one voice at all times.

The end of the fugue in C minor of Johann Ludwig Krebs (1713–1780) appears in Example 15.11. The final dominant is replaced with a leading-tone diminished harmony. Note the jarring cross-relation between A and A♭ in measure 9.

Krebs' fugue in E♭ features a stretto over a tonic pedal that elides with the final cadence. The subject appears in Example 15.12 together with the pedal and stretto for comparison.

EXAMPLE 15.12 Pedal point in Krebs

EXAMPLE 15.13 Pedal point in Krebs

Krebs' fugue in F minor uses a descending chromatic soprano over a tonic pedal, elided with the final cadence. Example 15.13 demonstrates these measures.

In another F minor fugue, shown in Example 15.14, Krebs creates a cadenza before a very short concluding pedal point.

EXAMPLE 15.14 Pedal point in Krebs

Krebs was said to be J. S. Bach's favorite student. In the B♭ fugue, shown in Example 15.15, the student pays homage to the master by spelling his name over a tonic pedal. (B natural is called "H" in German.)

In Krebs' D major fugue, shown in Example 15.16, the pedal is restruck instead of sounding continuously.

Krebs' F minor fugue (different from both F minor pieces shown previously), shown in Example 15.17, has no pedal point or stretto, as these events are optional. But look: two measures of textbook Rule of the Octave lead up to a compound cadence. Krebs knew his RO.

The Cadenza

The *fugue d'école* tradition paid no attention to cadenzas, most likely because the cadenza does not require the same contrapuntal discipline as the exposition, episode, presentation, pedal point, or stretto. But in real music, cadenzas occur in fugues sometimes. They are easy to improvise and dramatic in affect. The examples in this chapter will provide some sense of the variety of techniques available.

EXAMPLE 15.15 Pedal point in Krebs

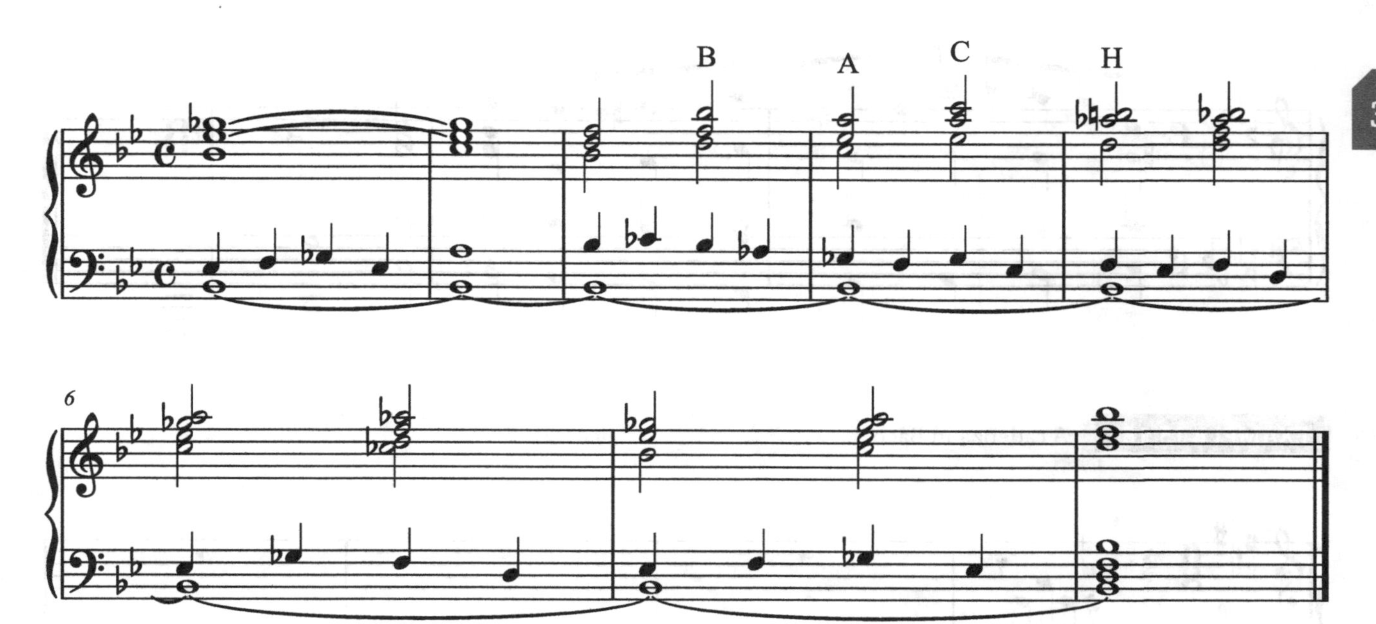

EXAMPLE 15.16 Pedal point in Krebs

EXAMPLE 15.17 Pedal point in Krebs

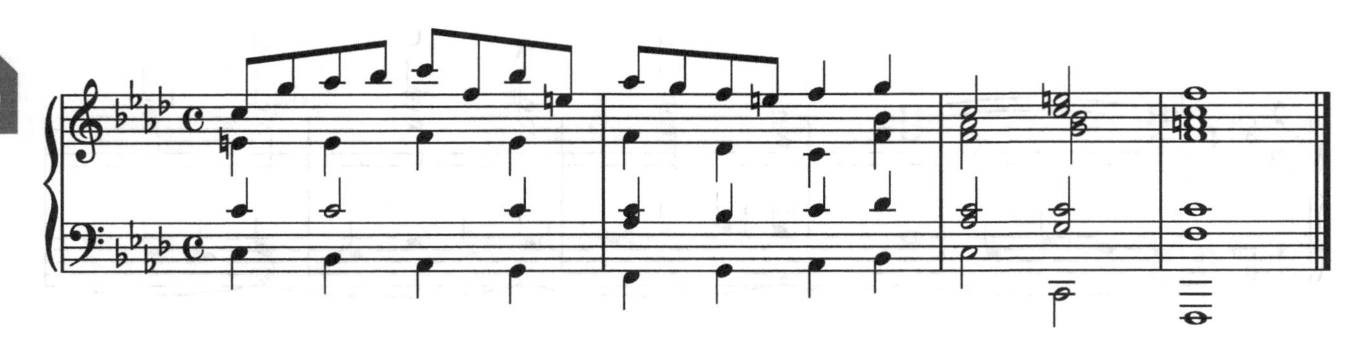

EXAMPLE 15.18 A cadenza in Bach

The toccatas for keyboard by J. S. Bach all conclude with fugues. Of the seven fugues, five end with cadenza-like passages. The end of the toccata in F♯ minor appears in Example 15.18. Its daring, exposed cadenza on the tonic triad precedes a final, harmonized subject statement.

The conclusion of the toccata in C minor, shown in Example 15.19, consists of a cadenza that begins at a slow tempo, is punctuated with chords, and then takes off at a fast tempo.

The cadenza at the end of the E minor toccata is smaller in scope, constructed of two measures that twist around the newly acquired parallel major tonality, as shown in Example 15.20.

EXAMPLE 15.19 A cadenza in Bach

The G minor toccata opens with a cadenza, and the same passage reappears as the conclusion of the fugue. Both are shown in Example 15.21.

As these examples of pedal points, cadenzas, and endings illustrate, no standard usage exists for any of them. These examples serve to convey a sense of the many possible approaches for the improviser.

EXAMPLE 15.21 A cadenza in Bach

Creating Pedal Points

Pedal points are not limited to fugue; they may be used in absolutely any kind of piece, provided they fit in musically. All the techniques you learn in this section may be freely adapted for use in other kinds of pieces.

When creating a pedal point, the improviser must ask what kind of things one can do over a sustained bass note on the tonic or dominant. The first limitation is tonality. In general, material over a pedal may "drift" one accidental in either direction. The drift toward one sharp fewer (or one more flat) is very common, and is the same harmonic move associated with the Quiescenza. In the other direction, a sharp is added (or a flat subtracted), which takes us to the harmonic region of the "secondary dominant" (as we called it in theory class). In minor keys, the leading tones of the neighboring tonalities iv and v may be present. Chromaticism is also possible, as seen in some examples in this chapter. When starting out with pedal points, the improviser need not overachieve and include every available harmonic area. One can stay completely diatonic and make a great pedal point.

Even though the pedal point may involve all sorts of dissonances of the upper voices against each other and against the bass, the beginning of the pedal point must occur according to normal harmonic procedures. That is, the voices must arrive at the first "chord" by following the same rules that apply elsewhere in eighteenth-century music: no illegal parallels and no unprepared dissonances. Likewise, the last sounding event within the pedal point must exit by the same rules. This can happen in many ways. If the pedal is on the dominant, it might terminate in a cadence or cadence evasion. On the tonic, the most likely result is a resolution that remains on the tonic. Pedal points on tonic or dominant may exit by providing $^{\#4}_{2}$ in the upper voices, in which case the bass would resolve by descending a step. This move will take you away from any imminent cadence, and make the piece longer.

On the organ, quite obviously, pedal tones are played on the pedals. (Hence the name.) On other keyboard instruments (excluding the very rare pedal harpsichord and pedal piano) the left hand is responsible to sound the bass note. Several techniques may serve this purpose. One may hold a single note or octave and leave everything else to the right hand. One may sound a single note with the fifth finger and use the other available digits to assist with upper voices. On a suitably equipped piano, one may also use the sostenuto pedal to capture a single note or octave, which then frees both hands to manage the upper voices. Many older pianos, particularly in Europe, do not have sostenuto pedals. (I once failed to foresee this when giving a concert in Russia. Having practiced the use of the sostenuto for a dramatic pedal point in a Bach-Feinberg transcription, I arrived at the concert hall to see not three, but two pedals staring up at me. The horror! This was before I started improvising. It wouldn't bother me now.)

Stylistic devices provide alternatives to simply holding a long bass note. Gedalge calls this approach "ornamented pedal." The pedal point may be restruck, with or without rests in between, which still functions as a pedal point. The bass may even be restruck with rhythms that echo activity in the upper voices, heightening the sense of contrapuntal interplay without adding any new structural pitches. The pedal point may be decorated with neighbor tones, turns, perpetual rhythmic activity, or trills. The bass note of the pedal point may alternate with another pitch or moving line in the manner of compound melody. Instances of techniques appear in Example 15.22.

As Gedalge has pointed out, pedal points may be used in multitudinous ways (or not used at all), making it difficult to discuss every possible role in fugue. The following exercises provide practice in some of the most common uses.

EXERCISE. One of the easiest ways to use a pedal point is to create a sequential pattern of two voices in the right hand while the left holds the bass note. The sequential pattern need not contain the subject or any important thematic material. Play ⑤ in the bass. Commence a 7-6 pattern in the right hand. At the end of the pedal point, the bass should move to ① and the right hand should resolve to tonic harmony. Transpose this exercise. In minor keys, use the natural form until you need the leading tone near the end.

EXAMPLE 15.22 Pedal point techniques

EXAMPLE 15.23 Pedal point exercises

EXERCISE. Repeat the exercise above. Instead of 7-6, use 2-3. Both exercises are demonstrated in Example 15.23.

EXERCISE. The exercises above may be elaborated by adding diminutions to 7-6 and 2-3 (Offset Scales). Such diminutions will be somewhat limited if the right hand is dealing with both voices; larger intervals and greater virtuosity becomes possible when the left hand is free by means of the sostenuto. Try some diminutions on Offset Scales in the right hand alone, and with left hand. Example 15.24 illustrates these ideas.

EXAMPLE 15.24 Offset scales over pedal points

EXAMPLE 15.25 Offset scales with thematic fragments

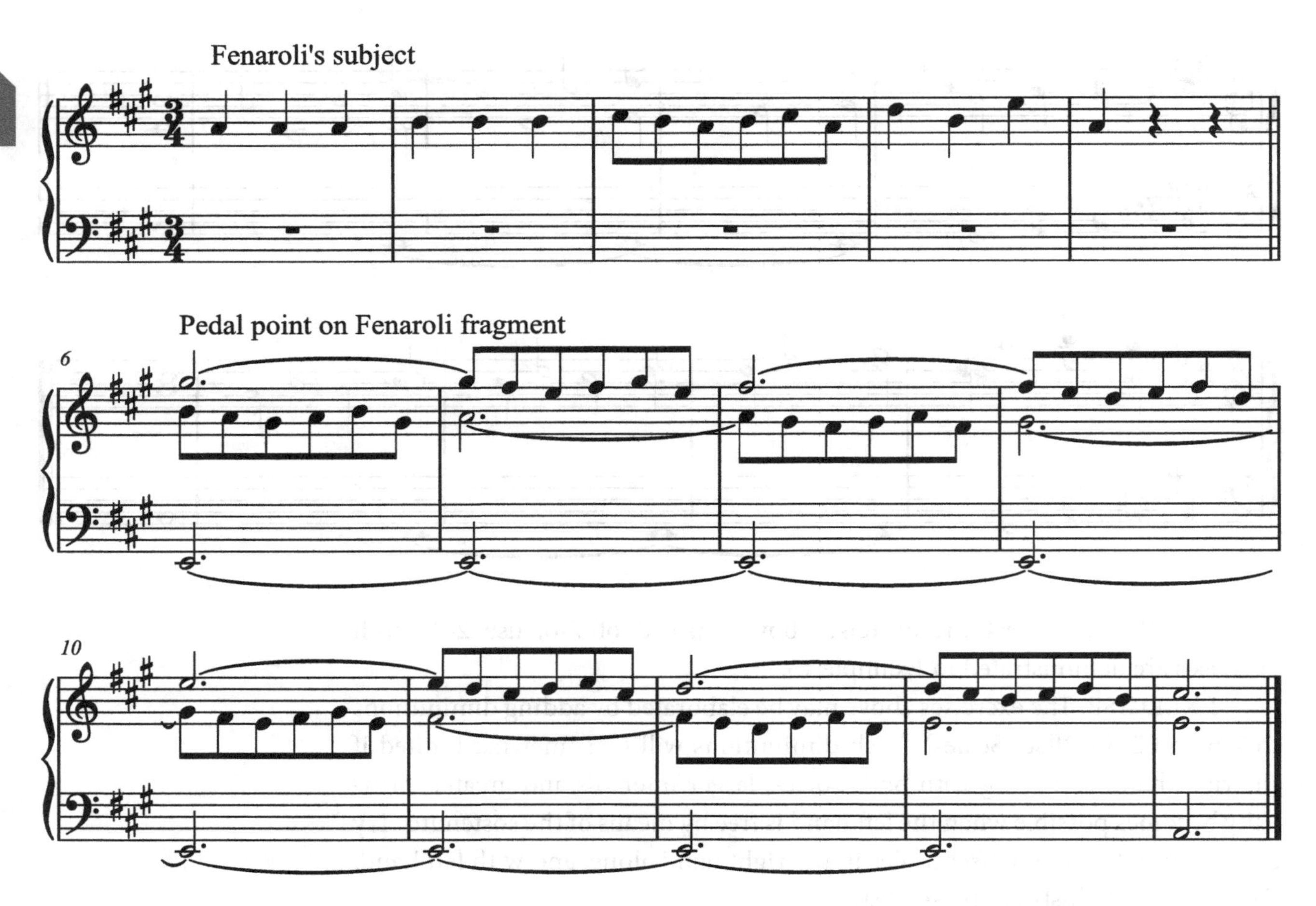

EXERCISE. Short fragments from the fugue subject or other significant thematic material may be grafted onto Offset Scales, as seen in Example 15.25, using a familiar subject of Fenaroli. Take fragments from many fugue subjects and deploy them in this manner. If the fragments are short and use small intervals, they will work best.

EXERCISE. A stretto over a dominant pedal is an impressive musical event. Most subjects will not lend themselves to being played and imitated in one hand, so this would be a good opportunity to use the sostenuto pedal, if available. See Example 15.26, where the Prix de Rome subject of Reber is placed in stretto over a dominant pedal point.

EXERCISE. Revisit the cadenzas from J. S. Bach's keyboard toccatas, shown previously in Examples 15.18–21. Develop several cadenza strategies that you can readily deploy in any key. Cadenzas may be harmonically very simple, perhaps outlining just a single chord. However, they must sound virtuosic. They should convey a sense of breaking free from the confines of the preceding music; they should sound somewhat out of time. Practice playing your own, and then moving seamlessly into a final cadence.

EXAMPLE 15.26 Stretto in Reber

Chapter 16

Improvising Fugue

Having studied and practiced all the individual elements of fugue, we will now proceed to put them all together in complete improvised fugues. First, a review of fugue subjects is in order, so you that may create your own to use with the exercises in this chapter if desired.

Subjects

Subjects for improvisation should be relatively short to allow for quick memorization. A fugue can be made on almost any tune, but the music will be far better if the subject has an interesting rhythmic feature or an engaging melodic shape. It should provide one or two motivic fragments for episodes and stretti. Building a subject around a well-known bass motion will make harmonization and development very easy, especially if the motion is one that combines easily with other motions in invertible counterpoint.

In designing a subject, the improviser should determine whether it takes a real or tonal answer, and whether it modulates or remains in the home key. For more ambitious fugues, the possibilities for stretto at the octave, fourth, and fifth should be investigated.

The best way to acquire skill at creating fugue subjects is, of course, to get down to the business of inventing and improvising upon them, and to do so repeatedly over a long period of time. I particularly recommend creating your subjects according to Martini's andamento model.

Review of an Introductory Model

Previous exercises have already provided guidance for creating very simple fugues, consisting only of expositions, episodes, and presentations, so we will revisit that introductory level only briefly here. Thereafter, we will begin to incorporate pedal points and stretti in various orders and increasing levels of difficulty.

EXERCISE. The flexible plan below is intended for review of the basic fugue sections, without pedal point or stretto. You may use it to "choose your own adventure," selecting from the various options to create ever-changing musical structures. Use any subject from this book, choose one from the literature, invent your own, or choose from the subjects shown in Example 16.1, selected from Pachelbel's Magnificat fugues.

Key: Major/Minor
Exposition: Ascending/Descending/Staggered
Answer: Real/Tonal
Number of Subject Entries: 3/4
Episode modulating to ii/iii/IV/V/vi OR III/iv/v/VI/VII
Presentation in ii/iii/IV/V/vi OR III/iv/v/VI/VII in High/Middle/Low Voice
Episode modulating to ii/iii/IV/V/vi OR III/iv/v/VI/VII
Presentation in ii/iii/IV/V/vi OR III/iv/v/VI/VII in High/Middle/Low Voice
Episode modulating to ii/iii/IV/V/vi OR III/iv/v/VI/VII
Presentation in ii/iii/IV/V/vi OR III/iv/v/VI/VII in High/Middle/Low Voice
Episode modulating to I/i
Final presentation in High/Low Voice in I/i
Final Cadence

Adding Advanced Techniques to Fugues

EXERCISE. Choose from among your own fugue subjects or those in Example 16.1. Starting with the flexible plan shown above, insert a pedal point on ⑤ before the final cadence. Over this pedal, add two-voice sequential patterns in the right hand. If necessary, start with material that is not thematically important. Once you are confident in getting through a complete fugue, derive thematic fragments from your subject and add them to the upper voices in the pedal point. Improvise complete fugues on this plan.

EXERCISE. Building off the flexible plan shown above, add a stretto in two voices before the final presentation in the tonic. As with any stretto, you will need to determine to what extent the subject is suitable before you attempt to improvise. It may be possible to layer the entire subject over itself, or a fragment only. If it is only possible to use fragments, create several entrances and imitations so that the stretto is not too brief. You can also use your own subjects, if they are suitable for stretto. Remember that any passage in two voices will follow the procedures of bicinium, and will consist primarily of thirds and sixths, with some diminutions and prepared dissonances. You may need to compose your stretto and drop it into your otherwise improvised fugue.

EXERCISE. Using fugue subjects from Example 16.1 or your own, improvise fugues according to the flexible plan shown above, but insert a pedal point

EXAMPLE 16.1 Fugue subjects

followed immediately by a stretto. These two events should take place before the final presentation in the tonic. Try reversing the two new events, placing the stretto before the pedal point. If desired, you can put the final subject presentation over a tonic or dominant pedal point. Finally, the stretto may occur over the pedal point. If you choose this last option, the stretto should be on a dominant pedal, allowing for the use of a tonic pedal with the final presentation. The tonic pedal could even continue into the final cadence. Do not stretch out the pedal until it becomes ridiculous, though. Your sense of artistry will tell you when enough is enough.

EXERCISE. Review your strategies for improvising cadenzas. Add a cadenza to the flexible plan shown above. The cadenza should occur before the final cadence. Then create an ambitious plan for a fugue, based on the flexible model, which includes everything we have studied: exposition, episodes, presentations, pedal point, stretto, cadenza, and ending. Practice improvising fugues with your plan until you are confident.

The flexible plan below includes all the fugue elements we have studied in this book. Of course, the order of events may be changed. In particular, the order of the pedal point, stretto, cadenza, and final presentation is arbitrary.

Key: Major/Minor
Exposition: Ascending/Descending/Staggered
Answer: Real/Tonal
Number of Subject Entries: 3/4
Episode modulating to ii/iii/IV/V/vi OR III/iv/v/VI/VII
Presentation in ii/iii/IV/V/vi OR III/iv/v/VI/VII in High/Middle/Low Voice
Episode modulating to ii/iii/IV/V/vi OR III/iv/v/VI/VII
Presentation in ii/iii/IV/V/vi OR III/iv/v/VI/VII in High/Middle/Low Voice
Episode modulating to ii/iii/IV/V/vi OR III/iv/v/VI/VII
Presentation in ii/iii/IV/V/vi OR III/iv/v/VI/VII in High/Middle/Low Voice
Episode modulating to ii/iii/IV/V/vi OR III/iv/v/VI/VII
Presentation in ii/iii/IV/V/vi OR III/iv/v/VI/VII in High/Middle/Low Voice
Pedal Point/Stretto
Final presentation in High/Low Voice in I/i
Cadenza

Final Cadence

Example 16.2 demonstrates just one possible fugue that could be improvised according to the flexible plan above. The subject is from the second of Handel's *7 kleine Fugen*. Notating a piece that is supposed to be a model of improvisation is a contradiction, of course, but I have tried to write very closely to the way I would improvise. I simply wrote down the first idea that came into

EXAMPLE 16.2 A fugue on a subject of Handel

EXAMPLE 16.2 Continued

my mind for each section, and resisted the urge to revise anything. The stretto took a few minutes of figuring; were I preparing to improvise at the keyboard, a stretto like this would probably take five or ten minutes of thinking, and a few minutes more to make sure the hands know what to do when the time comes (and to commit all of it to memory for later recall). The episodes are all based on familiar motions, and are short-lived and business-like. (In concert I might draw out these episodes longer.) The harmonic language doesn't try anything clever. The cadenza is the simplest technique I could come up with, a diminished arpeggio.

EXERCISE. Improvise complete fugues according to your own adaptations of the complete plan shown above.

The Two-Voice Fugue

Before concluding we should play attention to the two-voice fugue for a moment. Fugues in two voices are considerably less common than those in three or four. J. S. Bach's *Well-Tempered Clavier* includes only one out of the forty-eight. The *fugue d'école* tradition paid no attention to them at all; their standard was four voices. The skills of two-voice fugue may prove valuable for the improviser as a worthwhile musical challenge unto itself, but perhaps also for creating short imitative sections within the structure of larger pieces.

Such fugues have no complete chords and follow the procedures of bicinium from beginning to end. Like anything in two voices, they may imply fuller harmonies, without actually sounding them, by means of compound melody. While improvised fugue in three or more layers need not keep a strict accounting of the number of voices, the two-voice fugue loses its character if it adds any additional parts. This represents a significant but worthwhile challenge for the improviser, as the impulse to throw in supplemental parts to fill out harmonies can be difficult to resist.

One may improvise two-voice fugue with or without a fixed countersubject. If the countersubject is fixed, each presentation of the subject is largely determined in advance: one voice will take the subject, and the other the countersubject. Since no other voices are present, little else remains to be figured out. Pachelbel's fugue in G major from the Magnificat fugue collection is shown in its entirety in Example 16.3. This fugue has a fixed countersubject. Note that the majority of this piece consists of presentations of the subject and countersubject in either of two possible inversions. Once the subject and countersubject are worked out, most of the fugue is "prefabricated."

EXAMPLE 16.3 A fugue of Pachelbel

EXAMPLE 16.3 Continued

EXERCISE. Improvise two-voice fugues. Begin by working out a subject and countersubject in invertible counterpoint. Try to make the fugue as "prefabricated" as possible.

EXAMPLE 16.4 A fugue of John Stanley

EXAMPLE 16.4 Continued

EXAMPLE 16.4 Continued

EXAMPLE 16.4 Continued

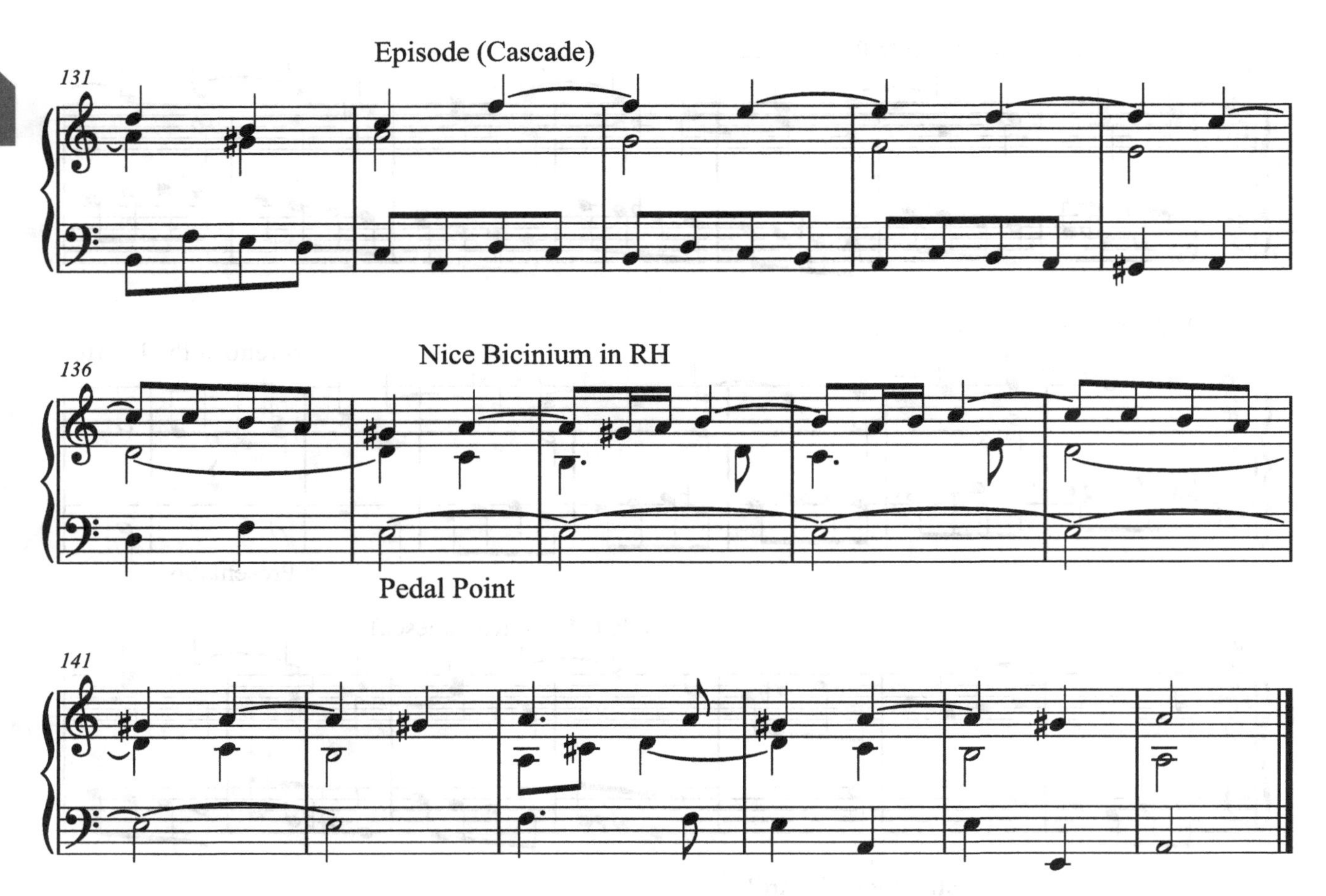

Self-Imitating Subjects

Speaking of things prefabricated, the fugue in A minor of John Stanley (1712–1786) from the Voluntary, Op. 7, no. 8 (shown in Example 16.4), uses a subject that conveniently imitates itself after two measures. It also works in double counterpoint. Stanley takes full advantage of this quality, placing several short stretto-like passages throughout the fugue before a final, more extended stretto. The little stretti that appear with each subject presentation may be a new idea to you, but most or all of the remaining techniques in this piece you already know. The episodes are made of familiar bass motions and set up modulations to new key areas. The pedal point features textbook bicinium in the upper voices. Stanley's setting of the Monte Romanesca connects the rising fifths in the bass with stepwise diminutions, so that the motion takes place entirely over ascending scales, as seen in measures 67, 85, and 103. Despite certain oddities of voice leading (such as the dissonant D in m. 77—perhaps a copying error), the composition presents some good ideas for improvisers. It is interesting to find so many familiar partimento bass motions in an English fugue.

EXAMPLE 16.5 Fugue subjects

EXERCISE. Invent subjects that may be placed in double counterpoint with themselves. You may wish to follow Stanley and fashion the tune around rising steps (as we also observed in some stretti in Chapter 14). Descending steps will also work. Practice playing your subjects with their own imitations above and below, in major and minor keys. Improvise fugues, placing your subjects in brief stretti in some of the presentations. Subjects that function in double counterpoint against themselves appear in Example 16.5.

Conclusion

The aim of this book has been to map out the long adventure that leaves behind score dependency, ventures through partimento, and arrives finally at fugue improvisation. At this point, you have everything you need to create pieces in fugal style, although fluency can take years to achieve, and you may find it necessary to revisit certain topics for additional study and practice. However, with sustained effort, a devoted musician can surely develop the skills of improvising fugue.

Glossary of Persons and Terms

10-9-8 A variant of the 8-7-6 bass motion.

3-♯4-6 A bass motion over a descending scale.

8-7-6 A bass motion over a rising scale.

Ascending 5-6 A bass motion over a rising scale.

Bariolage Rapidly alternating notes, often in sevenths and sixths, derived from violin technique.

Bass Motion A pattern of intervals in a bass line, indicating upper voice harmonic solutions.

Benoist, François (1794–1878) Organist and professor of improvisation at the Paris Conservatoire.

C5 Also Circle of Fifths. A bass motion over falling fifths.

Cadenza A section of a fugue which departs from strict part writing and engages in virtuosic display as a closing gesture.

Cascade A bass motion that descends a third and rises a second.

Cherubini, Luigi (1760–1842) Composer, teacher, and head of the Paris Conservatoire.

Chromatic Fauxbourdon Chords of the sixth over a descending chromatic scale.

Coda A short interlude in the midst of a fugue exposition.

Complete RO The complete version of Rule of the Octave as taught by the partimento masters.

Compound melody A single melodic line implying two lines by leaping between registers.

Corelli, Arcangelo (1653–1713) Influential composer, primarily of music for strings.

Corelli Leapfrog A bass motion over a rising scale, characterized by voice-crossings.

Cotumacci, Carlo (1709–1785) Composer, partimento teacher, and author of *Partimenti, fughe e disposizione al contrapunto.*

Descending 7-6 A bass motion over a descending scale.

Diminution The process of filling in decorative notes between structural notes.

Dolareti A bass motion over a falling third and rising fourth.

Domirefa A bass motion over a rising third and falling second.

Doublefrog A variant of the Corelli Leapfrog, with four voices.

DP10 A variant of Descending 7-6, with four voices.

Dupré, Marcel (1886–1971) Organist at the Paris Conservatoire and improviser.

Durante, Francesco (1684–1755) Composer and prominent teacher in the partimento tradition.

Episode A section of a fugue departing from a full statement of the subject and setting up a modulation.

Exposition The opening section of a fugue in which vocal entries occur.

Falling Thirds A bass motion over descending thirds.

Fauxbourdon A bass motion of parallel chords of the sixth over a rising or falling scale.

Fenaroli, Fedele (1730–1818) A leading partimento teacher and composer, and author of *Regole musicali per i principianti di cembalo.*

Fenaroli Chromatic Ascent A bass motion with over nearly complete ascending chromatic scale.

Figuration prelude A keyboard piece made of chords broken into consistent figuration.

Fixed countersubject A theme that consistently accompanies a fugue subject.

Fugue d'école The academic or school fugue, a pedagogical tradition of strict fugal creation from the Paris Conservatoire.

Furno, Giovanni (1748–1837) Prominent teacher in the partimento tradition and author of *Metodo facile breve e chiaro delle prime ed essensiali regole per accompagnare partimento senza numero.*

Gedalge, André (1856–1926) Professor of fugue at the Paris Conservatoire and author of *Traité de la fugue.*

Herz, Henri (1803–1888) Professor of piano at the Paris Conservatoire and author of *Henri Herz's New and Complete Pianoforte School.*

Insanguine, Giacomo (1728–1795) Composer, teacher, and author of *Regole con moto di basso partimenti e fuge.*

Lamento A minor-key descending bass motion over a chromatic scale.

Leaping Romanesca A bass motion over a falling fourth and rising second.

Leo, Leonardo (1694–1744) Composer of opera and sacred music, and respected partimento teacher.

Marpurg, Friedrich Wilhelm (1818–1895) Composer and author of *Abhandlung von der Fuge.*

Martini, Giovanni Battista (1706–1784) Composer, highly regarded teacher, and author of *Esemplare, o sia saggio fondamentale pratico di contrappunto.* His epithet was "Padre".

Mattei Canon A canonic solution over a rising scale, named after Stanislao Mattei.

Mattheson, Johann (1681–1764) Composer of *Die Wohlklingende Fingersprache.*

Monte A bass motion over an ascending chromatic scale.

Monte Principale A bass motion over a rising fourth and falling third.

Monte Romanesca A bass motion over rising fifths.

Offset Scales Two descending scales in patterns of 7-6 or 2-3.

Pachelbel, Johann (1653–1706) Prominent composer and organist.

Paisiello, Giovanni (1740–1816) Composer and author of *Regole per ben accompagnare il partimento.*

Paralique Author's invented word denoting two voices moving in parallel motion and one static voice.

Passacaglia A minor-key bass motion over a descending scale.

Pedal Point A section of a fugue with a sustained note in the bass.

Perfidia A variant of Leaping Romanesca, characterized by suspensions.

Presentation Section of a fugue in which one or more iterations of the fugue subject appears.

Real answer A fugal answer that maintains the subject's intervals exactly.

Scale mutation An accidental, usually indicating a key change.

Scarlatti, Alessandro (1660–1725) Composer of many operas and partimenti.

Simple RO A simple version of Rule of the Octave consisting of three voices in chords of the fifth and sixth only.

Stepwise Romanesca A bass motion over a descending scale.

Stretto A section of a fugue in which the subject overlaps itself.

Structural notes The important notes that determine harmonic events.

Subdominant answer A fugal answer at the subdominant rather than the typical dominant.

Termination Also modulation. A change of key.

Tied Bass A bass motion over a descending syncopated scale.

Tonal answer A fugal answer that changes one or more intervals in the fugue subject.

Tritto, Giacomo (1733–1824) Composer and author of *Scuola di contrappunto ossia teoria musicale*.

Über-Lamento A nearly complete descending minor-key chromatic bass motion.

Umpadeeda Author's invented word describing a typical eighteenth-century keyboard figuration of four sixteenth notes.

Unmeasured fantasia A keyboard piece consisting of chords of vaguely defined metrical value, to be arpeggiated freely in performance.

Valente Chromatic Ascents Various bass motions over ascending chromatic scales.

Zibaldone A personal notebook of musical observations.

Zimmerman, Pierre-Joseph-Guillaume (1785–1853) Professor of piano at the Paris Conservatoire and author of *Encyclopédie du pianiste compositeur*.

Zingarelli, Niccolò (1752–1837) Composer of sacred music and partimenti.

Bibliography

Bach, Carl Philipp Emanuel. Letter to J. N. Forkel, probably from December 1774, trans. in *The New Bach Reader*, ed. Hans T. David and Arthur Mendel, rev. Christoph Wolff (1998). W. W. Norton.

Bach, J. S., Irmer, O. von, & Theopold, H.-M. (1978). *Das wohltemperierte Klavier*. G. Henle Verlag.

Bach, J. S., Steglich, R., & Theopold, H.-M. (1990). *Toccaten*. G. Henle Verlag.

Cherubini, L., Clarke, M. C., & Bennett, J. (n.d.). *A Treatise on Counterpoint & Fugue*. Novello and Company.

Dupré, M. (1938). *Cours complèt de fugue*. A. Leduc.

Durante, F., & Giarraffa, R. (2004). *Toccate e fughe: Per organo o clavicembalo*. Armelin Musica.

Durante, F., & Machella, M. (2007). *Esercizio, ovvero, Sonata per organo*. Armelin.

Furno, Giovanni. (c. 1817). *Metodo facile breve e chiara ed essensiali regole per accompagnare Partimenti senza numeri.* http://partimenti.org/partimenti/collections/furno/the_method_1817.pdf.

Fux, J. J. (1971). *The Study of Counterpoint: From Johann Joseph Fux's Gradus ad Parnassum*. Translated and edited by A. Mann. W. W. Norton.

Gedalge, A., & Davis, F. (1965). *[Traité de la fugue.] Treatise on the Fugue. By André Gedalge. Translated and edited by Ferdinand Davis*. Norman: University of Oklahoma Press.

Gjerdingen, R. O. (n.d.). Partimenti of Fenaroli. Retrieved November 23, 2021, from http://partimenti.org/partimenti/collections/durante/index.html.

Gjerdingen, R. O. (n.d.). Partimenti of Insanguine. http://partimenti.org/partimenti/collections/leo/index.html.

Gjerdingen, R. O. (n.d.). Partimenti of Leo. http://partimenti.org/partimenti/collections/leo/index.html.

Gjerdingen, R. O. (n.d.). Partimenti of Mattei. http://partimenti.org/partimenti/collections/leo/index.html.

Gjerdingen, R. O. (n.d.). Partimenti of Paisiello. http://partimenti.org/partimenti/collections/leo/index.html.

Gjerdingen, R. O. (n.d.). The Fugue of Adolphe Deslandres, 1858. http://partimenti.org/fugue/collections/appr_paris/1858/deslandres.html.

Gjerdingen, R. O. (n.d.). Various Partimento Collections. Monuments of Partimenti. http://partimenti.org/partimenti/index.html.

Gjerdingen, R. O. (2007). *Music in the Galant style*. Oxford University Press.

Gjerdingen, R. O. (2020). *Child Composers in the Old Conservatories*. Oxford University Press.

Gooley, D. A. (2018). *Fantasies of Improvisation: Free Playing in Nineteenth-Century Music*. Oxford University Press.

Handel, G. F. (n.d.). *Six Fugues pour le clavecin ou l'orgue*. https://s9.imslp.org/files/imglnks/usimg/7/7f/IMSLP365081-PMLP298270-Handel_-_Six_Fugues_pour_le_Clavecin_ou_l'Orgue.pdf.

Herz, Henri. (1844). *Henri Herz's New and Complete Pianoforte School*. John F. Nunns.

Marchant, A. W. (1892). *500 Fugue Subjects and Answers, Ancient and Modern*. H. W. Gray.

Marpurg, F. W. (1970). *Abhandlung von der Fuge*. G. Olms.

Martini, G. B. (n.d.). *Esemplare, o sia saggio fondamentale pratico di contrappunto sopra il canto fermo*. https://s9.imslp.org/files/imglnks/usimg/c/c2/IMSLP186275-PMLP323483-parte_prima.pdf.

Martini, G. B. (n.d.). *12 Sonate d'intavolatura*. https://s9.imslp.org/files/imglnks/usimg/8/8e/IMSLP347076-PMLP90923-Martini_12Sonate.pdf.

Mattheson, Johann (1735). *Die wohlklingende Fingersprache*. Verlage des Versassers.

McCarthy, David. Organ Teaching at the Paris Conservatoire. (n.d.). https://www.davidmccarthymusic.com/technique/conservatoire_organ_class.pdf

Mortensen, J. J. (2020). *The Pianist's Guide to Historic Improvisation*. Oxford University Press.

Mulvey, M. N. (2014, March 24). *The School Fugue: Its Place in the Organ Repertoire of the French Symphonic School*. UNT Digital Library. https://digital.library.unt.edu/ark:/67531/metadc278639.

Ouseley, F. A. G. (1869). *A Treatise on Counterpoint, Canon and Fugue*. Clarendon Press.

Pachelbel, J., Botstiber, H., & Seiffert, M. (1986). *The Fugues on the Magnificat: For Organ or Keyboard*. Dover.

Renwick, W. (2007). *The Langloz Manuscript: Fugal Improvisation through Figured Bass*. Oxford University Press.

Sanguinetti, G. (2012). *The Art of Partimento*. New York: Oxford University Press.

Scarlatti, A., & Macinanti, A. (2009). *Opera omnia per strumento a tastiera*. Ut Orpheus Ed.

Tritto, Giacomo. (n.d.) Digital Collections. *Scoula di contrappunto ossia teoria musicale*. http://digital.lib.buffalo.edu/items/show/20093.

Van Tour, Peter, ed. (2017). *The 189 Partimenti of Nicola Sala: Complete Edition with Critical Commentary*. Uppsala: Acta Universitatis Upsaliensis.

Zimmerman, J. (1840). *Encyclopédie du pianiste compositeur*. L'Auteur.

Zingarelli, Nicolò. (1833). *Partimenti del Signor Maestro don Zingarelli*. Ricordi.

Index

Printed in the USA/Agawam, MA
May 22, 2023

810382.017